Without Troops & Tanks

Without Troops & Tanks

The Emergency Relief Desk and the Cross Border Operation into Eritrea and Tigray

Mark Duffield
*School of Public Policy
University of Birmingham, UK*

&

John Prendergast
*Center of Concern
Washington DC*

THE RED SEA PRESS
Publishers and Distributors of Third World Books
11 Princess Road, Suite D
Lawrenceville, NJ 08648

The Red Sea Press, Inc.
11-D Princess Rd.
Lawrenceville, NJ 08648

First Printing, 1994

Book and Cover Design: Jonathan Gullery

Library of Congress Cataloging-in-Publication Data

Duffield, Mark R.
Without troops and tanks : humanitarian intervention in Ethiopia and Eritrea / by Mark Duffield and John Prendergast.
p. cm
Includes bibliographical references and index.
ISBN 1-56902-002-7 (cloth). -- ISBN 1-56902-003-5 (pbk.)
1. International relief--Ethiopia. 2. International relief--Eritrea. I. Prendergast, John. II. Title.
HV555.E8D84 1994
361.2'6'0963--dc20 94-28293
CIP

Contents

Foreword

My first trip to Khartoum took place in early 1981. For some years previously, I had been counselling Eritrean refugees in Holland. This experience had helped to shape my knowledge of the war and its human impact. My introduction to the Eritrea Relief Association (ERA) was through Kiros, who was then preparing for a grain purchase mission in Gedaref. Regrettably, a couple of weeks later while on that mission, he was killed in a car crash.

The history of Emergency Relief Desk (ERD), despite the consortium's great achievements is also a sad history. It is a story of friends and friends of their friends who have been lost. This book pays tribute to the thousands of anonymous Eritreans and Tigrayans who staffed the distribution stations, worked on the roads or repaired trucks, often with no tools except their brains and bare hands. Those who kept the community records in the village committees should also be remembered. They had the awful task of selecting beneficiaries. The book likewise salutes the many acts of selfless heroism on the part of ordinary people. The courageous Tigrayan drivers, for example, who sacrificed their lives driving during daylight when the MiGs were out hunting them down. In 1984 and 1985 the starving people of Tigray needed the food desperately and driving by day was a lot faster than at night!

The turbulent history of ERD is in this book. The wrangling amongst the member agencies in their attempts to stick together; the struggle to convince donor governments to supply food aid and transport capacity. In the last analysis, how-ever, it is the story of a group of non-governmental organisations and indigenous implementing agencies that learned to work together. Often against all odds!

Protestant church agencies, which formed the basis of ERD, and the humanitarian arms of liberation movements are not natural allies. This was even more the case under the prevailing political conditions in the Horn toward the end of the 1970s. It took the far-sighted welfare policies of the Fronts and the perseverance of a number of ERD members to mould the consortium into what it became: the largest humanitarian operation ever undertaken by church agencies! It also took a savage war with indescribable human suffering to teach the ERD family that they had a wider responsibility than just supplying humanitarian aid.

None of us in the mid eighties could foresee that the war would be over in 1991; that Eritrea would gain its independence after 30 years of struggle and that the TPLF\EPRDF would break the backbone of the mightiest army on the African continent. ERD for most of its life had to deal with an unfavourable political climate in Europe and North America. The UN and even major sectors of the NGO community kept their distance, if not being openly hostile. As late as 1988 a donor representative responded to my plea for more food aid for ERA by claiming that "you are asking us to feed the enemies of our friend. We don't do that." I can assure you that this conversation did not take place in the Kremlin!

In many ways, ERD was a war consortium. Continually beleaguered by demands for cash and aid in kind which surmounted our combined capacity to respond. Battered by organisational and management problems resulting from the strained environment in which we worked. Embattled by pressures from the implementing agencies and Fronts to be a vocal solidarity movement while checked by our real doubts about such a role.

So what kept this disparate group of agencies with different traditions and approaches together for more than a decade? I think it was a deep conviction, a true faith for some of us, and ecumenical solidarity. A faith that we should not abandon God's suffering people in the wartorn areas of Eritrea and Ethiopia as long as we had the means to assist them.

And a strongly felt sense of ecumenical solidarity by the individuals involved. Spurred on in the knowledge that other agencies would do their share, again and again, they managed to convince their own organisations that yet another even higher assistance budget was needed! General Secretaries regularly overstepped their authorities and boards and committees recognised the added value of this ecumenical spirit in which ERD operated.

For the above reasons and more, it was necessary that ERD's history be written in the wider context of humanitarian assistance in situations of conflict. Unfortunately, in the post Cold War era, conflict is becoming even more prevalent. I honestly believe that this history will help the ecumenical movement and NGO's in general to rethink the role they have to play collectively. As this book shows, we somewhat stumbled into our role and had to learn a lot by trial and error. Some mistakes can be avoided by studying this history. The underlying faith of the ERD family, however, is more true today than ever: people in conflict situations have a right to humanitarian assistance!

Jacques Willemse,
Dutch Interchurch Aid
(Twice Chairman of the Emergency Relief Desk)

Utrecht
1 October 1993

Preface and Acknowledgements

The Emergency Relief Desk (ERD) was formed in 1981 as an ecumenical NGO consortium to facilitate cross-border humanitarian assistance from Sudan into Eritrea and Tigray. It arose from the tragic effects of war and the indifference of the international community to dire conditions in non-government areas due to an overriding respect accorded Ethiopian sovereignty. From its inception to the fall of the Ethiopian government in 1991, ERD played a pivotal and often controversial role in channelling emergency aid into these areas. Following the end of the war and the decision to close ERD, its member agencies decided to commission a history of the operation so that its accomplishments and wider significance would not be lost. Norwegian Church Aid, a key member of ERD, provided the administrative support for this undertaking. The collection of material began in America in October and then Europe in December 1992. Part of January and February 1993 were spent in Ethiopia and Eritrea gathering more information, especially from the main ERD archive in Asmara. Further interviewing took place in Europe and a first draft was completed in May. The draft was discussed in Asmara during the formal closure of ERD in June 1993 and a corrected version forms the basis of this book.

It would be a lengthy task to thank individually all the people who have contributed to the completion of this history. The bibliography contains a list of those consulted. In all places visited the authors have been made welcome and generously provided with the help they requested. Special thanks, however, must be extended to Kosti Manibe who arranged the interviews in Addis Ababa and Asmara together with facilitating the accessing of information in these places. Mention must also be made of Gayle Smith, Jacque Willemse, Trish Silkin, Fiona Meehan, Arild Jacobsen, Synnove Vinsrygg, Jan Erichsen and Stein

Villumstad who in various ways, from prodigious knowledge to kind encouragement and incisive observations, have made this study possible. We would also like to thank the members of the ERD Editorial Committee for their invaluable comments and advice on the initial draft. Those not already cited include: Jeff Whisenant, Sarah Hughes, Teklewoini Assefa, Nerayo Teklemichael and Ayyaanaa Leencaa. Finally, an acknowledgement is due of Janne Svartberg for her efficient administration of the project. The authors would like to stress, however, that the responsibility for any factual errors, together with the interpretation of events, is theirs alone.

Mark Duffield and John Prendergast

Birmingham and Washington
October 1993

Figures

Glossary of Acronyms

BFW	Brot Fur Die Welt
CA	Christian Aid
CBO	Cross-Border Operation
CDAA/E	Churches Drought Action Africa/Ethiopia
CLWR	Canadian Lutheran World Relief
COR	Commission for Refugees
CRDA	Christian Relief and Development Association
CRS	Catholic Relief Services
DCA	Danchurch Aid
DDW	Diakonisches Werk
DIA	Dutch Interchurch Aid
ECS	Ethiopian Catholic Secretariat
EECMY	Ethiopian Evangelical Church Mekane Yesus
EIAC	Eritrean Inter-Agency Agricultural Consortium
ELF	Eritrean Liberation Front
EOC	Ethiopian Orthodox Church
EPDM	Ethiopian Peoples Democratic Movement
EPLF	Eritrean Peoples Liberation Front
EPRDF	Ethiopian Peoples Revolutionary Democratic Front
ERA	Eritrean Relief Association
ERCCS	Eritrean Red Cross and Red Crescent Society
ERD	Emergency Relief Desk
ERRA	Eritrean Relief and Rehabilitation Association
FCA	Finnchurchaid
IA	Implementing Agency
ICCO	International Coordination Committee for Development Projects
ICRC	International Committee of the Red Cross
JRP	Joint Relief Programme
LWF	Lutheran World Federation

LWR	Lutheran World Relief
MCC	Mennonite Central Committee
NCA	Norwegian Church Aid
OLF	Oromo Liberation Front
ORA	Oromo Relief Association
REST	Relief Society of Tigray
SCC	Sudan Council of Churches
SCR	Swedish Church Relief
TPLF	Tigrayan Peoples Liberation Front
TTAC	Tigray Transport and Agricultural Consortium
WCC	World Council of Churches

Maps

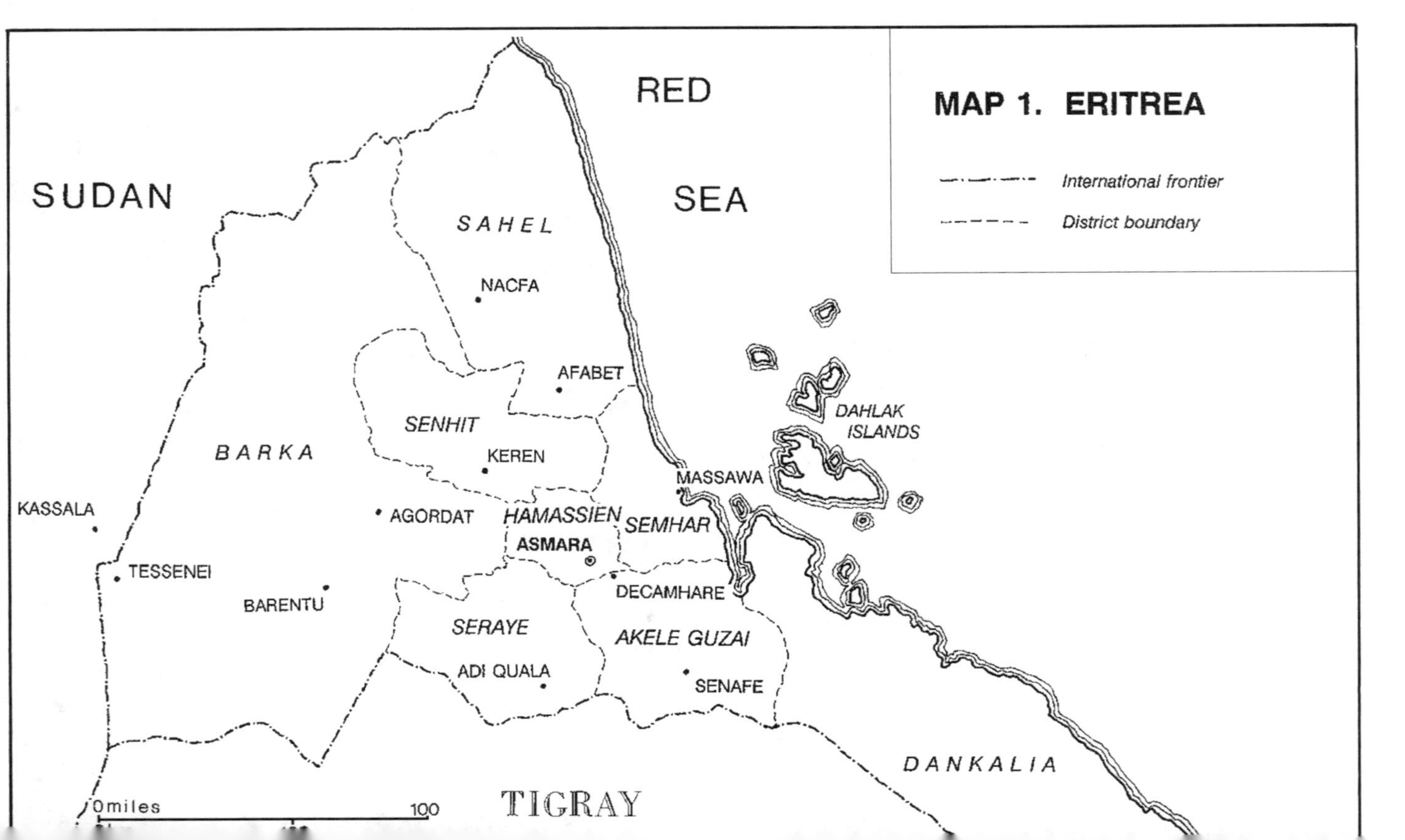

MAP 1. ERITREA
International frontier
District boundary
RED
SEA
SUDAN
SAHEL
NACFA
AFABET
SENHIT
KEREN
BARKA
KASSALA
AGORDAT
HAMASSIEN
SEMHAR
MASSAWA
DAHLAK ISLANDS
ASMARA
TESSENEI
BARENTU
DECAMHARE
SERAYE
AKELE GUZAI
ADI QUALA
SENAFE
DANKALIA
TIGRAY
0 miles
100

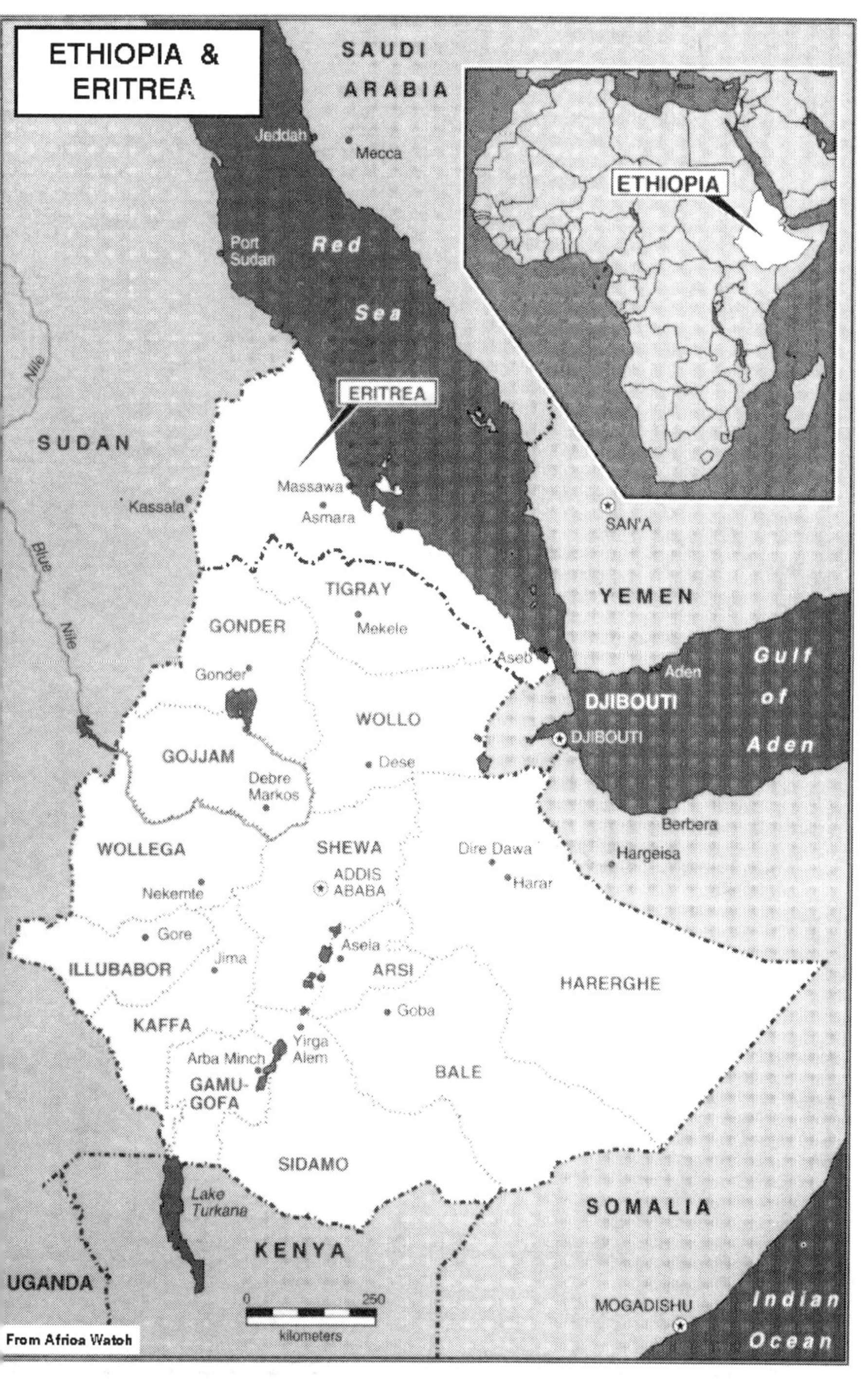

From Africa Watch

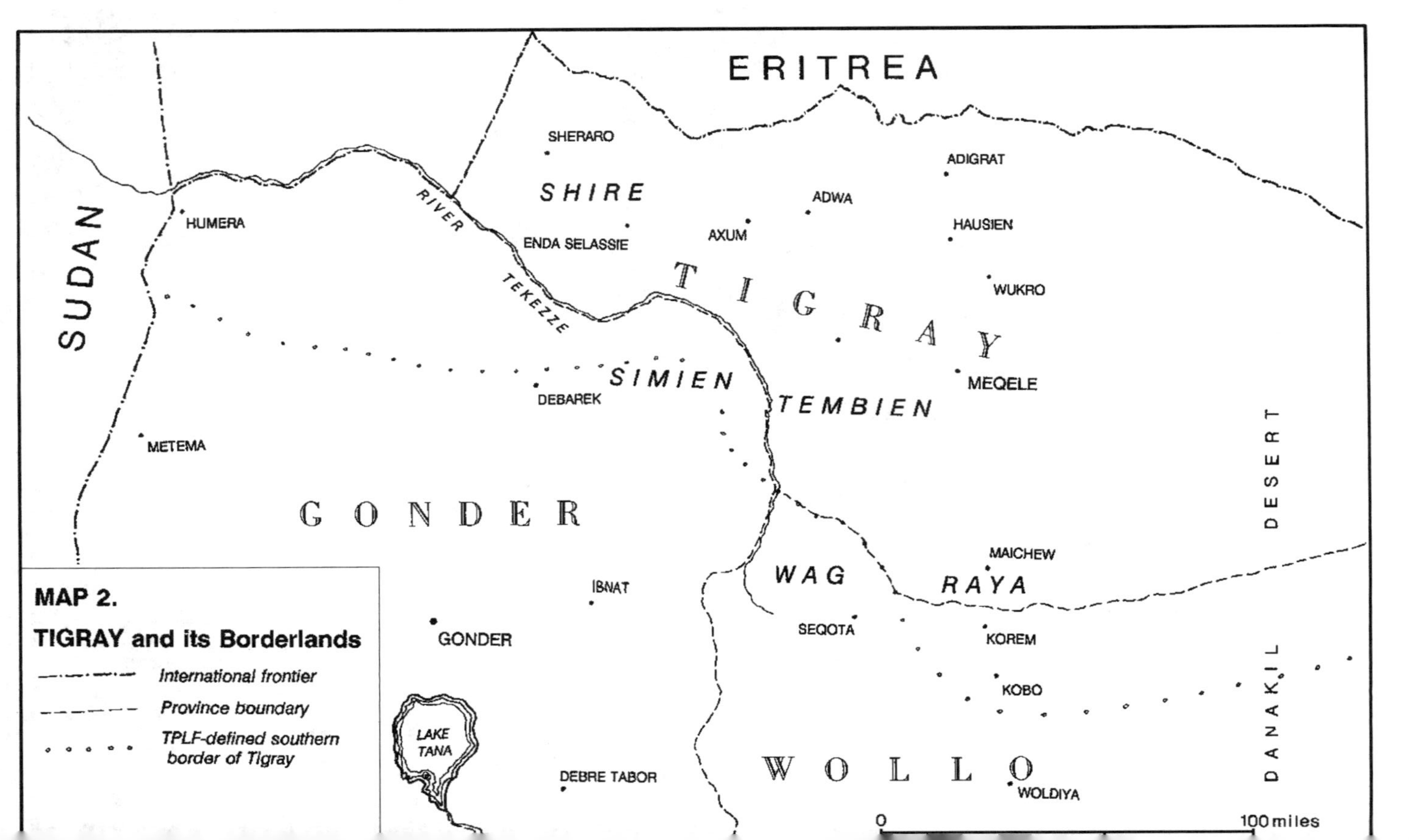

MAP 2.

TIGRAY and its Borderlands

International frontier

Province boundary

TPLF-defined southern border of Tigray

CHAPTER ONE

Introduction: The Historical Significance of the Emergency Relief Desk

Complex Emergencies and Internal War

There is a widespread feeling amongst commentators, politicians and practitioners that the world has entered a period of profound change in the nature of international relations. While the long-term implications of this shift are not fully understood, its basic contours are now well established. These range from a weakening of the principle of sovereignty as a means of structuring global affairs, the emergence of political conditionality to support the West's humanitarian and environmental policies and, largely through the reform of the UN, a trend toward selective military intervention as a means of international crisis management. Such developments can be seen as part of an historic reshaping of North-South relations. At the centre of this process, indeed, the base upon which the main features of this re-working is taking place, lies the emerging phenomenon of complex humanitarian emergencies.

In relation to Africa, the emergence of complex emergencies can be related to three broad factors, that is (a) the problems associated with the formation and development of the post-colonial state (b) the regionalisation of the global economy and the consequent marginalisation of the Africa's formal economy and (c) the end of the cold war and the reassessment of the North's political and aid priorities. The interplay between the unresolved problems of de-colonisation and the often radical response to economic decline has provided a framework for many of the internal wars[1] that have characterised Africa over the decades.

One of the defining features of the more recent literature on conflict in Africa has been to establish its relation to famine. This association, however, has been part of a more general move away from understanding famine as the result of natural causes, such as drought, to isolating its gender, economic and political determinants.[2–5] African famine and its various modalities is now increasingly understood, for example, in terms of the results of environmental degradation as rural producers respond to economic marginalisation; the restructuring of households through migration and other coping mechanisms; ethnic competition prompted by a shrinking resource base; and, in extreme cases, the use of physical force to seize subsistence assets.

It is in relation to internal war, in particular, that the political origin of famine, as opposed to natural events, is most easily seen. As will be shown in the text, the liberation movements in Eritrea and Tigray were aware of this connection in the 1970s. Here, it was the counter-insurgency strategy of the central government to directly target the civilian population which was the central cause of the chronic humanitarian crisis of the 1980s. The famine-causing strategy pursued by the Ethiopian government has been well documented.[6–11] Tactics primarily included measures to damage or destroy the agricultural, pastoralist and commercial economy of Eritrea and Tigray, disrupt population and limit the flow of food aid to non-government areas.

Counter-insurgency measures involved the planting of land mines; destroying crops and livestock; poisoning wells; and the bombing of markets in order to disrupt commerce, especially agricultural trade. Other measures included heavy taxation of civilians and tribute taking which depleted stores; forcing civilians to join militia or work on government lands during peak agricultural seasons which inhibited local production; terrorizing civilian populations through executions, torture, rape, forced conscription and resettlement; and undertaking major offensives aimed at displacing civilians, often with the purpose of drawing them into government held towns in order to restrict movement and provide easier monitoring and control. In addition, the Ethiopian government used the denial of relief assistance to non-government areas as a weapon to displace and starve populations at the same time as using food aid to draw civilians from these areas and into garrison towns. Government aircraft also strafed relief convoys coming cross-border from Sudan in an attempt to further curtail humanitarian assistance reaching non-government areas.

The effects of war-related famines are more egregious than those caused by drought alone. It has been argued that,

> ...warfare intervenes to destroy the means of subsistence and to prevent the strategies which people adopt to withstand scarcity engendered by environmental factors. Ultimately, war-related famines lead to social collapse with the associated phenomena of frank starvation and generalised migration, exemplified by events in Eritrea and Tigray in 1983-85.[12]

Internal war strategies not only prevent civilian coping mechanisms, they often target them as the primary means of destroying the support base of opposition movements. Warring parties are usually more ingenious in creating humanitarian emergencies for areas controlled by opponents than donors are in analyzing the causes and responding to these emergencies. The long term consequences are just as profound. Asset transfer and depletion are debilitating to vulnerable pastoral and farming communities, which complicate restoration strategies already compromised by ecological degradation and economies warped by years of militarisation and emergency relief. Post-war Eritrea and Ethiopia, in which millions of people still subsist in conditions of food insecurity, demonstrate that years of conflict do not produce cyclical emergencies, but rather semi-permanent ones.

The Problem of Access

During the cold war the official respect accorded sovereignty was an important element in the West's aid related sponsorship of an anticommunist alliance in what was then known as the Third World. The effects of internal war were as real then as they are today, the main difference is that Western donor governments were more inclined to disregard evidence of human rights abuse or other forms of malpractice on the part of recipient states if they were perceived as allies within the international arena. The end of the cold war, which in Africa was effectively over by the mid-1980s,[13] has served to unravel this web of relations. Political alliances have weakened as Africa has ceased to be a region of super-power contention. This has allowed the West the ability, so to speak, to choose to see authoritarianism, especially if, in a period of declining aid budgets, this new enlightenment helps to redefine strategic interests. Since the mid 1980s, the humanitarian consequences of internal war have increasingly become a subject of attention in official circles. Although these consequences have been a problem for decades and were clearly manifest in the Nigerian civil war at the end of the 1960s, it is only now that they have become an issue which is helping change the nature of international relations.

Complex emergencies, especially those associated with internal war, have usually been defined in terms of problems of accessing humanitarian relief. Towards the end of the 1980s, access had become a manifest problem for international aid agencies in several African emergencies.[14] This difficulty led to a growing critical appraisal of the principles of sovereignty and non-interference as established in the UN Charter. In effect, these principles mean that international humanitarian assistance is politically confined to areas under the jurisdiction of the recognised state. In cases of internal war or divided governance this poses particular problems in terms of helping civilians in non-government areas. Prior to the outbreak of the Gulf War in 1991, some NGOs had already called into question nation state sovereignty, especially when its institutional enaction was being used to bar the victims of internal war receiving humanitarian assistance.[15] The subsequent allied action to secure a safe haven in Kurdistan, together with the more recent American intervention in Somalia, has served to bring this debate fully into the public domain.

Since the mid-1980s, the growing involvement of NGOs in disaster relief, together with the end of the cold war, has had a profound effect on North-South relations. NGOs by their mandates have the ability to form a contract with 'people' rather than 'states'. Their enhanced role in the South is a practical manifestation of the challenge to sovereignty which has occurred in recent years. One aspect of this is that NGO humanitarian involvement in Africa's internal wars has sometimes acted, in terms of their representing the plight of the victims, to bypass the state and bring the desperate situation of civilians directly into the international arena. Many oppressed African groups, for example, are now better represented in Washington than in Khartoum or Nairobi. In other words, the consequences of internal war now impact directly on the institutions and conventions of global governance.

This re-working of North-South relations has promoted a crisis within the international political system because it is still largely based upon cold war foundations. This state of affairs is evinced, for example, in the contentious and halting reform of the UN together with the breathtaking escalation of its global crisis management role.

Internal War in the Horn

The origins of the war between Eritrea and Ethiopia can be traced to the failure of decolonisation in the Horn. Following the end of WWII which had seen the removal of the Italian colonial administration, despite Eritrea's popular and historic claim to independence, the UN, with the support of a number of Western governments, federated Eritrea to Ethiopia.[16] Ethiopia's subsequent abrogation of that agreement and the assumption of direct rule sparked the beginning of three decades of war in 1962. By the mid-1970s, the political leadership of the struggle for independence had been assumed by the Eritrean Peoples Liberation Front (EPLF). In the case of Tigray, the social and political convulsion which saw the overthrow of the autocratic regime of Haile Selassie in 1974 and the assumption of power by the Dergue, gave rise in Tigray, under the leadership of the Tigrayan Peoples Liberation Front (TPLF), to a struggle for national self-determination which shifted focus over time to unity and equality within a federated and decentralised Ethiopia. Other liberation groups, including the Oromo Liberation Front (OLF) also emerged. Towards the end of the 1970s, the Ethiopian government was able to significantly escalate the war with the help of Soviet military assistance. Despite this help, together with receiving a disproportionate amount of Western relief aid, the EPLF and TPLF, who were allied apart from a period in the mid 1980s, eventually toppled the Dergue in May 1991.

The complexity of the humanitarian situation prior to the mid 1980s, can be described as the opposition between popular democratic struggles in Eritrea and Tigray and an authoritarian military regime in Ethiopia which, since it constituted the internationally recognised government, enjoyed the material and moral support of important international donors, especially the European Community (EC) and its members. Soviet military assistance encouraged the West to compete with developmental aid and, increasingly, humanitarian relief. In contrast, since the Dergue claimed effective jurisdiction, the peoples of Eritrea and Tigray were isolated and most international agencies were reluctant to provide assistance.

The Emergency Relief Desk: An Overview

Having its origins in the late 1970s, the Emergency Relief Desk (ERD) was established in 1981 in Sudan as an ecumenical NGO consortium delivering cross border humanitarian assistance into the war ravaged, non-government areas of Eritrea and northern Ethiopia. With an administrative base in Khartoum, its nine core members were:

Brot Fur Die Welt/Diachonisches Werk (BFW), Germany
Christian Aid (CA), UK
Danchurch Aid (DCA), Denmark
Dutch Interchurch Aid (DIA), The Netherlands
International Coordination Committee for Development Projects (ICCO), The Netherlands
Lutheran World Relief (LWR), USA
Norwegian Church Aid (NCA), Norway
Sudan Council of Churches (SCC), Sudan
Swedish Church Relief (SCR), Sweden

Apart from SCC and the American LWR, the remaining agencies were European Protestant organisations. After its formation, the only new members were Canadian Lutheran World Relief (CLWR) which joined in 1989 and the Mennonite Central Committee (MCC) and Finnchurchaid (FCA) which both joined in 1990. Before its formal closure in June 1993, from its own resources and, especially after the mid-1980s from donor governments, ERD had mobilized around 3/4 million mt of food aid for Eritrea and Tigray together with other relief assistance and the necessary finance to transport these commodities. The total value of ERD's cash and in kind assistance was in the region of $350 million. Although only a fraction of the aid that was channelled through the government side, ERD efforts accounted for more than half of the total assistance accruing from the cross border operation (CBO) from Sudan. Until 1991 the ERD programme was implemented without any coordination or assistance from the UN, usually the lead operational body in an emergency response. In fact, until 1990 there was no mechanism for communication between the ERD assisted cross border operation and the UN led operation on the government side. The UN did not use information accessed by ERD, nor did the UN attempt to share its information about conditions in government held areas with ERD.

An important feature of the CBO was that ERD created partnerships with indigenous relief agencies, that is, the Eritrean Relief Association (ERA), the Relief Society of Tigray (REST) and the Oromo Relief Association (ORA). These organisations, in collaboration with the civilian departments established by the Fronts, played a decisive role in coordinating, implementing and delivering all programmes and assistance. ERD resources therefore helped support the development and expansion of locally managed relief systems. Unusual in present day emergency operations, no expatriate staff or outside operational agencies were involved in actual programme operations. Further, the indigenous agencies to which ERD channelled its assistance maximized the participation and responsibility of local communities in identifying beneficiaries and distributing food aid through elected councils. These locally managed, participatory systems allowed for a high degree of operational flexibility. They also created a "capacity to manage disasters at the community and regional levels."[17]

By contrast, the emergency operation on the government side was centrally organised and increasingly managed by international agencies which developed a more managerial and top down approach to relief assistance. The relationship between ERD and the indigenous relief agencies also differed sharply with the arrangements that developed from 1990 between the UN and these agencies. Representatives from ERA, REST, and ORA assert that onerous demands relating to mistrust and simple bureaucracy made dealing with the UN much more unwieldy and inefficient than with ERD. ERD had a much greater ability to raise and release funds quickly. Its consortium structure meant that as a fund-raising body, its sum was much greater than its individual parts.

Due to suspicions of partisanship or the politicisation of aid, the influence of Ethiopian sovereignty limited the ability of many international NGOs to raise support for the CBO. ERD largely avoided these allegations due to its conscious avoidance of direct publicity and its identity as a consortium of church organisations responding to relief needs, and responding only within a strict humanitarian mandate. Especially from the mid-1980s, ERD provided donor governments with a legitimate, if unorthodox, channel for their resources into Front held territories. Most governments would not have provided aid directly to the indigenous relief agencies because of the sovereignty issue, as well as legal or preferential restrictions on providing direct assistance to local organisations. ERD therefore served as a quiet buffer for some donors who otherwise would not have assisted the cross border operation.

Initially, ERD assistance largely comprised the local purchase of sorghum in Sudan and its transport to the border. As the humanitarian crisis deepened, this assistance was overtaken by foreign relief aid and, especially in Tigray, an innovative internal purchase programme which made cash available to buy and transport grain from surplus to deficit areas. Due to streamlined management, low administrative overheads, and extensive use of local and internal purchase programmes, ERD was a cost-efficient operation relative to larger UN initiatives. For example, ERA was able to move over three times as much food as Operation Lifeline Sudan for roughly the same amount of money.[18] It therefore provided ERD with an efficient vehicle for external inputs.

ERD's programme was partially a response to a growing frustration at dealing with symptoms, such as the influx of refugees into Sudan, rather than causes; that is, food insecurity within Front held territories. Until the mid-1980s, the humanitarian crisis in Eritrea and Tigray had been characterised by large-scale population movements which, amongst other things, manifest itself in a growing refugee population in Sudan. From this period, however, due to the increase in emergency assistance and, importantly, the development and strengthening of indigenous relief management capacity, the return and internal stabilisation of the civilian population in Front held areas proved possible. If a long term rationale for ERD assistance can be described, it was this prevention of migration together with the stabilisation of the local situation. Dr. Norman Barth, Executive Director of Lutheran World Relief, testified to this effect at a 1987 Congressional hearing:

> It is much better to keep farmers on their land so they can maintain their strength, their tools, furniture, and homes. It is much better to keep the pastoralists with their animals so they do not feel the pressure to sell them. This is a way to escape the horrors of feeding camps and the disruption of the fragile subsistence economies of the area.[19]

Apart from providing otherwise reluctant donor governments with an acceptable conduit for humanitarian assistance, the issue of accessing information in Front held territory was critical in developing a humanitarian response. ERD monitoring and assessment missions, as well as the ERD commissioned 1987[20] and 1991[21] Leeds University studies of food security in Eritrea, provided donors with reports to which they could respond at a higher volume than if the information came directly from ERA, REST, or ORA. ERD's relationship with and commitment to these indigenous agencies allowed them to access information more comprehensively and consistently than would have been the case in ERD's absence.

Although ERD adopted a low profile in public, it was active behind the scenes in making known to donor governments the humanitarian plight of civilians in Eritrea and Tigray.

The Structure and Themes of the History

Apart from relying on indigenous implementation capacity, since it was operational throughout the 1980s, an important feature of ERD is that it spans the re-working of North-South relations outlined above. That is, from a cold war system based upon nation-state sovereignty to an emerging balance of power characterised by the enhanced role of NGOs, in which such things as the principle of non-interference, especially in relation to humanitarian aid, is less firmly supported. Apart from its intrinsic merits, unravelling the history of ERD therefore provides an important opportunity to document this transition and judge the present direction of humanitarian politics.

Part of the difficulty in writing this history is that within a complex emergency there are numerous intersecting actors, agendas and underlying pressures. Moreover, although united around a humanitarian mandate, ERD had nine core members between which important differences over policy and approach existed. A work of this type has, of necessity, to be selective if a coherent sense of analysis is to be maintained. ERD's development has been divided into distinct historical stages which, it can be argued, constitute definite historical moments. That is, the early years of ERD from 1981 to 1983; the internationalisation of the crisis between 1984 and 1986; the growing ascendancy of the Fronts from 1987 and 1989; and, finally, the end of the war and phasing out of ERD between 1990 and 1993. The chapter format roughly follows this structure. In each of these stages, we have concentrated on those institutions, events and issues which it is felt best illustrates the essence and debates of each period. It has not been possible, or desirable, to produce an exhaustive chronology of the contribution of each of ERD's members or the indigenous relief associations.

(a) The Importance of Indigenous Political Structures

The book begins by looking at those internal factors which were necessary for the subsequent development of ERD. That is, the emergence in Eritrea and Tigray during the 1970s of a political practice amongst the Fronts which linked the provision of public welfare with mass political mobilization. Part of this practice involved the creation of relief associations, that is, the Eritrean Relief Association (ERA) and the Relief Society of Tigray (REST) for the purpose of accessing international humanitarian aid and reallocating internal resources. The relative efficiency of the integrated and participatory disaster management systems that the Fronts and their relief associations developed have already been mentioned briefly. ERD became a conduit of outside assistance for these structures and enjoyed their support. The result was an NGO relief operation of a scale and type with few parallels. The other necessary factor behind the emergence of ERD was the long standing animosity between Sudan and Ethiopia and the fears on the part of the former that the war would increase the flow of refugees into Sudan. Such factors effectively allowed the violation of Ethiopian sovereignty from Sudanese territory. From its inception, the CBO had the tacit agreement of the Sudanese state.

Despite a supportive local context, during the late 1970s and early 1980s, the international community was not favourably disposed to cross-border assistance. Initial CBO activity was largely the prerogative of Swedish Church Relief (SCR) and Norwegian Church Aid (NCA). Following the formation of ERD in 1981, this Scandinavian predominance continued for a further couple of years. During this period, ERD faced many difficulties including problems in raising official relief aid and the misgiving of other NGOs and partner agencies working in Ethiopia. The World Council of Churches (WCC) and the Lutheran World Federation (LWF), for example, out of concern for antagonising or otherwise compromising the Ethiopian Churches, gave no assistance. The UN, EC, USAID and many European donor governments were also unsympathetic and, especially USAID and the EC, had differing interests in the region. Such pressures dictated that ERD adopt a limited humanitarian mandate on the basis of an agreement between Sudan Council of Churches (SCC) and NCA. SCC, essentially, provided a local umbrella under which ERD could operate.

(b) Western Humanitarian Politics

In discussing ERD's relief mandate, it is argued that Western humanitarian politics revolve around a tension between 'neutrality' and 'involvement'. While situations vary, one can partly define this opposition as, on the one hand, actions limited to discrete, non-political and strictly humanitarian assistance, while on the other, ideas associated with advocacy or lobbying around one particular position, or set of positions, together with the provision of a wider range of help including development assistance and institution building. Another way of describing this contradiction is that the neutral approach usually attempts to work around indigenous political institutions with the primary humanitarian aim of saving lives. Involvement, however, is more concerned with seeking ways to work through indigenous institutions on a broader programme to reduce vulnerability. While not mutually exclusive, there is a tension between these two approaches. Within a complex emergency neutrality, for example, is often under pressure from sections of the relief community which seek greater commitment to one side or another, and from indigenous political structures which either demand association or accuse the humanitarian agency of partisan behaviour.

Prior to the ending of the cold war, the global balance, especially the dominance of sovereignty as a means of organising foreign policy, meant that a non-political or neutral stance to humanitarian assistance in conflict situations predominated, or at least, was required by donor governments. Although this still holds sway today, since the mid-1980s, the weakening of sovereignty has seen the issue of involvement, especially amongst some sections of the NGO community, move nearer to the fore and enter the realm of public debate.

Both neutrality and involvement have positive and negative attributes in terms of offering a framework for approaching complex emergencies. During most of the 1980s, ERD sought to adopt a neutral stance for its work. As the above overview suggests, in terms of attracting reluctant donor support to a sensitive cause, ERD's performance must be judged a success. ERD's neutrality, however, was compromised by the single factor which furnished the strength of the operation. That is, its reliance upon indigenous relief agencies. The work of ERA and REST, for example, would not have been possible without the material, institutional and political support of the Fronts. The response of ERD to this dilemma was to emphasise the efficiency and humanitarian credentials of ERA and REST as a means of playing down this connection. To a significant extent, ERA and REST were themselves portrayed as 'neutral' by ERD. To the degree that this view became accepted currency within the international community, therein lies a weakness of neutrality as a policy approach. While being able to access unwilling donor support, for example, it is weak on the internal analysis of indigenous political structures which are important and determinant factors. Arguably, it is around such structures that policy should be consciously woven. Towards the end of the 1980s, with the growing political ascendancy of the Fronts, this weakness became more manifest.

(c) The Internationalisation of Public Welfare

During the early 1980s, ERD began to change from a basically Scandinavian operation to an international consortium. This trend increasingly placed the original mandate under pressure, especially the umbrella role of SCC. This situation was brought to a head by a worsening of the humanitarian crisis during the mid-1980s and what can be described as the internationalisation of public welfare following a rapid expansion of foreign NGO activity.

From January 1984 to October 1985 when ERD was re-established as an international consortium, ERD operated without a formally agreed mandate. It was a period, moreover, of great change. Following the media exposure of 1984, the most important event was the support of the CBO by USAID and the EC. ERD neutrality shielded donors from the political consequences of their acknowledging the plight of civilians in non-government areas. The very fact of this assistance, however, was tantamount to a tacit recognition of the Fronts, or at least, that the Fronts controlled definite territory outside of the government's domain. More formal recognition, in the sense of direct contacts and negotiations between the Fronts and donors, would not develop until 1990. In some respects, donor assistance to the CBO, together with the increase in the number of NGOs working cross-border, can be seen as signalling the end of the cold war in the Horn. That is, it denoted a willingness by Western governments and the EC, although not the UN, to quietly disregard Ethiopian sovereignty. The existence of a low profile ERD allowed this development which, by the end of the 1980s, had become routinised.

When ERD was re-established in 1985, it was on the basis of NCA taking the lead administrative role. ERD, for its part, had no legal identity within Sudan and operated as a consequence, but not a formal part, of NCA's country agreement. Although a restricted humanitarian mandate was reaffirmed, albeit more broadly based since in included rehabilitation and transport costs, the debate within ERD highlighted the growing tension between neutrality and involvement. This was underscored by the fact that until the late 1980s ERA and REST were highly critical of ERD's lack of advocacy and its unwillingness to take a public stance on the effects of the war. This concern was despite the evidence that it was only ERD's discretion which allowed it to attract donor support. In order to overcome this contradiction and to establish a wider role, some ERD members, for example, sought bilateral development links with what by then had become known as the implementing agencies (IAs). This allowed some advocacy and public campaigning to develop during the mid 1980s. This was, however, strictly an individual agency responsibility.

(d) From Crisis to Stabilisation

The events of the mid-1980s saw a dramatic increase in the amount of humanitarian assistance being delivered through the CBO. At this stage, ERD was still the monopoly supplier. The increase in aid flow had a marked organisational impact upon ERD as well as ERA and REST. The latter especially, after a period of crisis had succeeded in establishing an adept and integrated system of disaster management. By 1987, the CBO was becoming more effective in meeting the requests of the IAs. As a consequence, the relief structures within Eritrea and Tigray, while not being able to prevent a continuing erosion of the asset base, had begun to stabilise the immediate food crisis amongst the civilian population. Within Sudan, buoyed by a feeling of professionalism, the ERD administration began to assert its independence from NCA and the existing ERD structure. At the same time, in seeking to establish a more formal relationship with the IAs, it came into conflict with ERA. This situation did not normalise until 1989 when NCA formally took responsibility for ERD activities in Sudan.

Coinciding with the stabilisation of the crisis, and after a period of non-collaboration during the mid 1980s, from 1987 the Fronts began to push back the Dergue forces. This had a number of consequences. It progressively increased the area and population under Front administration thereby creating new demands on the CBO. During this period, while remaining an important conduit, ERD lost its position as the monopoly supplier of food aid. Additional avenues of involvement, however, began to open up. Since the relief systems on both sides began to come into increasing contact, calls for aid coordination across the lines became more common. Some ERD members had been involved in behind the scenes peace diplomacy since the early 1980s. The Fronts' military successes during 1987 and 1988, however, had the effect of making all parties less inclined to a peaceful solution. This prompted renewed diplomatic efforts and ERD experience became an increasingly important factor in the negotiations to come.

(e) International Substitution of Indigenous Resource Capacity.

Between 1981 and 1991, ERD made available around 3/4 million mt of food aid, perhaps half the total, for use within Eritrea and Tigray. The total cash value of this food, together with the programmes supported by ERD members, amounted to around 350 million US dollars. While the existing literature generally agrees that the relief programme has not induced dependency amongst rural producers, this is less clear if one considers the possibility of a wider economic or institutional dependence. Given that the Fronts developed a political practice that combined the provision of public welfare with mass mobilization, it is argued that until the mid 1980s they provided the IAs with the bulk of their food aid and transport requirements. From this period, although still locally managed, the international relief system began to substitute for this provision as it became more efficient in meeting IA requests. This highlights a number of important issues, such as, what effect did CBO humanitarian assistance have on the dynamics of the war, and to what extent has substitution been transformed into international dependence in the post-war period.

(f) ERD and the War

Towards the end of the 1980s, ERD members became increasingly concerned as to whether ERD assistance was a contributory factor in the continuation of the war. While the direct military appropriation of relief assistance was never an intrinsic part of the political practice of the Fronts, through the fungibility of aid, the increasing resource substitution by the CBO probably did release Front energies for the war effort. This process was only possible, however, due to the participatory nature of the public welfare structures that had been established and the high degree of political mobilization amongst the civilian population. From this perspective, ERD's concern appears somewhat misplaced.

Any relief assistance within the context of an internal war will, simply by keeping people alive, have political and war related consequences. This is because the civilian population is simultaneously both a source of political support and a deliberate counter-insurgency target. Strictly speaking, it is impossible to be neutral in such circumstances. Assistance to one side is invariably seen as partisan by the other. ERD's concern would be more usefully phrased by asking whether its assistance was channelled through structures able to maximize its humanitarian impact. The answer has to be an unequivocal yes. This can be demonstrated, for example, if one compares the public welfare policies of the Fronts with the predatory practices of the neighbouring Sudan Peoples Liberation Front (SPLA). It must be stated, however, that given the tendency for those occupying the neutral ground to downplay political analysis, ERD's positive association with the Fronts and their relief associations was more by accident than design.

(g) The Phase Out of ERD and Re-assertion of Bilateral Relations

In practice, as a working consortium ERD did not survive the end of the war. During 1990 with the operation of the Ethiopia based Joint Relief Programme into Tigray and, especially the opening of Massawa in 1991 and the subsequent decision by USAID to route all aid shipments through Ethiopia, the CBO dramatically scaled down in favour of more conventional, UN managed supply routes. With the ending of the war in 1991 it was decided to phase out ERD by June 1993 at the latest, and in the meantime, to divide the remaining programme between Eritrea and Ethiopia. Without the countervailing pressure of the war many of the differences that separated ERD members quickly surfaced. It is in the context of the debate surrounding the phasing out of ERD that the difference between neutrality and involvement, particularly within Ethiopia, was most clearly put.

The end of the war brought together two contrasting modes of NGO operation within Ethiopia. REST is representative of a participatory approach developed in the context of a policy dialogue with the existing political authority. Within Ethiopia, however, most NGOs and church agencies have a more bureaucratic, centrally directed style of work. Moreover, historically they have little experience of policy debate, having generally attempted to keep clear of the Dergue. During the first part of 1992, a few ERD members advocated that in phasing out, ERD should attempt to establish a forum in Addis Ababa for reconciliation and policy dialogue. The issue of the relations between the new government and the donor and NGO communities, both in Ethiopia and Eritrea, was one of the suggested parts of this dialogue. The majority of members preferred, however, to maintain a more traditional and politically neutral stance, in many cases re-establishing bilateral links with long-standing Ethiopian church partners.

(h) Neutrality or Involvement

With regard to the opposition between neutrality and involvement, it can be argued that the positive attributes of neutrality have lessened with the end of the cold war. It is increasingly realised that, more than ever, NGOs and the international community need to discover new and innovative ways to positively engage the political reality of the African crisis. The agenda set forth by those seeking dialogue and involvement in the phasing out of ERD is a striking example of this thinking. The evidence of Somalia and Bosnia is that although the principle of sovereignty has been weakened, the West and the UN is responding to complex emergencies simply by developing 'neutral' institutions of humanitarian intervention which, if necessary, are protected by military force. Since this form of mediation avoids political engagement with the reality it confronts and eschews the need for supporting participatory and accountable structures, it has, arguably, little chance of improving matters.[22]

The history of ERD provides a singular insight into the changing nature of North-South relations and the key debates within the NGO community. The best of ERD was its involvement with indigenous political and humanitarian structures and its steadfast commitment to the politically disadvantaged within the international arena. As such, its experience is at the forefront of the call for a new framework for humanitarian assistance in the era of complex emergencies.

CHAPTER TWO

Public Welfare and the Politics of National Liberation

The Essential Foundations of the Cross-Border Operation

The manner in which the EPLF and TPLF fought the long-standing armed struggle in Eritrea and Ethiopia calls into question the conventional wisdom on the consequences of war and famine. That is, that war is the antithesis of development. Although the contribution of counterinsurgency activities to famine is increasingly acknowledged, what is less widely understood is that in the Horn, the Fronts successfully turned social dislocation and privation into a means of mass mobilization and political consolidation. In other words, the war, while visiting untold suffering on the Eritrean and Tigrayan peoples, also provided the basis for a process of internal development and social change having few parallels in contemporary Africa.

In writing the history of ERD, it is clear that the cross-border operation would not have taken place, or at least would have followed a much more limited trajectory, without (a) the active cooperation and support of the EPLF and TPLF and the relief organisations they established and (b) a background of long-standing regional animosity which effectively sanctioned the violation of Ethiopian sovereignty from Sudanese territory. The cooperation of the Fronts was of great importance and signifies the emergence, during the 1970s, of strong indigenous systems of disaster management in Eritrea and Tigray. These systems, with their emphasis on participation, planning and social and economic analysis, were not only in advance of the main approaches amongst international relief agencies; the political imperatives of the Fronts, which had public welfare as a central part, stood in strong contrast to the predatory relationship between combatant and non-combatant populations characteristic of successive Ethiopian regimes and, more widely, the logic of internal war that is, unfortunately, all too prevalent in Africa today.

A full appreciation of indigenous political response to public welfare and internal war has yet to be written. So far, much of the literature has concentrated on the role of the international community.[1-4] Given its importance to the success or failure of relief operations, the need for such internal political analysis is vital. In order to understand the subsequent development of ERD and its role, it is necessary to briefly consider the public welfare policies of the EPLF and TPLF.

In the solidarity literature that has grown up around the Fronts there is a good deal of material demonstrating their effectivity and organisational skills. Less often encountered are references to how the Fronts were able to sustain themselves economically and, at the same time, pursue a programme of political mobilization. The argument developed in this section is that the available evidence suggests that the Fronts, using similar strategies but with different aims, established a political economy of liberation capable of simultaneously providing effective famine relief, engendering political support and pressing the war. The strength of this economy was its essential duality in which political support and public welfare were organically linked, often through the same organisations, in a mutually reinforcing structure: public assistance cemented political support and growing political success facilitated increased humanitarian aid. When pitched against the divisive politics of the opposition, this 'virtuous circle' has had proven effect. Therein, however, lie the seeds of present concerns. That is, the ability of such a directed structure to manage a transition to peace and reconstruction.

Public Welfare and National Liberation

For both the EPLF and TPLF, a political economy of liberation had it roots in the political struggles following the end of World War II which eventually came to fruition in the 1970s. In the case of the EPLF, apart from the war, its approach to public assistance was shaped by its emergence from, and political struggle with, the Eritrean Liberation

Front (ELF) during the 1960s and 1970s. The ELF was formed in 1961, having origins which can partly be traced to the Muslim League of the 1940s. Initially, it was an anti-feudal, pro-Arab and religious organisation gathering most of its support from the Western Lowlands. As an organisation, it began to expand during the mid-1960s. This was helped by the fall of the Abboud regime in Sudan which saw the new Nimiery government sanctioning ELF activity from within Sudan. In addition, the soliciting of Israeli support by the Ethiopian government served to swing sections of Arab opinion behind Eritrea. The final factor was that, again having reference to earlier opposition movements, highland Christians began to join the ELF in increasing numbers. By the end of the 1960s, the ELF had become a force to be reckoned with.

The growth of the ELF, especially the wide social and economic origins of its membership, served to highlight a number of internal contradictions. These included that (a) its leadership resided outside Eritrea (b) it was pro-Arab and asserted a Muslim identity despite that half the population of Eritrea was Christian, and (c) its guerilla army was divided between five autonomous regions and, in effect, constituted five tribal armies.[5] During the latter part of the 1960s, these tensions led to splits and purges which eventually saw the emergence of the EPLF in 1970. This struggle was a complex process and is not easily reduced to a straight opposition between conservative and progressive opinion. Before its effective demise in 1981, to a certain extent, political struggle also saw the marginalisation of the more traditional and tribal elements within the ELF. It even developed its own public welfare programmes. During the 1970s, a political dynamic emerged which involved periods of alliance and conflict linking the two Fronts.

By 1969, the progressive forces had succeeded in unifying three of the five regions and had created a leadership internal to Eritrea. As a result, the ELF lost all influence in the Highland plateaux. The political programme developed by the EPLF during the 1970s, was argued to be representative of a second wave of African independence.[6] The first wave, from which the ELF drew much of its political doctrine, was associated with the conventional nationalism of decolonisation which placed the need for political independence ahead of social transformation. By contrast, the second wave brought these two factors together: rather than being separate issues, national and social questions had to be solved simultaneously. This was an important development since, rather than an afterthought as reflected in much of African post-colonial politics, it placed public welfare at the heart of the political agenda.

In relation to famine, part of this fusion was an analysis of the historical susceptibility of Eritrea and Ethiopia to social dislocation and famine as resulting from natural and, importantly, political factors, such as, the increasing impact of counterinsurgency violence and predatory war preparations since the 1960s.[7] That it would be more than a decade before a similar analysis was respectable in Western academic circles is worthy of note. The clear evidence that civilians were increasingly having to endure hardship and impoverishment as a result of deliberate government action forged the perception that not only was there a need for effective defense, it was vital that the civilian population was assisted if the mould of past political action was to be broken.[8] The revolution, in contrast to the policies pursed by the Ethiopian government, became "a movement with profoundly human aims."[9]

As the effects of counterinsurgency began to be felt, especially on the nomadic population, the responsibility for an increasing number of displaced and destitute fell on the ELF during the latter part of the 1960s. The ELF, described in EPLF sources as an organisation dependent upon foreign assistance and unable to overcome ethnic divisions and personal interests, was argued to have neither the will nor capacity to properly address this problem.[10] Reflecting, to some extent, today's predatory guerilla movements in South Sudan, Mozambique and Angola,[11] despite having its own relief wing, it is asserted that the ELF alienated large sections of the population due to its un-reciprocated exactions of food and assistance. These allegations may be overstated, the picture, however, is useful since it serves to locate the EPLF's commitment to self-reliance and public assistance.

Self-Reliance and Reciprocity

Self-reliance is more than a slogan. Since it implies popular participation in problem solving, it is primarily a question of organisation. In the case of the EPLF and TPLF, this involved establishing a system of civilian administration which could serve as both a means of organisation and a channel for voluntary material and political support. The economy of internal war is dependent upon the productive capacity of the civilian population. For this reason, civilians are the main target of counterinsurgency campaigns. When, as under semi-subsistence conditions, productive assets are thinly spread, such campaigns can assume genocidal proportions. Since the process of political evolution within the EPLF and TPLF had propelled them to harness civilian productive capacity through voluntary means rather than exaction, it underscored the need for organisation, education and civilian assistance.

From the mid-1970s, in Eritrea and Tigray zonal geographical structures were created, in which elective village committees were linked through to area organisations. Where they were controlled, large towns had a similar elective administration. Interconnecting with these vertical structures, both Fronts developed civilian departments responsible for the main aspects of public policy: health, education, transport, economy, social welfare, and so forth. For example, the EPLF's Agricultural Department carried out programmes in water supply, afforestation, soil conservation, terracing, seed collection and agricultural extension. The TPLF's Agricultural Department initiated projects in animal husbandry, poultry, irrigation and afforestation.[12] Finally, the EPLF and TPLF established horizontal mass political organisations based on the main socio-economic groups, for example, women, peasants, workers and professionals. Not only did the mass organisations provide a link between administrative and public structures, they were the means through which more ambitious social issues, such as land reform and women's equality, were progressed.

The pursuit of liberation through self-reliance demands structures through which civilian productive capacity and political support can be voluntarily accessed. In the case of Eritrea, contributions destined for civilian relief were handled by the village committees. Contributions to the military struggle, due to their more political nature, went through the mass associations. Assistance which had not passed through such popular channels would not be accepted.[13] It should be realised that without this voluntarism, the virtuous circle collapses. Literacy programmes and political education meant that civilians could understand the nature of their situation. Voluntarism, however, demanded reciprocity on the part of the EPLF and TPLF. In addition to a programme of political and economic reform favourable to the main agricultural and commercial classes, reforms which were vulnerable to the vicissitudes of the war, reciprocity necessitated urgent attention to public welfare. Early developments in health, for example, meant that toward the end of the 1970s, despite the conflict, both Eritrea and Tigray had achieved historically unprecedented levels of health coverage.[14] In 1975, the EPLF was spending 20% of its total budget on medicines, 80% of which were being dispensed to the civilians within its jurisdiction.[15]

Reciprocity also involved food aid and other relief assistance. In the early 1970s, the EPLF established the principle of fighters sharing their rations with destitute war victims. As social dislocation grew, this direct assistance became more systematic, with the Fronts devoting what transport and other resources that could be spared for relief purposes.[16]

It is likely that up to the mid-1980s, the Fronts and the civilian population were supplying the bulk of the limited amounts of food relief available in Eritrea and Tigray. In Tigray, for example, in 1983, as famine began to peak but before international assistance became significant, the TPLF with civilian help managed to supply 55% of the 11,200 mt of food aid distributed.[17] By this stage, however, this was only a fraction of the assistance that was necessary.

The Economy of Liberation

While ultimately dependent upon the civilian population, self-reliance and the principle of reciprocity demanded that the Fronts establish an economy which provided a strategic resource base independent from an already hard-pressed civilian population. Although Middle East support for the ELF, for example, can be readily discerned, both the EPLF and TPLF avoided direct dependence on foreign political backers. For both the EPLF and TPLF, the extensive Ethiopian losses on the battlefield were a major source of military hardware. Information on the nature and extent of the Front economies, however, is sketchy and impressionistic. Despite the fact that a number of sources of income can be identified, material has yet to be released which would enable a confident quantitative appraisal to be made.

With regard to the EPLF, contributions from the mass associations within and, especially, outside Eritrea were very important. In the mid-1970s, there were an estimated 450,000 exiles, 270,000 living in Ethiopia and the remaining 180,000 scattered in the Middle East, Europe and USA. From this period, the support of the latter group, especially, was increasingly mobilized.[18] In the early 1980s, REST also established a network of overseas support committees which supplied material assistance.

Through the participation of fighters, both the Fronts undertook significant agricultural operations. The EPLF also leased some of its trucks for commercial use in Sudan as a means of earning foreign currency. The EPLF was engaged in cereal, vegetable, coffee and fruit production. In 1975, with the help of the civilian population, it was said to be producing 50% of its cereal and vegetable needs. At this time, 70% of the fruit which the EPLF grew was consumed by the Front, the remainder being sold commercially.[19] It was also common for poultry and goats to be reared in military encampments. The TPLF farmed extensively up to around 1987, having sufficient fighters, themselves drawn from the peasantry, to devote to this task.[20] From this period, the large-scale operations necessary in the final stages of the war saw a reduction of such activities. Additional cereals together with essentials such as sugar and tea were regularly imported, especially by the EPLF, through Sudan. The TPLF was more easily able to engage in the internal purchase of grain from surplus areas within Tigray.

Both Fronts encouraged commercial activity either establishing markets themselves or, as in the case of TPLF, seeking strategic alliances with merchants and commercial farmers loyal to the Front. From the early days, the importance of maintaining commercial activity within Tigray as a means of resisting politically induced famine was fully realised. Unlike the Ethiopian government's high tax policy,[21] the Fronts imposed a progressive, graded system of taxes to encourage trade. Locally produced food in Tigray, for example, was not taxed and essential traded items only lightly. Taxes would also vary from area to area, reflecting local conditions.[22]

Significant amounts of foreign exchange were saved and a measure of self-sufficiency achieved by the Fronts through their extensive network of cottage industries whose facilities were cut into the sides of mountains or hidden under the tree cover of the valleys. Workshops carried out the repair of vehicles, watches and radios together with the production of spare parts, school materials and text books, processed foods, plastic sandals and sanitary towels. Despite these various forms of income, however, in the last analysis, the Fronts were dependent on contributions in kind from the civilian populations of Eritrea and Tigray. To a large extent, reciprocity involved the reallocation and moulding of this assistance into programmes of public provision.

Relief Associations and the Strategy Toward the International Humanitarian System

It has been argued that the political economy established by the EPLF and TPLF is singular in its reinforcement of political support through public assistance. It is also clear, however, that the surplus within these war economies was small and their ability to meet both the escalating military demand after the Dergue's seizure of power in 1974, and manage the resulting growth in social dislocation was increasingly strained. The problem which presented itself was of a twofold character: firstly, the disaster management capacity of the Fronts' civilian departments had to be improved. This would involve significant organisational evolution. Secondly, since demand increasingly outstripped available resources as large sections of the civilian population ceased production, it made necessary the formation of relief associations responsible, amongst other things, for approaching international humanitarian agencies for assistance. The establishment of the Eritrean Relief Association (1975) and the Relief Society of Tigray (1978) are significant in that their emergence is co-terminus with the main push for social and political reform in Eritrea and Tigray respectively. It would be a mistake therefore to see them as a late addition to this process: they were an organic part.

Before the establishment of ERA, by way of example, is briefly described, it is necessary to define the broad thrust of Front foreign policy. The main aim of external policy was to reduce political isolation while, at the same time, avoiding the trap of becoming dependent on one political backer or camp. A mistake particularly associated with first wave nationalists. This led to a pragmatic approach which sought at the international level "to modify the very conditions of the struggle."[23] With regard to the EPLF, this is illustrated in its approach to the former Soviet Union. From the mid-1970s, Soviet military support became increasingly important to the Dergue. Although having serious disagreements with Soviet policy, the EPLF refused to brand the Soviet Union an outright enemy.[24] Instead, it mounted a campaign to change the position of the other countries within the socialist bloc. This strategy led to the first weakening in Eritrea's isolation. In 1978, for example, the EPLF opened an office in Algeria and secured similar recognition in Guinea-Bissau and Mozambique. In the same year, although having military personnel in Ethiopia, Cuba expressed concern with Ethiopian policy and declined to assist the war in the North. The second and arguably the most important weakening of isolation began with the activities of ERA.

By the mid-1970s, the importance of relief assistance within Eritrea was well established.[25] Growing dislocation prompted an initial agreement between the ELF and EPLF that ERA should be created as a single organisation to publicize the effects of the war and appeal for external assistance. Between March and September 1975, when the original Board resigned, trips were made to Aden, Beirut, Damascus and Iraq, together with a number of Western countries, and initial contacts made with several international agencies including the ICRC. Eritrean exiles in Sudan were also organised and contributed a shipment of sorghum.

One of the reasons for the resignation of the Board concerned problems with the ELF.[26] It is alleged that it wished the committee structure of ERA to be firmly under political control. This was opposed by the ERA Board and the EPLF which recognised the political importance of a more independent body. In response to this split, the ELF subsequently formed the Eritrean Red Cross and Crescent Society (ERCCS) as its relief wing. In December 1975, ERA was asked by the EPLF to re-establish itself and present a strategy for increasing the supply of urgently required relief assistance.

ERA recommended that the West, as opposed to the Middle East, should be the main focus of its external activities.[27] The reason for this was that in the West the public was capable of organising independent of government. The Vietnam War, for example, had shown that public opinion could be mobilized to directly counter government policy. In planning relief requests "the public must be the target and its capacity must never be under-estimated whatever the policy of its government may be."[28] This was important given the high level of official support that Ethiopia was attracting. At this time, since most of the main humanitarian agencies in Europe and the USA were either church organised or church related, the main church networks were an important target. A number of preliminary contacts had already been made either directly or through the Sudan Council of Churches (SCC). These included the World Council of Churches (WCC), Brot Fur Die Welt (BFW), Christian Aid (CA) and Norwegian Church Aid (NCA).

It was clearly realised, however, that the central problem in sustaining a successful public campaign in the West was the complexity of the Eritrean situation.[29] It was a political emergency having origins in the competing claims of Ethiopian sovereignty and Eritrean self-determination. Because international agencies were wary of association with political causes, it necessitated careful thought on how the origins and the aims of the Eritrean case were presented. In this respect, Eritrean exiles in the West, already valued for their material contributions, also acquired a vital role in helping publicize the Eritrean situation. Additional sensitivity arose from the fact that, due to ELF associations, the EPLF was perceived by some as an Arab influenced movement, intent on spreading Islam into Christian Ethiopia. The strategy argued that any campaign should be directed to counter these weaknesses. In this respect, it was indicated that WCC had been approached through Sudan's SCC which, in effect, had acted in place of an indigenous national church.

Finally, the growing need for external relief assistance demanded a clear understanding of ERA's relationship with the EPLF. ERA argued that the EPLF should act as its guardian and guarantor of its credibility as a humanitarian organisation. The EPLF should appoint an auditor and, until a public assembly could be organised for the task, it should also nominate ERA's Board Members and its Field Coordinator. Apart from stipulating that ERA should be accountable to donors for all assistance given, the strategy envisaged that ERA would establish a system of village and regional relief committees which would work in association with the civilian departments of the EPLF. In practice, as we shall see, ERA did not establish such a clearly defined internal organisation. To a large extent, it worked through the structures and institutions established by the EPLF.

REST was established in 1978 with similar aims to ERA and, although ERA had the largest network, both developed external branches for support work in Europe and the USA. Apart from material assistance, these played an important role in mobilizing public opinion in the early and mid-1980s.

The Development of Relief Assistance in Eritrea and Tigray

The severity of the famine in the mid-1980s, resulted in both ERA and REST increasing their organisational and logistical capacity. In the case of ERA, despite its 1976 proposal to establish separate village and regional relief committees working in association with the EPLF, such a distinct structure did not emerge and research on relief needs, for example, which took place regularly from 1978, was handled by the Department of Social Affairs.[30-31] ERA mainly concentrated on mobilizing and delivering external relief aid.[32] REST, on the other hand, was involved in the assessment of relief needs since its inception.[33] By around 1983, however, ERA, due to the growing crisis, also became involved in needs assessment. Moreover, the method of food targeting employed by ERA and REST could now be seen as broadly similar.

Reflecting the different conditions within Eritrea and Tigray, ERA and REST related in different operational ways to their respective Fronts. At the risk of over-simplification, the EPLF was distinguished by its consolidation of a liberated area, including towns, which was defended and expanded by means of conventional battles. Although both the EPLF and TPLF developed extensive logistical operations and food targeting systems based upon village committees and the use of socio-economic information to distinguish those families in most need; from 1975, the EPLF was characterised by its establishment of internal self-managing camps for the displaced.[34] The TPLF on the other hand, controlled a larger, changing sphere of influence, surrounding government held towns, and engaged in mobile guerilla warfare rather than conventional battles. From the early 1980s, TPLF relief policy was defined by the management of large-scale migration and repatriation and the internal purchase and allocation of surplus sorghum.

While having similar aims, ERA was more of a logistical organisation geared to the supply of relief goods to the civilian departments of the EPLF which organised the affected populations. Together with the supply of relief commodities, REST, on the other hand, with the support of the TPLF had a greater direct organisational role in relation to those in need.[35]

The Participatory Targeting of Food Aid

In both Eritrea and Tigray[36] village committees played an important role in the collection of socio-economic information on household productive capacity and needs. ERA, for example, working with the village committees regularly collected such information on a standard form. Apart from location, this included the names of all family members in the village; ages; clan names; children; marital status; numbers of dependents; total number of family heads in a household; and so on, together with an appraisal of existing and past assets, such as, family income; site and size of farm; livestock owned; livestock lost and relief provisions distributed to the household. With this information, which was checked by the EPLF, an assessment of those households in need was made in discussion and with the agreement of the village committee. The committee kept a copy of the form and the original was passed through to ERA's central body where the separate reports were integrated into an overall needs assessment.

In the early 1980s, for purposes of distribution in Eritrea, ERA followed the EPLF division into five zones. Once ERA had a consignment of food aid, a distribution plan was passed down the district and village committees of the zone, until the beneficiaries were notified of the time and place of the distribution. Only those notified would be eligible, and the amounts received would be duly recorded, in the presence of the village committee and EPLF, and the records passed back to produce a distribution report.[37]

In both Eritrea and Tigray, this method of food distribution was essentially pro-active in that it took account of expected trends and, unlike the collection of nutritional stress indicators favoured by many international relief agencies, it favoured attempts to conserve assets. Moreover, prior identification of beneficiaries is credited with reducing some of the worry at times of scarcity. The success of the system, which operated in different forms from the end of the 1970s until the finish of the war in 1991,[38] was largely dependent on the fact that it built on the participatory structures of civilian administration which in Eritrea were established by the EPLF and in Tigray were developed by the TPLF from a pre-existing local organisation called the Baito system. In Eritrea and Tigray, relief distributions were community managed and linked through relations of accountability to the political authority. As a form of relief management, it contrasted with the bureaucratic, centrally organised, family focused systems which were in operation on the government side.

The Political Use of Food Aid

For international agencies a key issue in consigning relief supplies to ERA and REST was concern over the possible diversion of that aid to military use. Donor governments frequently imposed accounting criteria on the cross-border operation in excess of that required in a conventional emergency. The result was that throughout the 1980s, a good deal of ERD, ERA and REST activity was consumed in furnishing monitoring reports and accounts to indicate how the aid was used. While onerous and one-sided, it can be argued that this pressure to continually prove accountability was practically useful in establishing the international credibility of ERA and REST. From an analytical point of view, however, the above analysis would suggest that concern was somewhat misplaced.

Political support for the Fronts largely sprang from their ability to defend civilian populations and meet their economic and welfare needs. From the mid-1970s, the possibility of supplying foreign relief assistance was seen as an important adjunct to this relation of reciprocity. Hence the conscious decision to establish relief associations. In fact, due to the international isolation of Eritrea and Tigray, foreign relief assistance became an important psychological boost for the stressed civilian population.[39] It indicated that some, at least, knew of their plight. ERA, for example, had the freedom to advertise the foreign origin of its relief supplies which was discussed with beneficiaries and on radio broadcasts. A perceptive visitor in the early 1980s noted that the distribution of foreign relief assistance gave the EPLF political credibility,

> ...the only 'trick' I have seen (the EPLF) use ... is being very helpful to the operation. This, I think, hardly amounts to something we should ask them to stop doing.[40]

It can be argued that the diversion of relief commodities not only contradicted the political logic of the Fronts, should it have occurred on any significant scale, it would have undermined their political base and hence the ability to press their aims. The historic and political significance of the Front's welfare policies have yet to be fully appreciated. It is clear that in choosing to assist civilians with various public welfare programmes, they effectively reversed the Asian model of guerilla warfare in which the rural producers were the source of material support for the political and military movement.[41] To the degree that this shift is representative of the second wave of liberation, it would suggest that this approach is of central importance in charting an indigenous solution to the wider African crisis.

Although the direct appropriation and control of food aid by the military establishment was not a feature of the Fronts' political dynamic, it can be argued that international relief assistance did allow them to stabilise populations and expand their resource base. In this context, fungibility or the ability to redeploy resources freed in one area to another, has to be taken into account. In so far as the CBO reduced the Fronts' burden of public assistance, the principle of the fungibility would suggest that their military capability would be enhanced.

Fungibility, however, together with voluntary civilian donations, should not be confused with direct military appropriation or diversion of relief assistance which was a significant practice of the Ethiopian government (see Chapter Five). Rather than the extensive cooperation which the relief associations and Fronts extended to the international community, direct military appropriation would have been tantamount to weakening the participatory relief management structures which had been established. Civilian productive capacity would have declined even further and the levels of suffering been worse. Given the kinship ties between fighters and the peasantry direct appropriation would, therefore, have undermined the Fronts' political base and hence its aspirations.

The Position of Sudan and the Sudan Council of Churches

This chapter began with the proposition that the cross-border relief operation would not have been possible without the active cooperation of the Fronts and their relief associations. It is also the case, however, that successive Sudanese governments chose to keep the border open and, eventually, to allow ERD to operate from Khartoum. As ERA put it in 1975, the position of Sudan was "paramount in all our relief operations".[42] The several occasions when the border was temporarily closed indicates that the Sudanese could have curtailed operations should they have seriously wished to. That they did not, like the political economy of Fronts, is another singular aspect which needs to be briefly considered.

Since the expansionary wars of the 19th century, there has been a long-standing distrust between Sudan and Ethiopia. Although rarely appearing as open conflict, it is a suspicion which even today is manifest in the consolidation of an Islamic fundamentalist regime in Sudan at the same time as attempts to establish secular, democratic regimes in Eritrea and Ethiopia are underway. In recent years, the level of distrust between Sudan and Ethiopia has tended to vary. In the mid-1960s, with the toppling of the Abboud regime, Sudanese opinion swung in favour of the Eritrean struggle following Ethiopian involvement in the first civil war in South Sudan. With the ending of that war in 1972, this support ended and the Khartoum offices of the Eritrean Fronts were temporarily closed.

When the Dergue came to power in 1974, however, Sudan once more lent support to the liberation movements. On several occasions President Nimiery spoke out publicly in support of the Eritrean cause.[43] When ERA was established in 1975, therefore, it was a good time to organise within Sudan. The difficulty, however, was that the Sudanese government preferred the ELF and, during the late 1970s, was active in attempting to broker peace between it and the EPLF. Day to day relations with the Fronts were handled through the Liberation Movement Section of State Security. For the ELF in particular, this was one channel of Middle East financial backing.[44] Besides the regional political linkages that Sudanese support created, it was not without its material gains in the shape of the considerable scope for corruption that the informal taxing of the Fronts' Port Sudan and border activities allowed. Certainly, in 1977, when international agencies first began to work seriously with ERA in a cross-border capacity, although no written records were kept, the operation was known and sanctioned in Sudan at the highest political level.[45]

From the mid 1970s, the increased military activity of the Dergue also produced concerns over the growing number of Eritrean and Tigrayan refugees in Sudan. By the late 1970s, these numbered around half a million, many of whom had settled spontaneously in northern towns.[46] Concern over the economic and security implications of this influx was another factor which disposed the authorities to accept activities, such as cross-border relief, which promised the containment of this situation.[47]

It is in this connection that the position of the Sudan Council of Churches should be examined. It has already been recorded how, in 1975, ERA viewed SCC as a gateway to the WCC and the wider international community. For its part, the Sudanese government, or at least the Commission For Refugees (COR), also held SCC in a particular light. During the late 1970s and early 1980s, SCC was regarded by COR as a leading Sudanese NGO. At this stage, there were no Islamic agencies of any count in North Sudan and, despite being a Christian organisation, the fact that it confined itself to refugee work in the North lessened any religious sensitivity. The elevation of SCC to national significance, however, was also partly political. COR was against the involvement of international NGOs in Sudan's growing refugee problem. As far as practical, it attempted to place SCC in this role.[48] That SCC should play an important part in the initial cross-border relief work and the subsequent formation of ERD in 1981, was therefore to be expected.

Sudan's attitude towards the Eritrean issue began a slow change from 1978. Growing Soviet military assistance to Ethiopia cast doubts on the viability of the liberation struggle and, furthermore, threatened to intensify the refugee influx. The widening rift between the EPLF and ELF, and the effective elimination of the latter in 1981, also served to distance the Sudanese government from the EPLF.[49] In 1982, coinciding with the launch of a fresh Ethiopian offensive, high level meetings began between Sudanese and Ethiopian officials in which the Ethiopians pushed for the closure of the CBO and the handing over of the Eritrean leaders. This is the nearest that the cross-border operation came to being seriously compromised by the Sudanese. In 1983, with the emergence of the Sudan Peoples Liberation Army (SPLA), civil war in South Sudan was again rekindled. Subsequent Ethiopian backing for the SPLA once again swung Sudanese support behind the EPLF and TPLF. From this period until the late 1980s ERD did not encounter any further official pressure.

CHAPTER THREE

The Horn and the Divergence of Donor Policy

WAR AND FAMINE SUMMARY (1975-1983)

(a) Eritrea

The significant decision of the Soviet Union in 1987 to abandon its principal Horn client, Somalia, and militarily assist the Dergue, decisively turned the tide of the Ogaden War against the Somalis. The Soviets replaced the United States as the Ethiopian government's main patron, and the amount of military aid flowing to Ethiopia dramatically increased, commensurately enhancing the government's ability to wreak havoc in Eritrea. By 1977, the EPLF and ELF were in control of roughly 90 per cent of Eritrea. In December 1977, however, an EPLF attack on the port of Massawa was soundly defeated and within half a year the government had launched a withering Soviet assisted counter-attack which, by the end of 1978, resulted in the near collapse of the ELF and the retreat of the EPLF to the Sahel district on the Sudan border.

Between May 1978 and July 1979, five offensives were launched by the Ethiopian government in Eritrea. The tactics used included saturation bombings of civilian centres and animal herds, mass detention, looting, and large scale ground assaults. In December 1979 a further government offensive was mounted which aimed at dislodging the EPLF from its stronghold in Nacfa, but instead the government was pushed back to its headquarters at Afabet. Between 1978 and 1980, between 70,000 and 80,000 people died as a result of the war in Eritrea and the refugee population in Sudan doubled to nearly 420,000. In 1982 the Red Star campaign was launched. This was the most destructive government offensive to date, utilising phosphorous and cluster bombs together with over 120,000 ground troops. By mid-year the Dergue abandoned the failed campaign, but not before approximately 40,000 government troops were killed.

(b) Tigray

From the beginning of the civil war in Tigray in 1975 until 1983, the Ethiopian government launched seven major offensives to check the expansion of the TPLF. Between 1976 and 1978, the nation wide Red Terror Campaign, aimed largely at wiping out urban based popular dissent, was waged with particular ferocity in Tigray. This government campaign drove many Tigrayans to support the newly formed TPLF. During the latter part of the decade, the government prioritised the wars in the Ogaden and Eritrea, and Tigray was relatively unscathed, leaving room for the TPLF to organise.

Two major offensives were launched by the government in Tigray in 1980 and 1983. During the 1980 offensive, the Dergue began to employ counter-population tactics, including the destruction of villages and grain stores, the burning of crops, the killing of cattle, aerial bombardment and the calculated displacement of agrarian communities.[1] One of the largest offensives was conducted in February and March of 1983, when the government attacked western Tigray to damage the economic and agricultural base of the TPLF. At least 100,000 people were displaced in this operation.[2] The TPLF, in coordination with the newly formed Ethiopian People's Democratic Movement (EPDM), launched its own offensive in Tigray and northern Wollo in 1982, leading to gains for these movements during 1983.

In Eritrea and Tigray, by 1983 at least 250,000 casualties had resulted from the war with around 500,000 civilians being made refugees in Sudan. Countless more were internally displaced. The war had contributed to growing famine conditions during the late 1970s and early 1980s. These conditions were more severe in Tigray than in Eritrea.[3] The reasons included (a) climatic changes were less severe in Eritrea than in Tigray (b) a positional war was fought in Eritrea which clearly defined the battle zones, whereas guerrilla warfare made Tigray's front more dispersed and civilian targets consequently more attractive (c) some reconstruction resources were directed to Eritrea as part of the government's counter-insurgency campaign. In Tigray counterinsurgency involved more anti-civilian violence and (d) black market trade continued in government garrison towns in Eritrea, whereas in Tigray trade was greatly restricted.

The Strategic Nature of United States Food Aid

From 1977 until the mid-1980s, the American approach to the crisis in Ethiopia was characterised by reservation and restriction. In this respect, the US position was singular in that the UN and the European Community, together with other Western donors, were generally supportive, in some cases significantly so, of the Ethiopian government. This chapter, amongst other things, examines some of these divergences.

The emphasis of US bilateral aid since the 1940s has been to maintain economic and political stability in friendly countries and to promote short term US foreign policy interests. In 1961, President Kennedy created the US Agency for International Development (USAID), and placed it within the State Department. This structure has left USAID primarily responsive to US security and economic interests, rather than the interests of the recipients overseas. A 1977 USAID task force concluded that,

> ...in practice, the 'voice for development' has too often been muted at the working level in confrontations between long term development interests and short term political exigencies.[4]

By the early 1980s, rather than weakening the connections between strategic concerns and American aid, USAID was strengthening its relationship to the State Department.[5]

Similar considerations have dominated US food aid commitments. Since its inception in 1954, the American food aid programme has usually operated in response to strategic concerns and US agribusiness interests. In 1966, the Food for Peace Act formally made the function of US food aid "to develop and expand export markets for United States agricultural commodities." The humanitarian intent of the Food for Peace programme was not written into the authorising legislation until that time. A 1978 report to the Secretary of Agriculture applauded the "maximum flexibility" of the Food for Peace programme, stating that many of the country programmes,

> ...are motivated in large part by our desire to further what are very clearly foreign policy interests.[6]

Historically, food aid has therefore been organised to play a geopolitical role. The Food for Peace Programme has been proactive in seeking to create new markets for US agricultural products abroad, and reactive in response to American foreign policy considerations. It is also increasingly amenable to pressure from segments of the public, the US Congress, the NGO community and the media when humanitarian emergencies develop or become publicized. When, for political reasons, all other forms of US assistance (economic and military) to a specific country is terminated, food aid assumes an even greater strategic importance.

The Geopolitical Context of United States Policy

Despite the strategic nature of US aid, the decision-making process in US foreign policy toward Ethiopia and Eritrea was complicated by a myriad confounding circumstances, for example, the containment of communist expansion in the strategically important Red Sea region; the lack of an ideologically acceptable alternative to the Soviet-backed government in Addis Ababa; US support for three non-democratic regimes to the east, west, and south of Ethiopia, that is, Somalia, Sudan, and Kenya; and the gradual deterioration in the status of vulnerable populations in northern Ethiopia and Eritrea, culminating in hundreds of thousands of deaths by the mid-1980s. Were it not for this last factor, US policy might have been marked by a much more aggressively anti-government approach.

When the Dergue began to consolidate its control of the Ethiopian state, US relations deteriorated rapidly. The Carter Administration decided to apply its new policy of human rights advocacy to Ethiopia, cutting bilateral aid in February, 1977. Other restrictions on aid followed. Because of a dispute over Ethiopian payments for past purchases of military equipment, the Brooke Amendment was invoked, forbidding bilateral non-humanitarian assistance to Ethiopia. Brooke Amendment sanctions were lifted in 1980, but then reinvoked in 1981.[7] To doubly reinforce the aid ban, in 1980 the Hickenlooper Amendment was applied to Ethiopia. This prohibits development aid to any country which nationalizes US property, as the Ethiopian government did in 1975 and 1976.[8] America, moreover, did not restrict its human rights activism to its own bilateral programme. Using the Gonzalez Amendment's applicability to multilateral disbursements, the US opposed loans to Ethiopia by the World Bank and the African Development Bank.[9]

Despite the above restrictions, the United States continued to provide humanitarian assistance. During the five years prior to 1983, US contributions averaged a relatively modest $9 million per annum through the PL-480 food aid programme administered from the USAID regional office in Nairobi (see Figure 1). Food aid was channelled through Catholic Relief Services (CRS), the World Food Programme (WFP), and some bilateral aid to the government. USAID also contributed to the development of a Famine Early Warning System.[10] At this stage, no aid was provided to the cross-border operation.

In early 1983, the CIA predicted famine in Ethiopia. As evidence of a growing food crisis continued to mount, the charge d'affaires of the US embassy in Addis declared a state of emergency in May. This was partly in response to Congressional pressure on the Reagan Administration. In June, a letter signed by 74 members of Congress was sent to USAID urging that PL-480 aid be channelled through the UN Disaster Relief Organisation (UNDRO). In July, resolutions in the House of Representatives and the Senate supported a continued relief effort.[11] These and other communiques were notable for, among other things, their lack of recognition of the significant territory in Tigray and Eritrea inaccessible through government and UN relief channels.

Growing humanitarian need in the context of an impending famine in 1983 created a thorny diplomatic problem for US policy toward Ethiopia. This situation was compounded by the uncertain applicability to Ethiopia of the so-called Reagan Doctrine, which called for assisting rebel movements against Soviet-supported regimes such as Afghanistan and Nicaragua. Fears surrounding the communist agendas of the EPLF and TPLF, as well as the hope of swaying the Ethiopian government to the West, limited the United States to token assistance to the Ethiopian Peoples Democratic Alliance (EPDA), a group with virtually no presence on the ground in Ethiopia.[12] The EPLF and TPLF received no American support. Assistance, however, was not token to Ethiopia's neighbours. US aid to Sudan, Kenya, and Somalia all increased during the Reagan administration's first term for the purpose of containing the suspected expansionist aims of Ethiopia and Libya.

Until 1984, despite the continuation of humanitarian aid on the government side, the American response to the growing Ethiopian crisis was hedged with restraint. The cross border operation, moreover, was not seen as an alternative. Aside from the above ideological debates, the US response within Ethiopia was contained by fears of large-scale government diversion and uncertainty over access. The question of diversion is discussed below in more detail in relation to European assistance. Some observers, however, have argued that US policy prior to

1984 represented an attempt to use the famine as a means to pressure the government to rejoin the Western sphere.[13-14] This is unlikely since, as is indicated below, other Western donors and the UN were not only providing more than the US, they were also increasing their assistance during this period. There was no united front amongst donor governments. On balance, it is more probable that the complexity of the Ethiopian situation dictated US hesitance rather than a lone and politically risky strategy of famine toleration. Certainly, following the outburst of public concern over the Ethiopian famine in 1984, the consequent sense of direction that American policy developed stands in contrast to this earlier period.

The United Nations and Sovereignty Constraints

The reluctance shown by America toward the Ethiopian government was not shared by the UN. In common with many Western bilateral donors, the major UN agencies, namely WFP, UNHCR, UNDP, and UNICEF, actually increased their assistance during the late 1970s and early 1980s. In 1977, total aid from these agencies stood at $13 million. It continued to grow over subsequent years until it had reached $67 million by 1981.[15] The first major UN appeal for famine relief was issued by UNDRO in March 1983, with UNICEF following in April with its own appeal.[16]

Due to sovereignty considerations, however, UN humanitarian assistance was not forthcoming in non-governmental areas. Because the Dergue denied that there were areas it did not control, the UN, by not publicly challenging this misrepresentation, tacitly helped limit aid to such areas. This created large structural disparities in the ratio of aid going into government as opposed to Front-held territory. It also placed the onus on ERD and other agencies involved in the cross border operation to have to legitimise their case. The UN further compounded these problems by not attempting to incorporate information gathered from CBO agencies with access to non-governmental areas.[17] Since donor aid packages normally rely on UN assessments, this omission significantly restricted the available information and consequently distorted donor perceptions of need and access.

The Developmental Role of the European Community

Similar to the UN, the European Community (EC) was supportive of the Ethiopian government and hence also diverged from US policy.

Unlike the US, rather than being organised to play a geopolitical role, the orientation of the EC toward the Third World was more of a developmental one through the Lome Conventions. The EC, which was formed in 1957, is primarily a trading and economic bloc for West European nations. For most of its history it has lacked therefore what could be considered an agreed foreign policy. Such matters were the concern of the member states. It is only now, with the discussions taking place on greater political union, that the structure for a common foreign policy is slowly and controversially emerging.

The main features of the EC's relationship with the Third World stemmed, in part, from the centralised, redistributive aid mechanisms that had been established within the community to overcome economic disparities between member states. Projected as an external relationship, this manifested itself from the late 1950s, as a series of special funds and trade agreements between the Commission of the EC and in the main the former colonies of member states. With the enlargement of the EC during the 1970s and, especially, the membership of Great Britain which retained numerous ties with its former colonies, a more formal arrangement was required.

Talks that began in the early 1970s eventually led to the signing of the Lome I agreement in February 1975 between the EC and 46 of what became known as the Africa, Caribbean and Pacific (ACP) countries. Ethiopia was amongst these founder signatories. In June 1979, this agreement was superseded by Lome II. The Lome conventions were enacted at a time when trade was beginning to stagnate between the EC and ACP countries. Indeed, it was largely as a measure to counteract this trend that the Lome conventions were signed. That they have failed in this mission is noteworthy. Nevertheless, at the time, Lome was seen as being at the forefront of progressive aid management.[18] It allowed ACP signatories market access within the EC, trade promotion measures, financial cooperation and export stabilisation funds. Since the aid was largely concessional, it was deemed to be of great benefit to poorer countries and its participatory provisions placed much of the implementing responsibility onto the recipient country. Lome I also made special provision for emergency aid to ACP signatories.

Ethiopia was one of the original Lome signatories in 1975. It is clear that the EC regarded Ethiopia as having great economic potential and a strategic developmental role within the region, if not the continent as a whole. Ethiopia's resistance to colonisation was seen as giving it "more experience" than other ACP countries.[19] It was a founder member of the UN and the non-aligned movement as well as Addis Ababa being the headquarters of the OAU and the UN Economic Commission for Africa. From the opening of its office in April 1976, in the space of several years Ethiopia became the EC's largest aid programme receiving some $225 million in financial assistance.[20] This contrasted strongly with the US position during this period. Reflecting its relationship with the EC, in 1979 the Ethiopian government appointed an ambassador extraordinary and plenipotentiary to the EC's Council of Ministers and Commission.

Within this context of high expectations and aid flows, the EC was public in its support for the government, even to the extent of offering its official journal as a platform for the Dergue's political programme.[21] Resettlement and villagisation, which had already begun by the end of the 1970s, were seen positively as promoting the effective provision of agricultural services through the concentration of population.[22] With the exception of the US, this supportive relationship was characteristic of Western bilateral donors.

The Diversion of Food Aid

The EC's position on food aid to Ethiopia and, increasingly, the non-government areas, was influenced by several factors. The Lome conventions made provision for emergency assistance but only to ACP signatory countries. This ruled out non-government areas. In many respects Lome was another reflection of the limitations imposed by sovereignty in cases of internal war. In addition, the participatory nature of Lome imparted great responsibility on the receiving state. Until the mid- 1980s, the Ethiopian government and the RRC were the main recipient of EC food aid. The elevation of Ethiopia in the EC's development thinking also meant that its Addis Ababa office became the EC's regional headquarters. It was to Addis Ababa that Brussels would turn for advice or comment on regional issues. Finally, the EC is not an open or democratic structure. The European Parliament has little control over the Commission which is mainly staffed by salaried officials and is responsible for administering Lome. In these circumstances, food aid provision tends to be led by rules and conventions. This can be contrasted with USAID, where not only can the decision making process be more public and hence sensitive to opinion, geopolitical considerations have evolved a structure which is able to respond quickly to changing needs when politically expedient.

Toward the end of the 1970s, the emerging famine in Ethiopia and Eritrea prompted a number of responses. Unlike Haile Selassie in 1973,

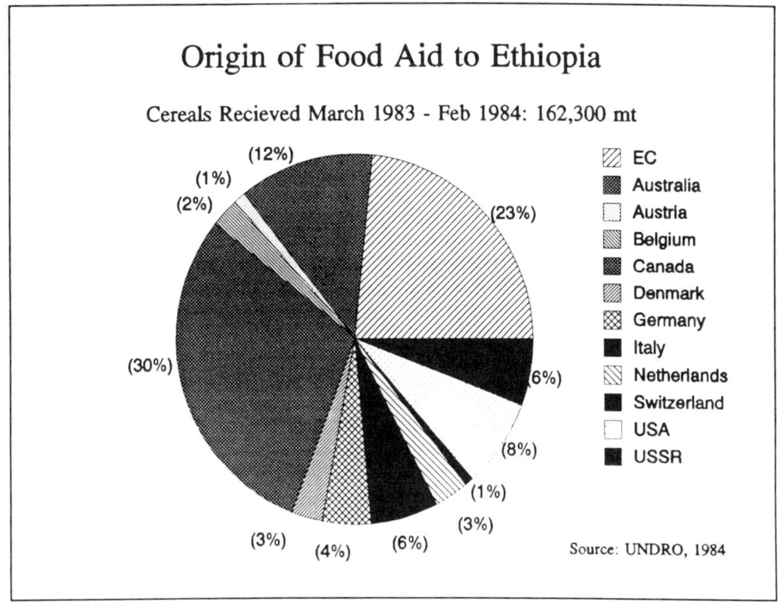

Figure 1

the Ethiopian government widely publicized this famine, largely blaming natural or environmental factors. It was only with the approach of the military regime's ten year anniversary celebrations in 1984 that official attempts to play down the situation occurred. Amongst the donor community, it had also become evident that the declining trend in food production meant that Ethiopia had a major structural problem in terms of feeding its 30 million population. It is against this background that initial donor support, including the EC, was obtained for the Dergue's resettlement and villagisation policy. Toward the end of the 1970s, non-US Western assistance to Ethiopia increased.[23] In 1978, the EC's first donation of food aid, some 80,000 mt, was consigned to the government.[24] Donations of increasing size continued. During 1983, for example, the EC donated approximately 38,000 mt of cereals or around 23% of total government receipts. In contrast, ERD handled only 17,400 mt in 1983 which, although a significant improvement on earlier years, was only about 10% of the aid being channelled to the government side.

Although the Ethiopian government blamed natural causes for the return of famine at the end of the 1970s, an explanation the donor community was willing to support, the EPLF had a different explanation. It argued that the reason for the Dergue's willingness to court publicity was that it hoped,

> ...to exploit the famine to raise large sums of money and huge quantities of food and other essentials from various governments and humanitarian organisations. Previous experience shows (it will be used) to feed a huge army of occupation and to pay its troops and workers in lieu of cash, which would be used to buy armaments.[25]

During the early 1980s, evidence of the widespread diversion of food aid, as predicted by the EPLF, slowly began to surface. Allegations were that not only did RRC feeding programmes concentrate in urban areas, they tended to favour the families of soldiers. Although never proven, it was even alleged that some international relief supplies never left the port of Assab, being re-shipped to the USSR as part-payment for arms. Toward the end of 1981, substantiated cases began to be recorded of donated food aid being used by the government to provision Ethiopian military campaigns. This included EC, WFP, UNICEF and ICRC food aid and medical supplies captured by the Fronts in Eritrea and Tigray and displayed to agency staff and independent observers.[26-28] At the end of 1983, an RRC official seeking political asylum, brought with him a memo signed in February 1982 by the RRC Commissioner instructing the RRC office in Wollega to falsify the records so as to hide the fact that WFP food had not been used for the intended beneficiaries.[29] Such disclosures fed the bad press that the government began to attract concerning its handling of food aid.

Response of the European Community to Diversion

The EC's response to such disclosures, together with the growing evidence of the ferocity of the war being waged by the government in Tigray and Eritrea, can be understood in terms of the division between the European Parliament and the Commission. Links between the two are weak and, in terms of helping garner support for ERD and the cross border operation, the contribution of Parliament was negligible.[30] While there were exceptions, the main Parliamentary support came from anti-communist MEPs or representatives of right wing nationalist factions. In November 1982, on the grounds of government aggression in the

North, the European Parliament voted to suspend aid to Ethiopia pending a full report by the Commission. The vote, however, was non-binding on the Commission which continued to supply aid. Indeed, following a visit by the head of the Development Division even more was pledged. It was widely rumoured that the Division was making a stand against the European conservative lobby which was seen as toeing the anti-government US foreign policy line.[31]

It should be noted that this position was symptomatic of a further level of complexity that faced ERD. That is, the left in Europe and the USA was split on the issue of whether the Dergue was pursuing a socialist alternative. Generally speaking, those groups supporting a more orthodox communist position were persuaded that it was. From this perspective, the Dergue had to be defended against predatory US moves and the damage the 'rebels', and their supporters, were claimed to be inflicting. A number of politicians, journalists, academics and political activists were involved in this loose alliance. It was given further shape as a consequence of the so-called Reagan Doctrine which counselled US support for political movements opposing communist regimes. Although never applied to the EPLF and TPLF, until the mid-1980s, it served to work against a more realistic understanding of what was happening in Eritrea and Tigray.

Hard evidence of the diversion and abuse of relief aid by the Ethiopian government, however, continued to grow and could not be ignored. Increasingly, donors were forced onto the defensive. In response to the evidence that the RRC in Wollega has falsified accounts relating to WFP food aid, for example, the Acting Chief of WFP's Emergency Division responded that the Ethiopian government was allowed to use certain bilateral aid as it saw fit. These were the rules of the game.[32] The EC Commissioner similarly claimed that since the RRC was the consignee, it could use the food as it wished. The problem was that of poor administrative practices within the RRC. In this case, WFP should have been informed beforehand of the change in use. The EC, however, had to admit the evidence indicated that in future it would have to strengthen "control of our food aid."[33] During 1984, stung by bad press, donor opinion began to change and, following the upsurge of public concern after the dramatic TV coverage of the famine in October 1984, an increasing proportion of donor assistance would be channelled through NGOs.

CHAPTER FOUR

Neutrality, Humanitarianism and the Formation of ERD

Early Cross-Border Assistance: (1977 - 1981)

By the late 1970s, it was evident that the World Council of Churches (WCC) and the Lutheran World Federation (LWF) were reluctant to become involved in cross border assistance. In some respects, one could argue that WCC and LWF, since they recognise a form of sovereignty as embodied in acknowledged national churches, resemble the UN system in that they find addressing situations of divided governance particularly difficult. LWF was initially concerned that CBO association would invite a government reprisal on the Ethiopian Evangelical Church Mekane Yesus. WCC, on the other hand, wished to be politically correct in the eyes of African governments and not be seen supporting the separatist agenda of the Eritreans.[1] It is also the case, however, that within Ethiopia, WCC made no efforts to bring the Ethiopian Orthodox Church, to which it is attached, into communication with the Catholic and Lutheran relief systems being organised from Addis Ababa.[2] Although WCC was periodically called upon by ERD to play a liaison and facilitator role during the 1980s, it offered no assistance to the cross border relief operation.

Until 1982, when other agencies became increasingly involved, it was the Protestant Scandinavian organisations Swedish Church Relief (SCR) and Norwegian Church Aid (NCA) which filled this lacuna (see Figure 2). Indeed, up to this time they were supplying almost all of the relief assistance reaching Eritrea and Tigray from international agencies.

Missionary and historical links, the independence of Scandinavian aid policy and the strong ties between church and state, all contributed to shape this involvement.

The initial pre-1981 years of the cross border operation are significant in several respects. Given the situation in Sudan, they confirmed the importance of SCC as the 'legal' conduit for relief operations. For ERA in 1975, as an agency recognised by the Sudanese government, the Relief Desk of SCC was an important conduit for outside assistance. Like the government, however, SCC's contacts were primarily with the ELF and its relief wing, the ERCCS.[3-4] It was not until 1977, through the auspices of SCR that the first of the agencies later to form ERD began to assist the Eritreans through SCC. The main element of this relief programme was medical supplies, clothing and sorghum locally purchased in Sudan. Indeed, this was the situation until the early 1980s.

Swedish missionaries had been active in Eritrea for many years. Escalating fighting in the mid-1970s weakened the links between them and their constituencies. Relief assistance was an important way of trying to maintain this contact. Like SCC, however, SCR's preferred contacts were with the ERCCS.[5] The result of this involvement was the formation of an Eritrea Relief Desk supported by SCR within SCC. Until 1981, SCR was the largest contributor to the cross border operation. As a means of establishing a balance,[6] in September 1977 the EPLF contacted NCA by letter, inviting it to work in Eritrea.[7] The invitation was accepted and in March 1978, after a field visit, NCA established an office in Khartoum as a basis for its work.

Although invited by the EPLF, the Norwegians had been asked to develop a coordinating group in which both ERA and ERCCS could be represented. REST was not involved at this stage. For several reasons, this was not easy and, until it was agreed to form ERD in 1981, SCR/SCC and NCA operated as two parallel systems mainly assisting the relief wings of the ELF and EPLF respectively. Pressure to increase coordination grew from a number of quarters. By 1979, it had become clear that the WCC and LWF were unwilling to become involved in Eritrea. At the same time, reflecting Scandinavian independence in aid and relief matters, NCA had decided not to let international church politics shape its actions and, largely using its own resources, its relief support to Eritrea had grown to eclipse its other programmes. A few other Protestant agencies, again using their own resources, had also become interested in providing relief assistance primarily through NCA. These included, Christian Aid (CA), Brot Fur Die Welt (BFW), Dutch Interchurch Aid (DIA) and the Interchurch Coordination Committee for Development Projects (ICCO). The latter two Dutch organisations in particular were sceptical of the credibility of the SCR/SCC operation.[8] Lutheran World Relief (LWR) made its first bilateral grant to REST in 1980.

The 1981 ERD Agreement

The negotiations to establish a coordinating group began in 1980. This represented a new departure for NCA which traditionally had worked independent of other agencies. At first, the proposal was opposed by SCC and ERA. The former wished to maintain the status quo while the latter feared that NCA may reduce its support once a wider group had been formed. The agreement to form the Emergency Relief Desk (ERD) was eventually signed in Khartoum on 21 February 1981.

The original organisation and mandate of ERD arose from the need to balance several conflicting agendas. The limitations of operating from Sudan, for example, had to be balanced with the Fronts' wish for wider international recognition and the difficulty of attracting donor support due to the political sensitivity of the issues involved. The end result was an organisation with a limited humanitarian brief with SCC giving a legitimate Sudanese base and NCA providing an office and, from September 1982 at least, executive management. Apart from SCR, the other supporting agencies were not formally involved in the organisational structure until 1985. By 1983, however, a couple of years after its formation, ERD had outgrown it original structure and severe organisational strains had begun to show. To understand the changes that took place in the mid-1980s, the contours of the original body have to be sketched in more detail.

ERD's Humanitarian Mandate

It is important to note that the agreement to form ERD was made between SCC and NCA. It was on the basis of this agreement, which established an ecumenical instrument for cross border relief work, that other church affiliated agencies were approached.[9] Apart from SCC, NCA and SCR, the initial group of donor agencies were Danechurch Aid (DCA), Dutch Interchurch Aid (DIA), Diakonisches Werk/Brot Fur Die Welt (DDW/BFW), Christian Aid (CA), Lutheran World Relief (LWR) and InterChurch Coordination Committee for Development Projects (ICCO). While all were Protestant church based organisations, apart from SCC, LWR was the only American group in an otherwise European consortium. Several of these NGOs had already been providing assistance to ERA and REST. Most, moreover, had previous working links in other relief consortia including the Relief and Development Group Somalia (RDGS) which was formed in 1980.

ERD was established as a "limited independent body within the SCC." The five person ERD Committee, which was to meet once a month and operate its own bank account, was divided between SCC and NCA. SCC filled three of these positions including the Ex-Officio Chairman and was also responsible for organising an annual audit and co-signing ERD cheques. In addition to providing the office, NCA furnished the remaining two committee members, one of which being the ERD Executive Secretary.[10] Until September 1982, when NCA filled the Executive Secretary position, SCR, with significant gaps when the post was unfilled, occupied this role. Other supporting agencies were not formally involved in the committee structure or management of ERD. Indeed, it was not until 1984, when negotiations concerning the reorganisation of ERD began, that all member agencies began to meet on a formal basis. Until 1985, apart from the SCC/NCA agreement, ERD was essentially an informal consortium.

Although this structure brought the ongoing cross border relief activities under one organisation and, therefore, was an improvement on the previous situation, it was also fraught with contradictions. With regard to SCC, due to the sensitivity of having to operate from Khartoum, the agreement establishes SCC as the 'legal' basis for ERD's operation. In practice, however, it was NCA and the ERD Executive Secretary which effectively ran the operation. This position was reinforced by the fact that NCA had been active in the informal briefing of the Sudanese government on the proposal to establish ERD.[11]

From the outset, ERD perceived itself as non-political and having a strictly humanitarian brief. It avoided publicity for its cross border relief activities and maintained a low profile in Khartoum. In relief terms, ERD was seen as being a "temporary instrument," subject to annual review and only providing aid in kind and at a "reasonable level." Transport, in the form of trucks, for example, which were in short supply in Eritrea and Tigray were not provided. The cost of transporting relief goods, moreover, was only met either to Port Sudan or the border. It was not covered to the point of distribution. Cash payments were also excluded. Within this limited brief, the indigenous "humanitarian organisations" were to be treated "on an equal basis." At this stage, for example, assistance to ERA and ERCCS was divided equally. In relation to ERA and REST, however, due to the prevalence of earmarked funds for the former, rough equality was not achieved until around 1986. The agreement also established no formal mechanism for the consultation or involvement of what later became known as the 'implementing agencies' (IAs).

Essentially, ERD was established as a logistical and monitoring organisation to receive requests from the IAs for assistance, to verify need through field visits, pass on requests to member agencies, when necessary arrange procurement in Sudan, clear shipments, keep regular accounts, receive distribution reports, provide members with information on developments in Eritrea and Tigray, and so on. In other words, ERD was primarily an ecumenical conduit for channelling relief assistance in kind to the IAs, verifying its legitimate distribution and disseminating information to its members.

Neutrality, Sovereignty and Western Humanitarian Politics

Apart from its ecumenical basis, the defining characteristics of the ERD mandate was (a) its restriction to relief items in kind and (b) its discrete and non-political style of work. These two features were linked by the belief that accepting a public solidarity role, or engaging in long term development work, would imply making a political assumption about the nature of the conflict and thereby jeopardize ERD's neutrality.[12]

The ERD mandate and its underlying assumptions is a good example of Western humanitarian politics. The political space for this practice is defined by the contradiction between 'neutrality' and what can be loosely termed 'involvement'. The former position holds that the international credibility of a humanitarian agency rests on its having a non-political stance. This often requires such things as establishing a distance from indigenous political relations, the avoidance of advocacy on behalf of specific parties, the treatment of all parties equally, and the monitored provision of basic relief items to civilians only. Rather than an involvement with the indigenous political reality that defines the emergency, such as, institution building, working through local political structures, advocacy for specific parties and positions, or providing a wide range of material assistance, the neutral position argues for what appears as political distance and quietism.

The self-image of ERD, which it projected effectively, was that of a neutral humanitarian consortium. Because ERD only worked on one side of the conflict and, moreover, collaborated with relief associations established by the Fronts, this image, it should be stressed, demanded an ideological sleight of hand in its construction. The basis of this was to cast ERA and REST as also being neutral humanitarian organisations or, to use ERD terminology, as simply Implementing Agencies. That they were also effective organisations helped in this matter. Chapter Two has indicated that rather than being neutral, however, ERA and REST were part of the political practice of the Fronts and heavily dependent on the support of their respective civilian administrations. They could have implemented little on their own. It is important to note, however, that it was only by treating them as neutral, as somehow above the political realities of Eritrea and Ethiopia, that ERD as a consortium of agencies with different agendas was able to form. In this respect, it was important that some ERD members also had long standing relations with Ethiopian church agencies. ERD's limited humanitarian mandate, which rested upon the portrayal of ERA and REST as having similar aims, provided therefore a neutral forum in which the differences between member agencies could themselves be subsumed.

This settlement, however, was fragile since ERD's neutrality was also constrained by the nature of the CBO itself. By the nature of the situation, it could only work on one side of the conflict. This contrasts to some extent with the "active neutrality" of the various Medecins Sans Frontieres (MSF) organisations which seek to work both sides of a military line. Apart from this, however, the only other difference with ERD's idea of neutrality is that the MSFs reserve the right to publicize cases of human rights abuse when appropriate.[13] The same attempt to maintain political distance however is observed. Indeed, working both sides strengthens this position. In the case of ERD, being confined to one side tended to heighten the tension between neutrality and involvement especially as some members developed a deeper understanding of what was happening in Eritrea and Tigray. Indeed, by the mid-1980s, while ERD's collective neutrality was confirmed, individual members had begun to go on public record on the consequences of the war. Although the terms of the debate would change during the course of ERD's existence, the contradiction between neutrality and involvement continued to shape the internal discourse and outward policy direction of ERD.

ERD's collective neutrality reflects the views on sovereignty which were prevalent when its members came together in the late 1970s and early 1980s. Basically, the reality of sovereignty, and its political and legal permanence, was then accepted by Western agencies and donors: it was not an issue. Until the mid-1980s, the hegemony of sovereignty in all major international institutions and conventions had a number of consequences. These included (a) it created conditions in which cross border relief work was seen as 'illegal' (b) it gave a strong incentive amongst donor governments and multilateral institutions to take the lead from 'legal' or nationally based interests or programmes and (c) with NGOs, the notion CBO illegality not only dissuaded many from involvement, even when agencies were active it was often at the price of the institutional segregation of the personnel involved. Through internal managerial means, organisations frequently attempted to maintain some form of political distance. This greatly reduced internal agency discussion of the issues raised by the CBO.

Until the mid-1980s, the hegemony of sovereignty meant that ERD defined itself in terms of meeting humanitarian need "in parts of Ethiopia which are not accessible from areas controlled by the Government of Ethiopia."[14] In other words, rather than see itself in relation to what could be done in Eritrea and Tigray, ERD was described negatively, as it were, in terms of what could not be done from the government side. To some extent, ERD's continued association with WCC fits into this framework. It was involved, for example, in an advisory capacity during ERD's 1984 evaluation. Although WCC gave no real assistance and was not involved in the establishment of ERD, for some considerable time it was nevertheless thought that WCC may be able to somehow liaise on the government side to improve ERD's effectivity and, presumably, its 'legal' standing.[15-16]

A central argument in the analysis of ERD is that neutrality together with involvement both have distinct strengths and weaknesses. Until the mid-1980s, as we shall see, ERD's neutral stance served it well in terms of being able to attract fickle donor support to an otherwise sensitive cause. ERD provided a discrete 'screen' for such assistance. It strengthened its diplomatic position with regard to a behind the scenes peace role which its members, on occasion, were able to play on behalf of the Fronts. In addition, ERD's attempts to maintain political distance allowed it to mediate the political differences which distinguished the Fronts and their respective relief associations. From the mid-1980s, however, with the support of USAID and EC for the CBO together with the greatly enhanced role of NGOs, the situation began to change.

The shape of Western humanitarian politics has been increasingly influenced by a weakening of the principle of sovereignty and a propensity toward more direct forms of intervention. Although the latter should not be confused with involvement as defined above; today, more that a decade after ERD was established, and especially since the end of the Gulf War in 1991, there has been a perceptible change in the manner in which sovereignty is seen in the West. Because neutrality as defined in relation to political distance is the essential product of the hegemony of sovereignty, when this hegemony weakens the limitations of neutrality as a policy become more manifest. One example is the growing gap between an increasing understanding of the complexity of a situation that close association develops and the limited response that neutrality dictates.

It is now accepted by many humanitarian agencies[17-18] together with the UN General Secretary,[19] that sovereignty is no longer an adequate excuse for a state to deny international access for humanitarian purposes. While enforcement is a different and vexed question, this change in the global balance has tended to highlight the political and structural nature of contemporary emergencies. At the same time, neutral humanitarian assistance has become open to the criticism that, at best, and this is still a crucial best, it simply keeps people alive while doing nothing to solve the structural causes of the emergency. In this emerging climate the need for new and radically different forms of involvement with the political complexity of the African crisis is gaining ground.

A singular, if not unique attribute of ERD is that its history as a humanitarian consortium spans this transition period. Differences amongst members, therefore, reflect the contradictions and tensions in the shifting balance between neutrality and involvement.

Western Humanitarian and Front Public Welfare Politics Contrasted

Insofar as neutral humanitarianism is able to develop an active political practice this is usually a complex process of quiet background work, behind the scenes advocacy and informal alliances. It is, essentially, a politics of working through others to influence events. Since it uses distinct means to achieve defined aims, one should be in no doubt that it is, indeed, a form of politics. It is also clear that it contrasts with the political practice and concerns over isolation characteristic of the Fronts. One could say that it falls short of the demands likely to arise from a process of national liberation. It has already been shown that by 1975, the EPLF and ERA were aware of the need for international assistance and recognition. Moreover, as evinced in ERA's understanding of public opinion in the Vietnam War, for the Eritreans, assistance and recognition were inextricably linked. Indeed, this can be argued to originate from the political practice of the Fronts which linked public assistance with the creation of political solidarity.

While Western humanitarianism and Front public welfare policies both had the same aim of saving lives, one can argue that two contrasting practices were involved. Not only does Western neutrality have its strengths and weaknesses, it would appear that, until the mid-1980s, there was a degree of mutual lack of understanding between the two systems. In 1979, for example, the General Secretary of the EPLF visited Norway where he strongly pressed NCA to show more open political support.[20] He was met with the implacable argument that, in order to garner humanitarian assistance, Western agencies needed to demonstrate impartiality and, in the case of Eritrea, a low profile. In relation to IA attitudes toward ERD, until the mid-1980s, if not longer, this can be summarised as follows. Although ERA and REST were appreciative of the material support provided by ERD, they lost no opportunity of firmly criticising its limited relief brief and, importantly, ERD's lack of advocacy and what were felt to be major shortcomings in its efforts to raise public awareness of what was happening in non-government areas.[21-22] For its part, the political distance demanded by neutrality tended to transform the differences between Eritrea and Tigray into similarities thus narrowing ERD's understanding of what in fact was happening.

At the same time, however, the non-political approach of ERD, by establishing an impartial ecumenical instrument that could be defended before Western donors worried over sovereignty, created the main conduit through which outside relief assistance was channelled during the 1980s. This was the main strength of the approach. The Norwegian government, for example, assisted on the basis of a neutral ERD from 1981. In 1982, help from the British government, via CA, was again only possible on this basis.[23] It was the same with the Dutch and American governments. The ability of being able to present an accountable ecumenical body as a neutral 'screen' between Western donors and the complex political reality of internal war was a strength of ERD. This was especially the case with regard to donor support for Tigray which did not develop until the mid-1980s. From this period, with the increasing involvement of USAID and EC, having a neutral screen became, if anything, even more essential.

The Involvement of Indigenous Relief Associations With ERD

ERD was primarily formed as a means of better coordinating the relief assistance already being channelled to ERA and ERCCS. REST and the Oromo Relief Association (ORA) were incorporated later. In the case of REST, it approached SCC/SCR in February 1981, shortly before the establishment of ERD.[24] At the time, it was regarded as being of unknown capacity and the decision was taken to assess its performance with a contribution of 200 mt of sorghum. By the end of 1981, it was an accepted implementing agency within ERD.[25] Since a number of the ERD members had assisted REST previously, that it should become a regular partner is perhaps not surprising. It should be pointed out, however, that since the TPLF were fighting not for independence like the Eritreans but a more decentralised Ethiopian state, support for REST was regarded by many agencies, especially European, as more sensitive than ERA. The EPLF was seen as having a territorial claim while the TPLF, however, represented a direct challenge to the integrity of the Ethiopian state. This position was somewhat reversed in the USA which historically had played a major role in denying Eritrean aspirations for independence and then had become increasingly hostile to the Ethiopian government once the Reagan administration assumed office. However, indicating the initial involvement of the Europeans, donor support for ERA grew from the early 1980s, while with REST, this would not occur until the mid-1980s and was associated with a major shift in donor policy.

ORA was established in 1979 as the relief association of the Oromo Liberation Front (OLF). It can be distinguished from ERA and REST on several accounts. In the first place, for most of the period ORA did not have a programme within Ethiopia but mainly took responsibility for Oromo refugees living in Sudan at Yabus, near Demazin. In terms of aid received, compared to ERA and REST, it took less than 10% of the total. In many respects, it was therefore a small player within ERD.[26] Finally, the OLF did not go on to develop the type of public welfare programmes that typified the EPLF and TPLF. Because of this position, ORA is not given a detailed focus in this history. ORA first approached ERD in October 1981, for assistance with Oromo refugees in the Demazin area of Sudan's Blue Nile Province.[27] Since the ERD Executive Committee knew little of ORA or the situation of the refugees, it was decided that the Executive Secretary should make a field trip to ascertain the situation. This proved favourable and, by mid-1982, ORA was an established recipient of ERD assistance.[28]

That fact that ORA was included alongside ERA and REST is worthy of note. ERA and, to a large extent, REST were involved due to historical association and the pressure of the IAs. ORA, on the other hand, can be seen as an inclusion owing more to the informal operation of member politics than comparability between the different situations of the IAs. The documentary evidence contains no indication of the criteria on which this inclusion took place. Indeed, some would argue that this was largely due to pressure from some ERD members with Oromo constituencies in Europe.[29]

The Criteria for Accepting Indigenous Relief Associations

It was, in fact, not until 1985 that ERD drew up guidelines for the evaluation of indigenous agencies seeking to become recipients. The criteria were that the applicant had to accept an ERD evaluation mission. This mission would be looking for such things as continuous presence in a target area; an administrative capacity; a monitoring capacity; a logistical capability and an ability to clearly identify the target population.[30]

It is interesting to note that these criteria do not include any reference to the participatory or community targeting systems that the EPLF and TPLF had developed or the relations of accountability and reciprocity linking rural producers to the political authorities. These are important considerations for the success of any public programme. ERD's criteria represent, essentially, a de-politicised lens since they rely on ideas of presence and efficiency. It is a good example of one of the weaknesses of neutrality as a means of informing policy. Since it tends to de-politicise complex realities it finds it difficult to produce a comprehensive analysis of an emergency situation. Attempting to define ERA and REST, for example, with the above criteria, while producing a result which would maintain the neutral image of the international agency, would result in a distorted view of the political dynamic in Eritrea and Tigray.

In the event, having received applications from the now fragmented ERCCS and the Ethiopian Relief Organisation (ERO) in October 1985 the inclusion of any further IAs was rejected on the pragmatic grounds that ERD lacked the capacity to work with any more.[31] Although ERD would periodically receive applications from other organisations, it would introduce no more than its 1981 complement of ERA, REST and ORA.

ERD and the European Community

ERD's first contact with the EC, at least indirectly, came at the beginning of 1981. The ICRC approached SCC's relief coordinator to see if it would act as a conduit for EC food aid in kind to Eritrea.[32] At this stage, relief assistance was being divided between ERA and ERCCS. The offer was for between 2,000 to 3,000 mt. Although only a modest amount, this would have doubled the tonnage that the cross border operation was moving into Eritrea. A good deal of hesitancy from the ERD side surrounded this offer. Partly this was due to the significant operational increase that this would represent and the added risk of exposure. At this stage, the Fronts were also reluctant to accept aid from donors which did not recognise them.[33] The result was that it took a year for ERD to agree in principle to accept the ICRC offer and begin serious negotiation.[34] It was then, in early 1982, that DIA came into the picture as the ERD member which would act as the EC/ERD link in Europe.[35] Inconclusive discussions were finally held in Brussels in June 1982. As a result, ICRC decided to carry on for the time being with its own operation and the initiative petered out.[36]

This contact with the EC, however, prompted DIA to make a trial approach on behalf of Eritrea since the 'legality' of the case could be more easily argued. ERD's approach was to the EC's Emergency Division which enjoyed a reputation for officiousness. This not only related to EC aid being ruled out but, importantly, that Emergency Division assistance was governed by Lome which restricted it to ACP countries. DIA argued along the lines that the UN had agreed Eritrean autonomy and that the case was one of a failure of de-colonisation.[37] A good deal of information was passed to the EC and meetings with people having first hand experience of Eritrea arranged. Eventually, the Emergency Division temporarily relented and, in April 1983, an application was made for $700,000 for local purchase within Sudan. Although agreed, the final grant was cut to $270,000.[38] Although the possibility of more assistance from the Emergency Division existed pending ERD's report back, this never materialised. The Division was not satisfied with the report it received, demanding in the eyes of ERD an unrealistic and unjustified level of detailed accounting. One will recall that this was a time when the Ethiopian government was diverting EC food aid wholesale.

Although ERD did not develop further its relations with the EC's Emergency Division, this contact was significant for several reasons. In 1983, the EC's grant (around 5% of ERD's total budget) was the start of ERD's widening of its donor base. Moreover, through this initiative, links were forged with the EC's Food Aid Division which was not constrained by Lome. It would be through this Division that increasing amounts of food aid would be accessed and, moreover, Tigray included.

The Emergence of Other Cross Border Consortia

By 1983, the growing need in Eritrea and Tigray had led to an increasing demand for relief inputs. It had also given rise to broader demands for rehabilitation, transport and development assistance. In 1983, for example, the transport situation was so bad that ERD appealed to non-ERD agencies to support the spiralling transport costs.[39] Because of its relief mandate, ERD was unable to fully address these needs. This became an issue of contention during 1984 and 1985 when the re-establishment of ERD was under discussion. During this period, ERD came under great pressure from the IAs to change its policy and buy trucks.[40] Prior to this, however, lobbying by ERA and REST drew other agencies into these fields. In particular, in 1983 the Eritrean Inter-agency Agricultural Consortium (EIAC) and the Tigray Transport and Agricultural Consortium (TTAC) were formed. Both of these consortia were non-denominational and drew their initial organisational impetus from some of the agencies associated with Euro-Action Accord (EAA).

In the late 1970s, EAA had drawn up plans for an integrated agricultural development programme in Eritrea.[41] The subsequent strategic withdrawal, plus the fact that some member agencies had programmes within Ethiopia, led to doubts and EEA's subsequent dropping of the proposal.[42] With an initial shared membership of some of the British members of EEA and with War on Want as the lead agency for both consortia, EIAC and TTAC were eventually formed. EIAC initially concentrated on agricultural, veterinary and water drilling programmes, while TTAC tackled transport and, from 1985, agriculture.[43] Other agencies including NOVIB were drawn into these consortia in the mid-1980s. Of the ERD members, CA was alone in being involved in both of these consortia.[44] CA, therefore, had a unique position in being a member of all the cross border consortia as well as supporting programmes within Ethiopia.

Having different mandates, EIAC and TTAC can be seen as complementing the relief work of ERD.[45] Until around 1987, however, when mutual observer status was established, there was little formal contact between these consortia and ERD. There were also a number of differences. EIAC and TTAC, for example, tended to have a closer organisational association with ERA and REST respectively. It was not until 1990, that the IAs became a formal part of ERD's committee structure, having achieved this status several years earlier in the other consortia. Some of the agencies, especially War on Want, also had more of a solidarity approach than ERD. In some respects, EIAC and TTAC went someway to satisfy the Fronts' need for wider inputs and contacts beyond that represented by ERD.

Growing Contradictions Within ERD

Apart from being unable to satisfy the demand for rehabilitation and development assistance, by 1983, other tensions and contradictions had emerged within ERD. Not only had relief needs clearly outstripped ERD's ability to respond, the local political conditions which had shaped the formation of ERD had changed. These changing relations will be briefly examined first.

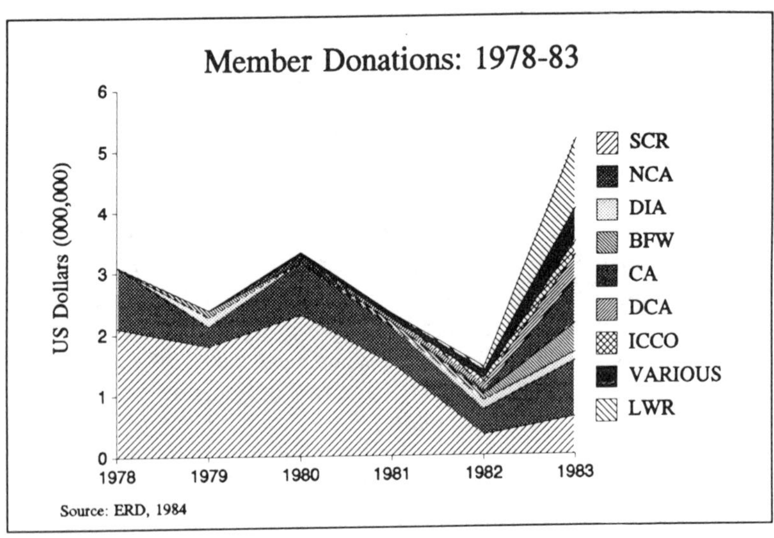

Figure 2

During 1980, open fighting developed between the EPLF and ELF. By mid-1981, the latter had been forced out of Eritrea and into Sudan where the ERCCS was confined to refugee work.[46] Given that ERCCS no longer operated in Eritrea, ERD decided to cease funding ERCCS in November 1981[47] at which stage ERA became the sole relief association operating within Eritrea. The defeat of the ELF coincided with a major reduction in Swedish funding which fell from over 60% of the total ERD budget in 1981 to 10% in 1983 (Figure 2). This was reflected in a significant decline in ERD's overall contribution. Although, in relation to ERA, ERD was meeting 15% of the total need claimed by ERA at the beginning of the 1980s, by 1983 this had fallen to 5%. For REST the comparable proportion was 1%.[48]

Despite this fall in performance, 1983 was also the year that the contributions of ERD members other than NCA and SCR first began to clearly manifest themselves. LWR, for example, at around $1 million was now providing 20% of ERD donations. In a sense, impressed with the IAs efficiency and concerned over US neglect of Eritrea,[49] it had begun to take over from the Swedes. The importance of LWR's material contributions would continue to grow. The structure of ERD, however, based upon an agreement between NCA and SCC did not adequately accommodate the demand which began to emerge for greater member representation. Mention has been made of the increasing request for rehabilitation, transport and development assistance which the IAs were also making. With regard to representation, not only was the original agreement increasingly seen as a limitation, the position of SCC had also begun to change.

It has been argued that SCC had risen to political significance in North Sudan largely as a result of the operation of Sudanese refugee and Ethiopia policies. One of the first events to change this was the defeat of the ELF. Given its association with ERCCS, ERA's relations with SCC were not good and did not improve with time.[50] It also appears that SCC, in its rise to national prominence, had perhaps been pushed beyond its organisational capacity.[51] Although responsible for arranging an annual audit of ERD, SCC never played this role. It was met by NCA. In the period until the end of 1983, although the ERD Executive Committee was supposed to meet monthly, on average, it only met four times a year. This meant that the role of the Executive Secretary, and hence NCA, became accentuated.[52] The original ERD became something of a one-sided organisation. Finally, with the introduction of Sharia Law in 1983 and the re-emergence of civil war in South Sudan, SCC, as an organisation with its roots in the South, also began to fall from official favour. Rather than being pushed to take on refugee work, a marginalisation of SCC began to develop.

Taken as a whole, these factors formed the background for the decision to evaluate the organisation and performance of ERD in order to assess the way forward. Although an evaluation should have taken place annually, it was not until November 1983 that the decision to go ahead was finally agreed.[53] This took place in early February 1984.

CHAPTER FIVE

The Internationalisation of the Crisis

War and Famine Summary (1984-1985)

The period between 1984-85 represented the peak in mortality rates due to war induced famine. Estimates regarding the number of such deaths range from a half million by Africa Watch to over a million by the United Nations. The Select Committee on Hunger in the US House of Representatives estimated 300,000 deaths between March and November of 1984.[1] Some analysts argue that death rates had already begun to decrease in late 1984 before massive food deliveries began.[2] The wide variation in these estimates is indicative of the great difficulty in assessing the real impact of war and famine in conditions as pertained in the Horn. Since they are open to manipulation, it is wise to treat all figures, unless of proven pedigree, with some caution.

When dramatic news coverage of the famine was broadcast by the BBC and US stations in October 1984, the Ethiopian government launched a year long offensive designed once again to destroy the support systems of the EPLF and TPLF. The government undertook the constant bombardment of ERA and REST supply routes from Sudan, especially during critical transport periods prior to the rainy season, when the pre-positioning and building of food stocks was a priority. It has been argued that the purpose of Ethiopian aerial bombardment campaigns during peak famine months was to herd people into government held areas and depopulate Front controlled regions.[3] In late 1984, Ethiopia's Foreign Minister admitted that "food is an element in our strategy" against the Fronts.[4]

In June, 1985, the Dergue undertook a renewed offensive aimed at capturing Nacfa in Eritrea. Around 200,000 troops and $1 billion in weapons were involved in the five month siege, resulting in 14,000 dead and injured. The spring of that year also saw heavy military activity in Tigray and in Oromo areas where the OLF was active.[5] War tactics wrought extensive environmental damage above and beyond continuing soil erosion, deforestation, locust infestation, and overgrazing. The bombing of civilian targets, the use of napalm and chemical defoliants, scorched earth bush clearance to remove ground cover for the Fronts, increased demand for fuel-wood around army garrison towns, use of depth charges by Soviet trawlers to harvest fish in the Red Sea, and the concentration of civilians around government held towns all conspired to devastate the ecological and subsistence base of Eritrea and Tigray.[6] Government policies of forcible resettlement also contributed to the suffering. MSF, for example, estimated that 100,000 deaths could be directly attributed to resettlement of civilians from Tigray and Wollo to the southwest.

As a result of the above factors, at least 200,000 Tigrayans moved across the border into Sudan beginning in late 1984, their movements organised and assisted by REST. Because of grossly inadequate funding for the cross border operation, and fears on the part of civilians of going into government held towns, people crossed into Sudan to become eligible for refugee assistance from international agencies. Because famine conditions were not as severe, a large scale refugee influx of Eritreans, however, did not take place. Prior to the spring rains in 1985, in a move unprecedented in the Horn, helped by REST Tigrayan refugees embarked upon a large-scale programme of voluntary repatriation to their home villages. Most international donors refused to help, arguing that since the war and famine were still raging, populations should not return. With the UN agencies such as UNHCR sidelined, a small number of NGOs and the Sudanese Commissioner for Refugees provided aid through REST to the repatriating Tigrayans.[7]

Between the moving BBC TV coverage of the Ethiopian famine in October 1984, and the end of 1985, more money was channelled to this disaster than any other previous emergency humanitarian operation.[8] Where these resources were delivered is one of the foremost controversies of the period. At the end of 1984, aid officials estimated that the Ethiopian government had access to only 22 per cent of at risk civilians. Despite this recognition, over 90 per cent of donated resources went to the government or NGOs working in government territory.[9] Publicly, though, the major multilaterals were putting a different gloss on the issue of access. The UN and ICRC alleged in mid-1985 that the Relief and Rehabilitation Commission of the Ethiopian government could reach 80 per cent of the Tigrayan population, and 76 per cent of civilians in Eritrea.[10] Throughout the period, main stream media coverage helped perpetuate the erroneous view that people in Front-controlled territories were being assisted through town based distributions in government held areas.[11]

US Strategic and Humanitarian Interests

If there were people hoping for a political edge as a result of US policy toward Ethiopia during the mid-1980s, they were in for disappointment. With regard to any idea that the Ethiopian government could be won back to the West with humanitarian assistance, for example, it soon became clear that the Dergue was taking Western food with one hand and Soviet arms with the other. Moreover, it was quite happy with the arrangement, even to the extent of publicly blaming the severity of the food crisis on the West's slow response.[12] On the other hand, if some felt that the TPLF could have provided a vehicle for US low intensity conflict against the Ethiopian government in the context of the Reagan Doctrine, their hopes were crushed with the open ascendancy of a Stalinist oriented Marxist-Leninist League of Tigray (MLLT) within the TPLF in the spring of 1985.

Largely on the basis of a humanitarian agenda, the media, public interest groups, NGOs, Congress, and USAID roared into the vacuum created by the political stalemate. News of the Ethiopian famine dominated the media, to the extent any African issue is capable, in late 1984, and Band Aid and Live Aid saw unparalleled celebrity activism in 1985. Operational NGOs were quite forceful in advocacy efforts with Congress and the administration. The consortium InterAction, for example, was formed in the Autumn of 1984 and was instrumental in maintaining momentum in Congress during the following year. A non-operational citizen's lobbying organisation addressing hunger issues, Bread for the World, was credited by the chief administrator for USAID as having forced onto the Reagan administration the policy line that "a hungry child knows no politics."[13] Congress itself was active in passing three emergency supplementary appropriation bills in 1984-85, as well as a comprehensive bill called the African Famine Relief and Recovery Act of 1985.[14] But when it came to US policy beyond humanitarian assistance, Congress appeared as divided internally as the administration. Some Democratic members of the House constantly pushed for dialogue with the Ethiopian government, while Republicans highlighted egregious human rights violations and pressed for sanctions, which were passed but never implemented.

USAID also registered strongly in the policy making process, ultimately dictating a humanitarian agenda which advocated delivering only emergency assistance, channelling relief through non-governmental or multilateral organisations and, importantly, serving people in both government and Front held areas. American aid swung behind the CBO. On this basis, from a position of restraint or absence, the US became the largest donor in Ethiopia and the non-government areas. In Ethiopia, almost all American assistance was directed through NGOs. This was different from many other western donors which, until this period at least, had largely channelled their aid through the government's Relief and Rehabilitation Commission. The US was also the only country to investigate the role of government human rights violations in the creation of famine, an issue which had been covered up by the UN and other large donors.[15] The 1985 investigation concluded that there was no "deliberate policy of starvation" being conducted by the government.[16] Later analysis has shown that American investigators failed to understand that the Ethiopian government had shifted to using the provision, rather than the denial, of food aid as part of its counter-insurgency strategy. Destroying the means of subsistence by civilians and then using internationally provided food aid to lure people into government held garrison towns was the new favoured war strategy.[17]

The large increase in humanitarian assistance combined with what was tantamount to the violation of Ethiopian sovereignty as a result of supporting the CBO was, in the final analysis, not motivated by perceived strategic exigencies, although such considerations softened any opposition the decision might have brought. The resulting aid flow to both sides of the conflict in Ethiopia and Eritrea can be seen as signalling the hesitant and uncertain beginning of a Western humanitarian agenda in North-South relations. By the mid-1980s the cold war in Africa was already on the wane. In Ethiopia and Angola where the Soviets still clung on, they were now on the defensive.[18] The historical significance of American and, subsequently, EC assistance to the cross border operation can be seen as a prelude to the dawning of the so-called New World Order in which humanitarianism has claimed an enhanced significance in international relations.

US Assistance to the Cross Border Operation

Several American NGOs, including LWR, were pushing USAID for assistance for months before it fully committed itself to the emergency. In relation to the cross border operation, LWR became the main conduit of USAID assistance. The timing of USAID's decision to back the CBO, although late, was still critical in sustaining ERD's programme as well as in helping to staunch the flow of even more refugees to Sudan. From the spring of 1984 it became apparent to ERD that it could no longer buy food from local merchants in Sudan due to the effects of drought. ERD decided to switch its strategy away from local purchase to external food donations.[19] In April 1984, USAID donated 5,000 MT of grain to LWR which ERD received in July.[20] In September, LWR also received cash to transport Canadian grain. It was following the media coverage of the famine in October, however, which saw the first large US food aid disbursements through LWR and hence ERD. In November, 23,000 mt was given and this was followed by another large disbursement in December.[21] Apart from food aid, transport capacity was also a major constraint for ERA and REST. ERD sought to address this when LWR approached USAID and the Office of Foreign Disaster Assistance (OFDA) about the possibility of providing trucks. Original concerns centred on ensuring that the trucks would only be moving humanitarian supplies, not people.[22] The National Security Council apparently turned down the first request due to the potential strategic uses of the trucks in late 1984. In early 1985, however, USAID approached LWR and encouraged the latter to submit a new proposal.[23] In mid-1985, USAID and OFDA approved a grant for 150 trucks.[24]

Besides LWR, for a time USAID also used Mercy Corps International and ICRC as conduits to Front held territory. In the case of the former, however, this was accessed through ERD. Thus, apart from relatively modest assistance to ICRC, ERD, through LWR, became the primary mechanism for channelling US relief to non-government areas. The Mennonite Central Committee also secured large quantities of wheat from the Canadian Foodgrain Bank for ERD.[25] It should be noted that USAID's reliance upon ERD stands in contrast to the European Community. While ERD was an important conduit for EC aid, the EC also came to use other CBO agencies, such as, OXFAM UK and Trocaire. Following its commitment at the end of 1984, the following year was pivotal for American involvement in the cross border operation. From 1985 through 1990, USAID supplied on average more than half of all relief assistance going through ERD (Figure 3). This represented a tremendous change in the sourcing of commodities for the operation, in essence clearly breaking the European monopoly. Although LWR played a key role as a credible conduit for US resources, this sudden dependence upon American assistance raised great concerns amongst other ERD members. This issue will be discussed further in Chapter Six.

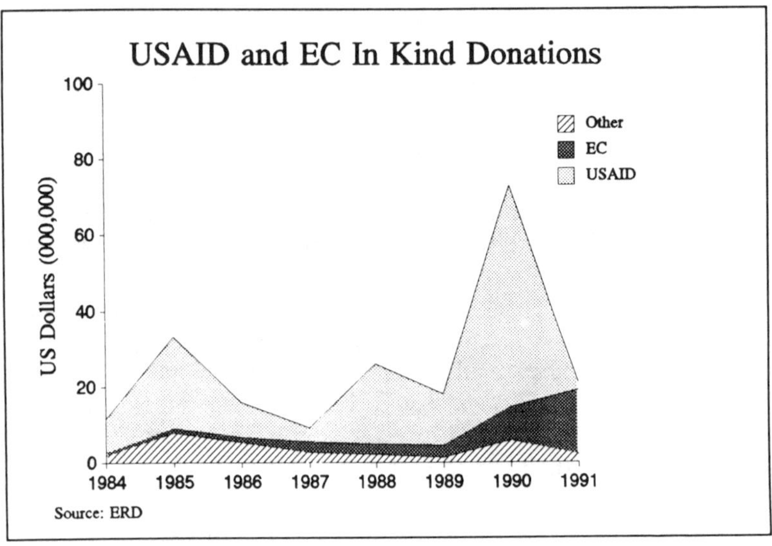

Figure 3

The Emergence of a Humanitarian Agenda

Similar to the interpretation of America's previous reluctance to become involved, contemporary commentaries often cite cold war motives behind the eventual US support for the cross border operation. A still widely quoted series by The Times of London analysed the visit to Sudan in early 1985 by the US Vice-President in rather mechanistic terms and concluded that it was primarily to use the threat of supporting the Fronts through the CBO as a means of prizing Ethiopia from the Soviet Union.[26] It is alleged that Bush discussed several options with the

Nimiery regime to bolster the CBO. These included road building and the provision of large amounts of food aid and trucks. US support for the CBO, however, can also be seen in relation to the American efforts then underway to pressure the Ethiopian government to feed civilians in contested areas. That is, if the government would not do this, the US would channel assistance through the CBO. By way of response, the Dergue launched an offensive in Tigray to convince the American government that REST could not deliver food safely to civilians in Tigray. Following the Sudan trip, however, the US Vice President met with the Ethiopian Foreign Minister and the broad outline of the Food for the North (FFN) initiative was agreed as a way of providing relief to contested areas from the government side.

In practice, the FFN initiative, rather than contested areas, became a mechanism for supplying relief commodities to government held towns. It has already been remarked that the control of food aid from garrison towns was an important tool in the Dergue's counter-insurgency strategy. In the case of FFN, large American NGOs, that is, Catholic Relief Services and World Vision were the principle operational agencies in Eritrea and Tigray respectively. Moreover, these agencies became the main channels of USAID assistance on the government side. The involvement of CRS and WV in FFN has given rise to allegations of a lack of impartiality and their being players in little more than a civilian pacification programme.[27] The merits of this case cannot detain us here. What is important, however, is that USAID assistance was flowing through ERD at the same time as FFN. Not only does this illustrate the complexity of the situation, it is difficult to reach a ready conclusion on how American strategic interest was supposed to be served. In fact, one could argue that this interest was cancelled out since both the Fronts and the Dergue were able to derive some benefit. The only common agenda for the US was a humanitarian one.

Although the US did significantly increase its assistance to the cross border operation, it did not do so to the extent allegedly promised. One ICRC official was quoted as saying,

> This US operation has been like the wind in Khartoum. One day it's in the West; the next day it's in the South - on and off like that.[28]

This volatility can partly be explained by the fact that, during the emergence of a new policy paradigm, the different sections of the American government were not working together. While USAID was attempting to respond to the humanitarian crisis, the State Department, National

Security Council and the CIA had conflicting agendas.[29] The policy making context was polarised. However, it can be argued that ethical imperatives won out over strategic and ideological considerations.[30] In such a divided and uncertain situation, internal pressures on the foreign policy apparatus from the media, NGOs, Congress, and public opinion pushed an anti-famine agenda to the fore. Beginning in Africa, this can be seen as the first stirring of humanitarian intervention as an element of Western foreign policy.

One element in the equation which did have strategic implications, however, was the importance of refugee prevention in Sudan. The Nimiery regime was an important US ally in the Red Sea region, and the threat of massive refugee flows into eastern Sudan was considered potentially destabilising.[31] Over 16,000 Tigrayan refugees crossed the Sudanese border on just one day in December 1984.[32] In this situation,

> The role of the cross border programme as a refugee prevention mechanism was used frequently in internal State Department discussions as a means to justify the questionable legality of the programme in relation to the Ethiopian government.[33]

This is important because it indicates that USAID lawyers had concerns over the legal ramifications of the CBO. It is interesting to note that USAID tackled the issue of illegality in a similar manner to ERD. That is, apart from maintaining political distance, a policy of trying to balance US donations to government and Front controlled areas also emerged.[34] The Canadian government also strove to maintain a semblance of balance in its aid programme.[35] It is unclear, however, to what extent balance was achieved. Figures cited in support of the contention that the CBO was grossly underfunded compared to government channels usually compare the amount of aid given to ERA and REST with the aid levels on the government side which account for the entire country, not just Eritrea and Tigray. The desire on the part of the US to be seen by the media as contributing to the relief effort made contributions to government areas more attractive because of easier accessibility, further clouding the extent to which balance was achieved.

Despite the opening of a new and important conduit for American aid into famine affected areas, US support for ERD remained discreet for a number of reasons. First and foremost was the sovereignty issue. Second was a fear that public support for the cross border operation would spur even more Ethiopian military activity against the supply lines from Sudan, or retaliation against US personnel or NGOs in government areas of Ethiopia.[36] Finally, there was some worry that a more public posture would encourage right wing organisations to advocate the escalation of US support into military assistance for the Fronts to topple the Ethiopian government.[37] The Canadians, on the other hand, encouraged public discussion about their role. The Canadian International Development Association (CIDA) told the Executive Director of the Canadian Lutheran World Relief that it "is expected that you will let the general public know about our involvement."[38]

The UN and the Continuing Silence

The US, and increasingly other Western donors, were ahead of the UN in terms of assessing and responding to humanitarian need in Ethiopia and Eritrea. The UN remained handcuffed by the issue of sovereignty. It was not only politically unable to change but, it was even hostile to those that suggested that change was needed. The UN Emergency Office for Ethiopia (UNEOE) was set up near the end of 1984 in order to coordinate the burgeoning relief response. Aside from ignoring the critical role of the cross border operation, the UNEOE repeatedly concealed evidence about egregious and systematic human rights abuses by the Ethiopian government. It has been argued that,

> UNEOE's main function was to act as a screening device, giving the appearance of competent action in response to famine but not compromising its actual position in Addis Ababa by unduly antagonising the host government... it would have been as embarrassing for the donors who had entrusted resources to the Ethiopian government as it was for the government itself to have aid misallocation exposed.[39]

It was not until 1990, and then with some difficulty, that the UN was drawn into aid negotiations involving non-government areas.

The Commitment of the European Community to the CBO

As famine conditions worsened during 1983, for humanitarian reasons, the Fronts changed their position and agreed to accept relief assistance from donor governments regardless of whether such governments provided recognition. By early 1984, the Fronts were willing to furnish any reasonable assistance in this respect.[40] Although many ERD members were concerned when USAID first indicated a willingness to become involved in 1984, the Fronts and IAs accepted this assistance on face value. It did, however, establish an incentive to ERD to encourage other European and Canadian donors to act as a counter balance to American aid.[41]

Between 1984 and the end of 1985, from initially being associated with the EC's Emergency Division, ERD became firmly attached to the Food Aid Division. This shift is significant and makes important changes in the role of NGOs generally. Chapter Four has described ERD's first approach to the EC's Emergency Division in 1983. While initially successful, by early 1984, the Division had shown itself to be unhappy with the nature of ERD's reporting. Apart from insisting on fine detail, the exact nature of its complaint is unclear. Growing familiarity however indicated that Lome restrictions were also involved. At this time, emergency assistance was governed by Article 137 of Lome II which demanded that such aid required the permission of the recipient government.[42] The Emergency Division's position was that this made EC assistance problematic in relation to Eritrea and, especially, Tigray. Further tension was created with ERD, however, by the fact that Emergency Division aid was administered under Article 950 which was a cost head supported by the EC's own budget. In theory, such aid could have been used in non-government areas despite Lome restrictions. Although unhelpful, the Emergency Division was seen by ERD as potentially more useful than the Food Aid Division because of its access to larger funds.

In mid-1984, these difficulties, together with the fact that approaches by ERD members to their governments had produced limited results, expressed themselves in ERD considering approaching WCC to help orchestrate a joint ecumenical approach to the EC.[43] DIA, however, was becoming increasingly familiar with the workings of the EC's Food Aid Division and making contacts with its staff. Alliances were also being formed with the NGO Division. Food Aid, unlike Emergency Division, was not governed by the Lome conventions and could therefore be more flexible. Its budget came from the EC and it had access to CAP agricultural surpluses.[44] During 1984, the increased publicity that the war and conditions within Eritrea and Tigray was attracting enabled ERD and other agencies to make use of this flexibility. Food Aid, for its part, was also able to chart a policy course independent of EC member governments owing to the weak links between the Commission and the European Parliament. This, however, created a situation of internal division within the Commission. Emergency Division, for example, channelled assistance to the government side, while Food Aid assisted the CBO. This led to tensions and internal turf wars. While EC total assistance to the CBO would grow steadily to become its single largest food aid programme, such internal rivalries gave the outward impression that EC assistance was fragile.

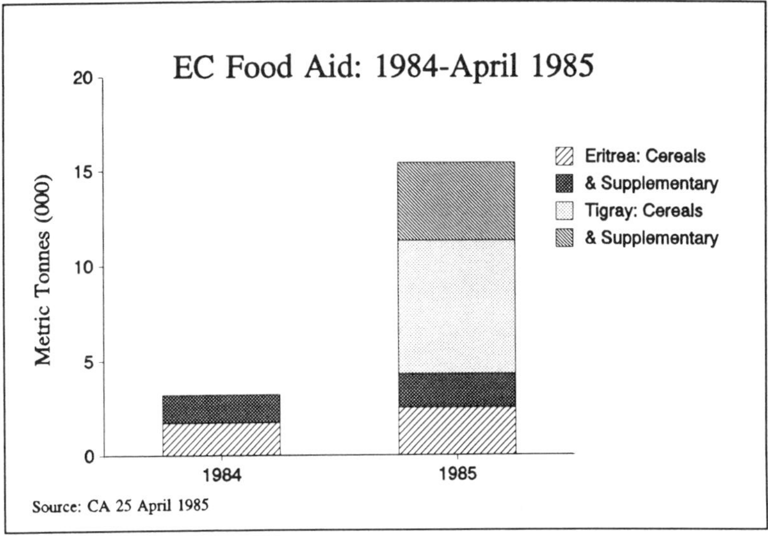

Figure 4

During 1984, DIA was successful in obtaining Food Aid Division support for ERD. In November, when DIA and ERD's Executive Secretary met the head of Emergency Division in Brussels to clear up the earlier reporting problem, the meeting became acrimonious. It emerged that Emergency Division was putting pressure on Food Aid Division to "throw the book at us too."[45] This threat, however, did not materialise and, by the beginning of 1985, other agencies, such as OXFAM Belgique and OXFAM UK, had also begun to work with Food Aid Division on the CBO.[46] Earlier requests that these agencies had made to Emergency Division had either been ignored or answered by Food Aid. By mid-1985, plans to attempt to work with the EC's Emergency Division, or bring further pressure to bear on it, had been dropped in favour of Food Aid.[47] Within a few months, the relationship with Food Aid was well established with DIA recognised as the agency presenting ERD's coordinated annual request to the EC. In October, ERD's Executive Secretary met the head of Food Aid Division to discuss long term arrangements and using ERD as a "buffer for EEC supply to ERA/REST".[48]

The erosion of sovereignty which began in the mid-1980s, can be seen in the changes within the EC. The fact that Food Aid and not Emergency Division took the lead on the cross border operation is symptomatic of the wider re-working of North-South relations that had begun. Governed by a now outdated sovereignty-based developmental paradigm, that is, the Lome Conventions, the Emergency Division lacked the flexibility to address the growing phenomenon of complex emergencies. Other Divisions, such as those governing Food Aid and NGOs, being free of these constraints were able to fill this vacuum. Although at one level personality differences played their part, one can detect similar hesitant steps toward a new policy paradigm as evinced with regard to USAID. As the unravelling effects of the end of the cold war began to be increasingly felt, these constraints resulted in eventual reform of the EC's emergency capacity with the formation of the European Community Humanitarian Office (ECHO) in 1991. This ongoing and, in the opinion of many NGOs, controversial reform process is akin to that currently taking place within the UN.

The Internationalisation of Public Welfare and De Facto Recognition

The changing position of USAID and the EC to the CBO should be seen in relation to the wider shift that was taking place in the relations linking donor and recipient governments and NGOs. Not only did USAID and the EC help ERD, they also assisted NGOs within Ethiopia on a scale not seen before. The establishment in Ethiopia of the Churches Drought Action Africa/Ethiopia (CDAA/E) consortium in 1984 from Catholic and Protestant agencies is a case in point. An important reason for this development was that donors regarded NGOs as giving them more control over the use and destination of their food aid. USAID, for its part, had long preferred NGOs to government agencies. Its wider development from the mid-1980s, was tantamount to a growing suspicion of indigenous political authority. Between 1984 and 1985, scores of NGOs set up shop in Ethiopia and Sudan. The evidence from Ethiopia suggests that part of the swing of donor policy toward NGOs was a response to the growing public realisation that the government was engaged in the widespread diversion and abuse of food aid. A piece by War on Want at the end of 1984[49] captures the spirit of the time. It describes the situation inside Ethiopia as characterised by widespread official abuse existing alongside accountable NGO operations. This contrast is further highlighted by the comparison with the efficiency of the IAs.

In some respects, this enhanced role of NGOs has emerged out of a process of political struggle between donor governments and recipient states. International NGOs are mandated to form contracts with people not government, and the growing interests in human rights is an important mechanism whereby NGOs have attempted to reflect popular interests at the global level. Many oppressed African groups, for example, are now better represented in Washington than Mogadishu or Luanda. The donor/NGO safety net systems which have developed from this period in many countries are, essentially, parallel constructions providing basic public welfare assistance with little or no recipient government control.[50] This internationalisation of public welfare denotes a weakening of sovereignty and has often undermined internal capacity. The main contrast with this development and ERD was that within Eritrea and Tigray the public welfare programme remained under indigenous management.

That donor/NGO safety nets should proliferate from the mid-1980s, is another indication that the cold war in Africa had effectively ended by this time. Recipient government attitudes toward donor/NGO safety nets has often been ambivalent. On the one had, they are an important source of resources, on the other, they represent an erosion of authority. The Dergue quickly learnt how to use NGOs within its political programme. In Sudan, however, until recently the relationship has been more antagonistic as ERD would eventually find out.

During the first part of the 1980s, assistance to Eritrea and Tigray was a sensitive issue for donor governments. By 1985, although still careful, the commitment of USAID and the EC to channel aid through ERD to ERA and REST was a most significant move. In the case of USAID, for example, Eritrea and Tigray were regarded as a single programme area subsumed under the heading of 'Ethiopian Refugees' and administered from Khartoum.[51] Until 1989, the EC also disguised CBO support as part of its Sudan programme. While still maintaining the cross border conventions of a low profile, Ethiopian sovereignty had nevertheless been ignored with the Fronts gaining implicit recognition through this assistance. Or at least, that they controlled areas that could not be reached through government channels. In distinction to earlier

NGO led operations, for example, in Nigeria and Cambodia, officially backed cross border aid to Eritrea and Tigray can be seen as the first international humanitarian intervention of the modern, post cold war era. The West had begun its hesitant and confused journey to Kurdistan and Somalia. With increased relief to non-government areas and a tightening of the control of aid to the Ethiopian government, the ultimate collapse of the Dergue was pre-figured in the events of 1984 and 1985.

CHAPTER SIX

The Re-Establishment of ERD

It has already been argued that the mid-1980s was a period of major change not only in terms of increasing media exposure concerning the situation in Eritrea and Tigray but, especially through the involvement of USAID facilitated by LWR, the amount of relief assistance channelled through ERD increased considerably. In terms of membership support and representation, it was also a time when ERD completed the transition from being a Scandinavian dominated consortium into a more broadly based ecumenical organisation. This section describes the changes introduced into ERD's structure and mandate to accommodate the beginning of a new era of enhanced NGO operations.

The February 1984 Evaluation

Arising out of the tensions that had been building up since its inception in 1981, by mid-1983, it was already felt that ERD had outgrown its original organisation. The short, nine day evaluation completed in February 1984[1], initiated a lengthy and sometimes difficult process of negotiation which would not be resolved until October 1985, when a new agreement was signed. This extended interregnum is notable for the fact that it corresponded with a substantial increase in the workload of ERD's Khartoum office which struggled to survive. The discussions also brought out many of the difficulties, including conflicting member views, which NGO consortia face.

The evaluation team was composed of representatives of SCC, NCA, SCR, LWR and WCC. The inclusion of WCC is indicative of a lingering belief that WCC could still play an important liaison role. The main finding of the evaluation can be treated under the following sub-headings:

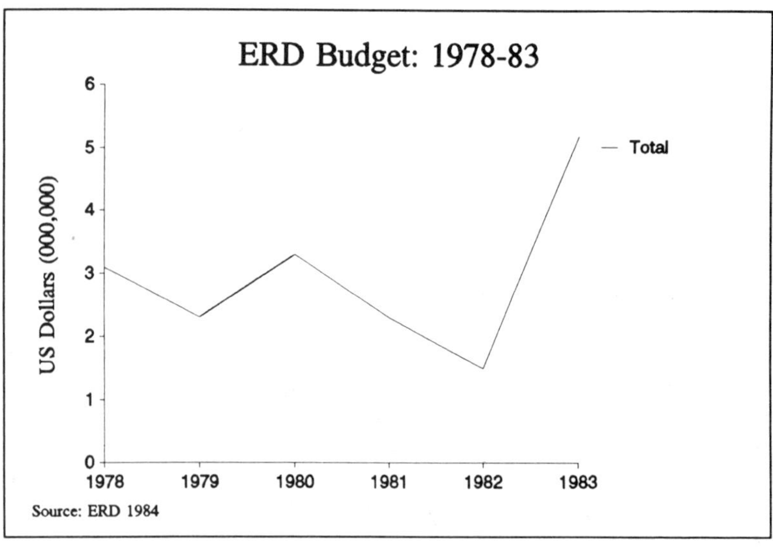

Figure 5

(a) Impact

It was clear that both the IAs and ERD had been able to meet only a small proportion of the needs that they had described. In 1983, for example, ERA had claimed that 1 million people in Eritrea had been at risk but, due to organisational constraints, had only requested 35% of the aid required. For its part, ERD could only deliver 17% of this or, about 5% of the estimated total requirement. For REST, its biggest constraint was transport, meaning that even if the food aid were available, it could only transport from Sudan around 8% of the estimated 75,000 mt required for the 1.2 million people deemed at risk. Including the internal purchase of surplus grain within Tigray, ERD managed to supply 4,360 mt in 1983 or, nearly 6% of the total estimate. If anything, the evaluation team noted that ERD's performance over the preceding years had stagnated in the face of growing need (Figure 5). Despite the fact that contributions had begun to grow, the budget was not keeping pace with demand. It recommended that the 1984 target budget for members be nearly doubled to $10 million. Out of this budget, ERD should be aiming to meet about half of the IA's requests.

(b) Administration

The evaluation reported on the growing workload in Khartoum and the inability of the existing staff numbers to adequately discharge the administrative and monitoring duties that the 1981 agreement had stipulated. In fact, little monitoring had been possible. Committee meetings and reporting had also tended to be ad hoc. The recruitment of an additional expatriate staff member to act as an Assistant Executive Secretary was recommended. This extra staffing was seen as necessary in order to increase the relief programme.

(c) Member Representation

It was realised that to improve the performance of ERD, its organisational structure needed to be widened to better represent the member agencies whose increased efforts were being sought. Although not describing in detail what this organisation would be, in relation to the NCA/SCC agreement, the evaluation talked in terms of an autonomous ERD having affiliation with SCC. In other words, widening ERD was at the expense of weakening the position of SCC. At the same time, the relation with the IA's was to be improved by incorporating a necessity for ERD to consult on matters directly affecting them.

(d) Rehabilitation and Development

The evaluation recommended that ERD's relief mandate should be broadened to include rehabilitation. This involved agricultural inputs such as seeds and tools, continued support for internal purchase and water resource development to increase food production and access to drinking water. The payment of transport costs to the point of distribution was also advocated. While the possibility of development work was not examined directly, the team felt that a future review of ERD ought to consider this issue and should look favourably at supporting community based development work.

(e) Neutrality and Public Profile

Although in several important areas the evaluation had recommended change, in relation to ERD's public profile, the team supported the view that had been in effect since the late 1970s. Discretion remained a key word and, although it has been shown that ERD was not having a significant impact, the evaluation advised against any sudden increase in the size of the programme should this alert or embarrass the Ethiopian or Sudanese governments. The criteria for the cross border operation were defined as need, the capacity of the IAs to deliver, and importantly, the lack of possible access from the government side. That ERD should take up human rights issues was ruled as being beyond its mandate. It was felt that such issues should go through SCC to WCC which would then encourage other Church agencies to take them up. ERD's neutral stance was therefore upheld. Indeed, the demands of USAID and EEC, once they became involved in the CBO, would strengthen the need for a discrete and neutral screen.

Initial Interpretation by ERD Members of the Evaluation

The ERD evaluation was discussed by member agencies in May 1984, in Geneva.[2] In addition to the core agencies of SCC, NCA, SCR, DCA, DDW/BFW, ICCO, DIA, CA and LWR, representatives from WCC where also present. This was the first occasion that members had all formally sat together on ERD business. Although the meeting did not resolve what quickly became the main issue raised, that is, the need to improve member representation and strengthen organisational capacity, it did set the scene for the lengthy process of meetings and discussions that was not finally resolved until October 1985. It also gave an important indication of the direction of ERD's development and the tensions within it.

The meeting accepted the fact that ERD had outgrown its organisational structure and that adaptation was needed. The need to substantially increase the budget was also accepted. In relation to the evaluation, however, some important contrasts became evident.

(a) Member Representation

The necessity of improving representation was accepted. It was pointed out that accessing EEC assistance, for example, was made all the more difficult by ERD's unrepresentative structure. The main organisational problem was the fact that any increase in member representation would be at the expense of SCC voting power. This necessitated some sensitive thinking. Although the need to consult IAs on matters directly affecting them was agreed, the question of SCC was left to an Interim Committee composed of ERD's Executive Secretary, SCC, SCR and CA to produce a discussion document by the autumn. It was then hoped that a new agreement would be signed in January 1985.

(b) Rehabilitation and Development

The suggestion that ERD should consider expanding its mandate to include development was discussed and, although not unanimously, it was rejected in favour of retaining and expanding its relief mandate to include rehabilitation inputs. This expansion, however, would be largely limited to improving food supply and production. The Scandinavian agencies, in particular, preferred a relief mandate. It was also agreed to pay transport costs to the point of delivery. While falling short of approving development work, however, the agreement to accept rehabilitation was important. With the exception of local purchase in Tigray, which began in 1983, the relief programme to date had largely figured around the supply of basic foodstuffs. From 1984, in both Eritrea and Tigray, the public welfare activities supported by ERD became more varied. This important development is discussed further in Chapter Seven. A tentative division of labour was discussed in which SCR, CA and WCC would concentrate on supplementary foodstuffs; CA would take responsibility for medicines and equipment; with DIA picking up other needs.

(c) Neutrality and Public Profile

The meeting confirmed the evaluation team's recommendation that ERD should maintain its non-political and neutral stance. Experience with donors had shown that international assistance could only be raised as long as ERD appeared impartial. Donor governments concerns over Ethiopian sovereignty necessitated this. Although it was agreed that a low media profile for ERD was necessary, the dilemma, given the growing crisis, was recognised. Some members discounted that exposure of the cross border operation would have adverse effects on the churches within Ethiopia on the grounds that their position could not become any worse than it already was. Up to this period, only a few of the ERD members, including DIA and CA, had been prepared to publicly acknowledge their involvement.[3] Indeed, DIA had been criticised by the evaluation team for publishing a couple of ERD monitoring reports towards the end of 1983. The situation was resolved by agreeing that while the neutrality of ERD as a consortium should be maintained, it was up to members what public position they took as individual agencies. In general, the IAs were unhappy with this situation. They wanted ERD itself to speak out and were often critical of individual member efforts in this respect.

The May 1984 to October 1985 Debate

Despite the fact that the need for a new structure was recognised, it took eighteen months before an agreement to re-establish ERD was concluded. This period was one of unprecedented change and development in the history of the emergency. These developments included the greatly increased media attention after October 1984; the increased member contributions that this made possible; the beginning of USAID's serious involvement; the fall of Nimiery in April 1985 and the exposure of the extent of the famine in North Sudan; and, beginning in 1985, the emergence of political differences between the EPLF and TPLF and the reorganisation of REST. The intensity of these developments, at a time when important questions concerning the structure of ERD remained unresolved, nearly forced its collapse in 1985.

That such an important agreement took so long to reach indicates the difficulty of some of the issues and, significantly, that once representation is increased then the different philosophies and preferences of the member NGOs come into play. One of the difficulties concerned the role of SCC and its reluctance to accept a reduced position. Other issues related to the continuing internal debate on the scope of ERD's mandate. For those agencies favouring development work, the period was one of forming bilateral links with the IAs. For their part, the IAs supported both the moves to internationalise ERD and for members and other agencies to establish bilateral relations with them. While appreciating the support of ERD, the IAs were always concerned lest ERD became a monopoly supplier. By 1983, ERA, for example, had established links of various forms with 120 international agencies. Internationalisation and bilateralism both increased their access and representation.

Even when humanitarian relief provides the common denominator, the history of ERD would suggest that collaboration through consortia is not a natural state for NGOs. For most of its history, ERD was kept afloat by the personalities involved. The fact that member representatives knew each other and had shared disappointment and success served as a bond and sense of solidarity which overlay the significant policy differences which often separated them. Apart from the ecumenical nature of the agencies, this fractious solidarity was maintained by the exigencies of the war and the shared dislike for the policies being pursued by the Ethiopian government.[4]

The Position of SCC and the Internationalisation of ERD

By early 1984, it had become evident that SCC's changing political fortunes with regard to the Sudanese government had become a potential liability for the ERD. By June 1984, the need for ERD to find a way in which it could distance itself from SCC was seen as pressing.[5] During August, discussions between some of the European members had produced a working proposal in which ERD should pragmatically seek whatever umbrella suited it best. In this context, it was suggested that NCA should be asked to take on the role of lead agency for a consortium in which SCC was simply represented rather than being connected to SCC by an "umbilical cord".[6] By October, a view had emerged in which ERD was pictured by some members as an international relief consortium working in Eritrea and Tigray alongside other consortia, that is, EIAC and TTAC, in a division of labour.[7] A full meeting had been scheduled for October 1984, in Woudschoten in the Netherlands to finally resolve the representation question.

The Woudschoten meeting, however, had to proceed without the attendance of SCC. Three possible solutions had been under discussion. Firstly, an ERD associated with SCC; secondly, associated with NCA; or, finally, an autonomous ERD. During the discussions earlier in the year, SCC had expressed its concern at having its role reduced.[8] Despite several requests, however, other than informally indicating that it preferred an autonomous ERD not under NCA, it never clearly articulated its position or wrote its views down.[9-10] The Woudschoten meeting recommended a continuing association with SCC but with NCA as a lead agency. This proved an unsatisfactory conclusion and, in December, the problem was defined as being unable to reach a text that was acceptable to all parties namely "the donors need for control - SCC's need for not losing anything."[11]

By February 1985, the impasse had reached crisis point. Delays on reaching an agreement had begun to affect donor confidence and had contributed to a marginalisation of ERD during the course of 1984.[12] The ERD Executive Secretary, in a letter of desperation to member agencies, argued that the time had now passed for any further meetings and discussions: an immediate resolution was required.[13] Delay on agreeing to a new structure was having a negative effect on the relief performance of ERD and, in Tigray in particular, this could increase suffering. He proposed a new structure which was partly designed to overcome the difficulties with SCC. Within this structure, the member agencies would elect a lead agency which in turn would appoint an additional member to the SCC dominated Executive Committee. The resulting administrative arrangement was to be seen as an interim measure which would be voted on at the next Board Meeting towards the end of 1985. In the meantime, NCA would provide the point of coordination outside Sudan. In many respects, this proposal was a holding measure which confirmed the status quo. The draft agreement was also re-written which, after further modification would serve as the final text.

In May 1985, CA hosted an ERD meeting in London in which a range of issues relating to the new agreement were discussed. By this time, the question of SCC had receded, it having become resigned to the prospect of having its role changed. Other issues, such as ERD's mandate were still under debate, however.

The Growth of Bilateral Development Links and the Attitude of the IAs

The inability of ERD to reach a decision on its re-establishment contributed, in some members' eyes, to its marginalisation during the momentous year of 1984. Besides EIAC and TTAC, other agencies began an involvement in the CBO and, while remaining the monopoly food aid supplier until around 1987, ERD's overall share of CBO activity began to decline. ICCO forcefully argued that events had shown that ERD's limited relief mandate was no longer appropriate.[14] Furthermore, in the face of continued lack of progress on a new agreement, several Dutch agencies had decided to form bilateral links with the IAs for the purpose of development work. It was even questioned whether ERD was, in fact, still necessary. During the course of 1984, however, this trend had been wider than the Dutch.[15] Since 1983, CA, for example, had supported EIAC and TTAC and in 1984, it had recognised ERA and REST as bilateral partner organisations and had supported some of their administrative costs.[16] In 1983, BFW also changed its policy and began channelling aid in kind directly to the IAs, at the same time as continuing to put cash contributions through ERD. This trend can be seen as contributing to the diversification of internationally supported programmes in Eritrea and Tigray then underway.

By the time of the May 1985 meeting, a division which had been developing for more than a year had emerged between the ERD agencies. Roughly speaking, this contrasted agencies wishing to widen ERD's mandate to include either development work, or work with refugees in

Sudan. This group included DIA, CA, ICCO and DCA. Some of these agencies, as we have seen, were also keen to develop bilateral relations with the IAs due to what were perceived as restrictions in the ERD mandate. The other group, which included NCA, SCR and LWR, for various reasons worked more or less exclusively through ERD on a relief basis.[17] While not having a monopoly of the argument, this group clearly articulated the need for a relief brief to maintain the neutrality of ERD. By mid-1985, discussions between these two groups had replaced the SCC as the main area of unresolved questions in moving toward a settlement.[18]

The eventual outcome of these discussions was significantly influenced by the attitude of the IAs. Broadly speaking, apart from the issue of allowing greater access and transport costs, which had been accepted without much difficulty, the interests of the IAs lay in transforming ERD into an international consortium but, at the same time, limiting any extension of its mandate lest ERD should become a monopoly supplier. The IAs therefore supported the restriction of ERD to a relief brief, preferring to handle development work on a bilateral basis. Since the process of re-establishing ERD was first initiated, ERA, for example, had supported moves to reduce the role of SCC.[19] Moreover, with regard to bilateral links, it was of the view that ERD's mandate should be restricted to those agencies which, for some reason, cannot work with ERA directly. Other agencies should be encouraged to form bilateral links. It was therefore against any unnecessary growth of ERD, including the widening of its mandate.[20] This position stemmed from the continuing criticism of ERD's failure to speak out about the real causes of the famine and Ethiopia's violation of human rights. Some ERD members were also felt lacking in this respect. An enlarged or monopoly ERD, apart from restricting the IA's external contacts, threatened to stifle the IA's long-standing aim of mobilizing Western public opinion.

Neutrality and ERD's Behind the Scenes Diplomacy

Although ERD had agreed to maintain its public non-political stance this did not preclude its members making public statements or, for that matter, playing a diplomatic liaison role on behalf of the Fronts. Indeed, this can be seen as part of the contradiction between neutrality and involvement. It has already been noted that the neutral stance of ERD during the early 1980s frequently drew criticism from the EPLF despite the fact that this was the only platform on which ERD could access donor assistance. By the early 1980s, with the worsening famine situation, the EPLF and TPLF became keen to press its proposal for a safe passage and attempted to establish links with the OAU in order to reduce its isolation. These were the first proposals to raise such a prospect in the contested areas. Both Fronts offered protection for relief convoys and relief workers. Within this context, the neutral humanitarian stance of ERD, rather than being a weakness, increasingly placed it in the position of an honest broker.

From 1983, two different lines of activity were developed, that is, efforts to establish relations with OAU and the Ethiopian government. Following the Red Star campaign in Eritrea, for example, attempts were first made to forge better links with the OAU and so reduce the isolation of the EPLF. A number of informal meetings took place between DIA, CA and NCA to discuss how relations could be established with African governments and low profile meetings where arranged on behalf of the EPLF. At the beginning of 1985, DDW also wrote to Julius Nyerere to solicit his help.[21] The Tanzanian government, in particular, was targeted but, by 1987, having failed to gain the support of the OAU, the initiative had petered out.[22]

With regard to links with the Ethiopian government, in early 1984, ERA contacted NCA on behalf of the EPLF with a request that it could act as a go-between.[23] In March 1984, NCA's General Secretary visited Addis Ababa and established contact with the Ministry of Foreign Affairs. He travelled there several times bearing messages, his point of contact moving from the Ministry to the RRC Commissioner. Despite the fact of having a programme in Ethiopia, in its meetings with the government NCA had decided to keep nothing back concerning its involvement in the cross border operation on the grounds that is was a purely humanitarian gesture. This is a rare move for an NGO. Any perceived threat to a country programme is usually sufficient to secure agency silence. Although strongly rebuked, the RRC did not move against NCA's programmes within Ethiopia. With the failure of the Ethiopian government to respond to the joint agency appeals for a safe passage at the end of 1984, these meetings came to a halt.

These initial diplomatic efforts by ERD members in order to broker peace are notable in that they are regarded as confirming the veracity of ERD's neutral approach. During the late 1970s and early 1980s, the Fronts were critical of what was seen as a lack of solidarity. By the mid-1980s, however, this very neutrality became a valuable asset since ERD, in the interests of peace, could present itself to all parties as an honest broker. This was also a reason why, unlike EIAC and TTAC which forged closer organisational ties with the IA's, ERD chose to keep more distance and, as far as possible, treat the IA's even handedly.

ERD Members and Public Opinion

The effects of the publicity during the early 1980s, surrounding the Ethiopian diversion of food aid has already been discussed. During the course of 1983, interest slowly grew in Eritrea and Tigray with more people, including a few media personnel, crossing the border from Sudan into the non-government areas.[24] ERD itself began to attract small donations from other agencies, such as Grassroots International, which tended to identify more directly with what was happening in these areas. Growing familiarity, however, also prompted some of the ERD agencies to become more active in drawing attention to the worsening situation. Towards the end of 1983, CA and DIA published a report which made use of information coming through ERD channels.[25] This public move, in which the agencies identified their involvement, was matched by BFW/DDW private attempts to elicit the support of the German government.[26] These developments, although to some extent they cut across the relief/development division within ERD, were another indication of differences amongst member agencies. Public comment, for example, drew concerned remarks from the evaluation team. The attitude of some critical members was that it was prudent not to rub the Ethiopian government's nose in the fact that a cross border operation existed.

During the course of 1984, however, the government's handling of the famine and its internal affairs began to draw an increasingly bad press. The extravagance of the Dergue's 10 year birthday celebrations in September, for example, drew sharp comment.[27] This, plus the worsening famine situation prompted some other NGOs to become more publicly active. The main event to stir public opinion, however, was the celebrated BBC TV report on the Ethiopian famine in October 1984. Oxfam UK immediately made a public appeal for a truce in the conflict to facilitate the distribution of relief.[28] The church networks involved on both sides were also becoming increasingly concerned. The Europe based Christian Disaster Assistance for Africa (CDAA), which comprised Caritas Internationales, Catholic Relief Services, Lutheran World Federation and WCC, issued a similar call. CDAA, which should not be confused with a local consortium with the same acronym, represented the main church agencies working on the government side.

This move was immediately followed on 1 November 1984 with a supporting resolution issued by ERD members and associated bodies from Woudschoten in the Netherlands.[29] The resolution pointed out that the geography of the war meant that the six to seven million people at risk in Eritrea, Tigray, Wollo and Gondor could not be adequately helped without a safe passage for relief supplies agreed by all parties. Moreover, the time for lengthy negotiations had passed, an immediate agreement was needed. It should be noted that these resolutions, in so far as they highlighted the war as a contributing factor to the famine, ran counter to the government view which emphasised drought and environmental degradation.

The initial BBC report plus such appeals fuelled a huge surge in public concern across Europe and the USA. This awakening of public opinion led Western donors to rapidly increase the amount of disaster assistance being channelled through NGOs working on both sides of the conflict. In many respects, it was also a turning point for ERD. In many Western countries, harrowing TV reports gave rise to national campaigns to raise private donations and press for increased government assistance. The fire of Western public opinion which, since the mid-1970s, the Fronts had wished to kindle, had now been lit. These campaigns affected ERD in several ways. The increase in private donations, for example, enabled members to expand ERD funding. More importantly, however, increased public interest in the famine had the consequence of enabling ERA and REST's affiliated support committees in Europe and the USA, together with sympathetic solidarity groups, to put the Eritrean and Tigrayan case to a more receptive audience.

Fuelled by concern and media interest, the number of agencies, independent observers and journalists crossing the border increased significantly toward the end of 1984. This gave rise to a noticeable increase in the publicly available reports and accounts from non-government areas. These accounts variously described the government aggression against the civilian population, the political factors in the famine, government abuse of food aid, its neglect of famine victims, and the contrasting effectiveness of the Front's and IA's public welfare policies. It involved such groups as War on Want[30-31], Grassroots International[32], Survival International[33], together with respected independent observers.[34-35] The analysis of the period is well represented in Cultural Survival's 1985 critique, *Politics and the Ethiopian Famine.*[36] Following the end of 1984, more informed press coverage also began to focus on the famine in non-government areas[37] and the importance and fragility of the cross border relief operation from Sudan.[38] Within a matter of months, the nature of public debate had undergone a perceptible sea change.

The effect of this increasing exposure had internal consequences for ERD and, importantly, how ERD was perceived by other NGOs, especially those working in government areas. Increasing public awareness of the complexity of the famine plus the failure of the Ethiopian government to respond to the free passage appeals, prompted those ERD members that had already been active, such as, CA, DIA, ICCO, and DDW, to renew their efforts. Since the Fronts had for some time indicated they would accept a free passage arrangement, the failure of the public appeals could, with some justification, be placed at the door of the Ethiopian government. In private DIA, for example, urged the ERD members to step up material assistance and start "an international campaign to break the Dergue's criminal inhumanity by publicity and combined diplomatic action."[39] In many respects, these three ingredients advocated in November 1984, that is, increased assistance, publicity and behind the scenes diplomacy, became the features of ERD, or at least some ERD members, during the latter part of the 1980s.

At the start of 1985, DDW renewed its diplomatic efforts with the German and Tanzanian governments. Within Germany, an NGO study group was established to focus on the problems of the Horn.[40] In March, DDW issued a report which, although still representing an even-handed or neutral approach to relief, disclosed that it was working on both sides of the conflict and criticised Western governments, the UN and OAU for their selective responses thereby putting politics before humanitarian considerations.[41]

The Polarisation of CBO and Non-CBO NGOs

In Britain and the USA, a notable feature of the increasing exposure of the cross border operation and the agencies associated with it, was the adoption of a defensive, even hostile attitude by those NGOs working exclusively on the government side. In Chapter 10 it is described how such feelings have persisted in Addis Ababa even following the end of the war. To some extent, this issue has to be seen in relation to the split within left opinion over the CBO which has already been mentioned. For several years, it was impossible for concerned agencies to get the CBO on the agenda in UN or US State Department meetings despite the fact that such meetings were often the site of Ethiopian misinformation. As early as August 1984, SCF in Britain had expressed its concern to CA over its public stance on Eritrea and Tigray. SCF's position was that to draw media attention to the conflict was having the effect of reducing donor confidence in the Ethiopian government and the RRC.[42] It was also alleged to be causing SCF problems in Ethiopia due to its being associated with a fellow British agency.

Such attitudes continued to develop and, as Ethiopia's brutal resettlement programme became more widely understood to outsiders, NGOs became increasingly defensive and apologetic. In March 1985, for example, Survival International arranged a meeting in London to discuss resettlement and sent out an extensive agency invitation list. No NGO working on the government side attended.[43] This polarisation, and the role that NGOs played in concealing the nature and effects of Ethiopian government policies has been extensively documented by Clay.[44]

The Attitude of ERD and the IAs to USAID and EC Assistance

The nature and significance of USAID and EC involvement is discussed in Chapter Five. Here it should be pointed out that, just as some ERD members were forging bilateral relations with the IA's, some members were developing their expertise and experience of dealing with such strategic donors.[45] This is perhaps less true of LWR since USAID had long had a policy of working through NGOs. Until the mid-1980s this was not the case in Europe. The era of enhanced NGO activity began with a mutual learning process. Certainly, in terms of agencies becoming more familiar with donor politics, USAID involvement did create a pressure within ERD to secure more European and Canadian assistance as a form of counter-balance.[46]

In 1985, with the advent of serious USAID support, many of ERD's European members were concerned as to whether or not the CBO had become a tool in US foreign policy. This worry reflected the press coverage of the time and translated into speculation concerning the possible role of LWR. A feeling exacerbated as LWR's position as a major facilitator grew (Figure 6). Such speculation led to some tension and contributed to LWR adopting a relatively low profile in terms of policy debate within ERD. In other words, despite its huge material contribution in channelling USAID assistance, sensitivity toward the European agencies meant that LWR never attempted to turn this position into one of political dominance.[47] It is important to note, however, that such concerns were not shared by the IAs. Providing no strings were attached, they welcomed USAID support at face value and appreciated the political risk that LWR was taking in terms of its procurement.[48]

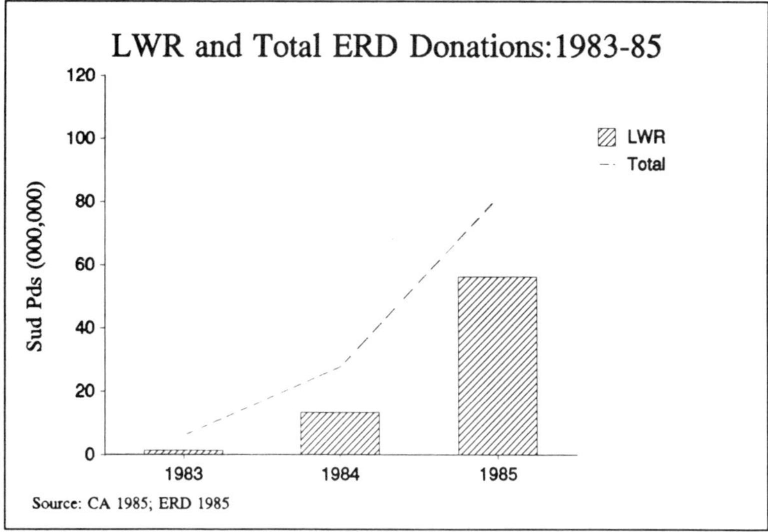

Figure 6

THE RE-ESTABLISHMENT OF ERD IN OCTOBER 1985

Between the evaluation at the beginning of 1984 and the signing of a new agreement in Khartoum on 14 October 1985, ERD members had come a long way. Apart from the organisational difficulties, due to the fast changing social and political climate, member agencies themselves were engaged in a media and political learning process. The increasing involvement of strategic donors increased the diplomatic links of agencies. At the same time, although ERD itself maintained a low profile, some members had established the precedent of more active individual campaigning. The events of 1984 and 1985, saw a loosening of some of the caution surrounding cross border work. The language of communication within ERD began to change, the term 'cross border', for example, increasingly began to be used to describe ERD activities. The polarisation amongst NGOs also served to give ERD itself more of an identity. Over this period, it became an international consortium working in Eritrea and Tigray not, as before, in areas that could not be reached from the government side.

At the same time, however, the prolonged negotiations had also shown that the member agencies had many differences of approach and philosophy. This ranged from the weight accorded partners' views in Ethiopia where they existed; differential preferences for relief and development; different attitudes to publicity and advocacy; varying positions in relation to the support of the main donors; and so on. Where the sense of common purpose came was in the revulsion at the effects of the war and determination to help the neglected peoples of Eritrea and Tigray. As a consortium, ERD was a product of the war in the same way as the humanitarian policies of the Fronts.

When the agreement was finally signed it was to re-establish, with the support of the IAs and the Scandinavian agencies, ERD's relief and rehabilitation brief.[49] NCA was elected the lead agency which, for the sake of political correctness, was phrased as the Coordinating Agency in the agreement. NCA's role was confirmed as giving general administrative support to ERD and, as appropriate, to member agencies. This included providing office space in Khartoum. While the agreement stated that NCA would provide administrative support in the recruitment of expatriate staff, in practice NCA furnished the Executive Secretary. In order to internationalise the organisation, the agreement established a Board which consisted of all signatory agencies, including SCC. The Board was charged with meeting once a year under a rotating Chairperson and deciding issues of general policy. It also elected an Executive Committee which in turn was to select ERD's Executive Secretary when the position fell vacant. This Committee consisted of the Chairperson, and a representative from SCC, NCA and two other member agencies with the Executive Secretary as a non-voting ex officio member. The responsibilities of the Executive Committee included the approval of reports, consulting regularly with IA's and arranging Board Meetings. The ERD Office, which in turn convened the Executive Committee meetings, was headed by the Executive Secretary and ran the day to day business of ERD: financial procedures; purchasing and transport; the clearance of goods; reporting and field visits; maintaining regular consultation with the IAs, and so on.

In terms of improved access, the agreement made some concessions to IA demands. They were given the right to approach the Executive Committee for consultation through the Executive Secretary. They could also request administrative assistance from the ERD Office and their opinions would be heard in the recruitment process when the outcome was of direct concern. Although the IAs were free to form bilateral links with member agencies, it was reiterated that ERD could not speak out on behalf of any IA.

Fault Lines in the New ERD

The new agreement weakened the link with SCC since, in effect, it became little more than an ordinary member. At the same time, it reconfirmed a limited relief and rehabilitation mandate as a necessary base for holding such a disparate group together. The main weakness lay in the fact that the 'legal' basis for ERD's existence in Sudan became NCA's country agreement which did not mention ERD. The existence of the consortium, in fact, remained an informal understanding with the Sudanese government. Through the process of widening member representation, however, the Board and therefore ERD itself, appeared as an independent body.[50] In the context of the enhanced role of NGOs during the latter part of the 1980s in Sudan, this spurious independence would grow having implications for member agencies, the IAs and the government of Sudan.

CHAPTER SEVEN

Front Ascendancy and the Vicissitudes of Donor Assistance

War and Famine Summary (1986-89)

Due to political differences, over the period of mid-1985 to early 1988, the Fronts operated independently of each other. From the beginning of 1986, the EPLF began to consolidate its territory in northwest Eritrea as a preparatory move to assuming an offensive stance. During this period of consolidation, the EPLF redoubled its attempts at political organisation and recruitment. Its military wing nearly tripled in size to 30,000 soldiers and the EPLF also substantially augmented its standing militias.[1] The TPLF pursued a similar strategy of retrenchment, consolidation, and then, by late 1987, the beginning of expansion. Its area of consolidation was western Tigray, with its precious access routes to Sudan. To keep government forces off balance, the TPLF frequently attacked garrison towns with the result that occasionally relief operations in government areas were disrupted. On March 8, 1986, for example, the TPLF joined with the Ethiopian People's Democratic Movement (EPDM) in attacking the garrison town of Alamata in north Wollo, killing two Ethiopian nationals employed by World Vision and wounding four others.[2]

By late 1987, both the EPLF and TPLF went on the offensive. The EPLF undertook a campaign which culminated in the capture of Nacfa, despite constant government bombing of civilian targets and continued pacification and villagisation campaigns.[3] In October of that year, the EPLF attacked a 34 truck food convoy, claiming that three trucks were carrying weapons. Despite the fact that for years the Dergue had been deliberately disrupting food aid supplies, this event, together with the Alamata incident, provoked widespread condemnation amongst Western donor governments. In a sense, this criticism was symptomatic of the slowly changing balance of military power. The TPLF began its fight back in September 1987, taking numerous towns in western and central Tigray.

Nineteen eighty-eight was one of the bloodiest years of fighting in the region and represented a pivotal turning point in the war.[4] Of central importance was the resumption of military coordination between the EPLF and TPLF after several years of non-communication. In March, the EPLF devastated the command centre of the Ethiopian army at Afabet, killing or wounding 15,000 soldiers, capturing significant quantities of weapons, and imprisoning three Soviet military advisors. The towns of Tessenei and Barentu were evacuated by the Ethiopian army soon afterward, and the EPLF followed up by pushing the government out of Halhal, Anseba, and Agordat.[5] By the end of the year, both Fronts had made significant gains on the battlefield. This resulted in greater access for the cross-border operation, creating a vastly increased area for which ERA and REST now had the ability, if not the means, to reach. It also created expanded responsibilities for civilian administration in the newly controlled areas.

Government counter-attacks in Eritrea and Tigray were largely aimed at civilian targets and caused widespread suffering. The signing of a peace accord between the Ethiopian and Somali governments helped the Dergue concentrate its counter-offensive. In 1988 Africa Watch estimates that 110,000 civilians were displaced in Eritrea, of whom over 70,000 came from the Sheib area alone. Forty thousand of these displaced moved across the border into Sudan.[6] Surveys carried out amongst refugees at the time found that mortality rates had doubled when the displaced were in transit to Sudan, and remained high, especially for younger children, in the camps of Sudan due to disease.[7] Tigray and Wollo also saw a tremendous upsurge in military activity. After a May 1988 offensive in which the TPLF overwhelmed numerous government garrison towns, the Ethiopian army counter-attacked with simultaneous aerial bombardment and ground campaigns. Tremendous death and displacement resulted although few Tigrayan refugees arrived in Sudan.

The first two months of 1989 witnessed the TPLF launching of one of its most successful campaigns to date, effectively taking control of all of Tigray save one government outpost at Maichew. This period also saw the TPLF and the EPDM merge to form the Ethiopian People's Revolutionary Democratic Front (EPRDF). The EPRDF emerged as a result of a shift from a struggle for regional self-determination which had broadly characterised the policy of the TPLF from the mid-1970s, to a movement with national aspirations. Part of this strategic change had envisaged the Oromo Liberation Front (OLF) as forming the Oromo wing within the EPRDF. The OLF, however, decided not to take part. In an attempt to maintain a national perspective, as a last resort, the TPLF encouraged the creation of a new Oromo organisation, the Oromo People's Democratic Organisation (OPDO) which came under the EPRDF umbrella.[8] The OPDO largely drew its original membership from Oromo prisoners of war and Oromos from Wollo. As the territory controlled by the TPLF grew throughout the late 1980s, tensions between it and the OLF had been growing. The OLF questioned the TPLF's territorial aspirations, and the TPLF doubted the OLF's military capacity. Nevertheless, by the end of 1989, the EPRDF had surged through parts of Wollo, and had taken towns in northern Shewa and southern Gonder.[9] Political differences between the EPRDF and OLF would remain and have continued into the post-war situation.

These military advances and ensuing government reprisals displaced thousands of civilians. By the end of 1989, the cross-border operation was serving a much larger area and much higher number of beneficiaries than ever before. Newly served populations included a large urban population, due to the numerous garrison towns abandoned by the government.[10] The Dergue's utilisation of food as a weapon was brought fully into play during the latter half of the 1980s as its position became increasingly desperate. The government burned grain stores and bombed food convoys, depots, and relief distribution centres. Other tactics were more subtle. It used food to restrict civilian movements as part of its counter-insurgency strategy and to control civilian populations through resettlement and villagisation policies.[11] It was also a period, however, during which ERD also became concerned about the effect of food and relief aid that it was channelling to non-government areas. The question arose as to whether this humanitarian assistance was itself helping support the continuing war.

The Volatility of US Cross-Border Assistance

USAID greatly decreased its food commitments to ERD from 45,000 metric tons in 1986 to 5,900 in 1987 (see Figure 3).[12-13] This decline had a number of causes of which the primary one was the growing gap between the perception of long term structural and emergency food deficits in the Horn. Although it had been known for some years that Ethiopia, for example, had a structural food deficit, by 1986, Western donors nevertheless felt that the 'emergency' was over in Sudan, Eritrea and Ethiopia when the rains and harvest proved better than average. This view was also common amongst NGOs and, as we shall see, ERD and it gave rise to a widespread feeling amongst the aid community that now was the time to turn from relief to development. In retrospect, one can see a lack of understanding of the complexity of the situation and that the reduction of productive capacity and asset depletion was now such that they constituted structural factors acting to maintain a situation of food insecurity even during years of good rainfall.

Reflecting this perceived return to normal, USAID expressed disbelief about the numbers of alleged recipients in Front controlled territories. This was symptomatic of a continuing lack of confidence in ERA and REST figures.[14] USAID felt that the November 1986 harvest was better than average and that ERD's requests were no longer based on emergency needs. The US subsequently challenged ERD to verify its numbers. This move, together with ERD's own concerns over what were the actual food aid requirements, led to the first University of Leeds assessment in Eritrea.[15] Another reason for USAID's reduced commitment was a considerable concern over increasing costs generally and, specifically, the escalation of internal transport costs in non-government areas. Both USAID and the State Department sought better checks and balances to keep a lid on this escalation and considered providing ear-marked funds for transport or reimbursing on a fixed-cost basis. Neither option, however, was acted upon.[16]

Other factors behind the onset of USAID hesitancy included the TPLF action against the garrison town of Alamata in 1986 which killed two World Vision employees and the 1987 EPLF attack on an Ethiopian food convoy. Despite the one-sidedness of donor concerns, some USAID officials advocated the cutting of CBO food aid in retaliation for these actions. In a meeting in Khartoum with USAID and British Embassy officials, ERD pointed out the potential for adverse donor publicity and the threatened complete cut-off never materialised.[17] Internal purchase contributions were also affected by USAID concerns. Through LWR, USAID contributed $2 million to ERD for internal purchase in 1985. This donation was not repeated because of REST's alleged poor reporting performance on these transfers.[18]

The fear of diversion of food to the Fronts also led to a fluctuating concern on the part of USAID regarding monitoring. While no direct evidence was given, numerous aid officials interviewed nevertheless felt that major diversion did take place. ERD monitoring missions, moreover, were described as being escorted and thus only seeing what the Fronts wished them to see.[19] ERD, however, was also aware of a problem in this respect. LWR, for example, also felt that monitoring was "impressionistic, not analytic"[20] and at times it pushed for increased frequency of missions and the improved reporting of findings.[21] Some saw political motives in USAID's erratic interest in monitoring and reporting. Because monitoring and reporting practices were never specifically codified by American and European donors, this has been argued to have "maximized the ability of back donors to exert political control and manipulation" of the CBO and, indirectly, the Fronts.[22]

Emphasising the volatility of US assistance, after 1987, the entire package of US aid to NGOs in both the government and Front held areas once again increased and never dipped below $150 million. Influential parts of the US government began to realise after the major offensives of 1988 that the Dergue was incapable of defeating the EPLF and it was thought that some form of political compromise would eventually prevail. EPLF leader Issias Aferwerkie visited America in May 1989, and later that year the US began pushing the UN to meet with the EPLF directly.[23-24] Although the public posture of US policy towards Eritrean independence did not officially change until 1991, privately some US officials were gradually preparing for the inevitable. Within this new climate, USAID concerns over monitoring considerably reduced.

The Continuity of EC Cross-Border Assistance

Unlike USAID, which used ERD as its major conduit for the CBO, the EC spread is assistance across a wider range of agencies. Besides ERD, in Eritrea the EC channelled aid through Oxfam Belgique and in Tigray through Oxfam UK. Indeed, by 1987, half of all EC assistance to Tigray was being delivered through Oxfam UK. The difference between USAID and the EC in this matter is not so much a policy difference as the fact the LWR was the only American NGO with a significant involvement in the CBO. Another contrast with USAID, however, is that rather than being subject to major swings, EC assistance through ERD exhibited a sustained, if slow, growth (see Figure 3).

Since the mid-1980s, ERD had continued to build up its relations with the Food Aid division of the EC. The internal divisions within the EC, however, especially that between the Food Aid and Emergency

Division, remained. In 1984, the Ethiopia government had complained about the EC's initial involvement in the CBO. Given the strength of public opinion at the time, Brussels chose to face off this criticism and the Dergue backed down. By 1988, the Ethiopian government once again began to pressure the EC to curtail its involvement.[25] The EC delegate in Addis Ababa was supportive of the government in this matter. The issue of policy differences between donor headquarters and field offices regarding the CBO also affected USAID and is discussed in Chapter Nine.

For ERD, this pressure plus attempts by ERA to establish direct links with the EC, raised the issue of the apparent fragility of EC assistance. In providing assistance to ERD, the Food Aid division was technically in breach of the Lome conventions which stipulate that all aid must be with government approval. In the case of the CBO, this had been finessed by the Food Aid division including CBO assistance within its Sudan programme. ERD, itself had also broken EC rules by using EC funds for local purchase without the EC having its own monitors to oversee the purchase. Although events of the mid-1980s had given the CBO some elements of recognition, factors such as this continued to demand that ERD retain a low profile. The fear at the time was that as a result of pressure from Addis Ababa, and the continuing differences between Food Aid and Emergency divisions, any mistake on the part of ERD or the IAs could furnish an administrative excuse for the curtailment of EC assistance.[26]

Despite these fears, however, EC assistance was not curtailed. In fact, the inherent institutional inertia within the EC proved it a more reliable source of assistance compared to the volatile USAID. By the end of the 1980s, the CBO had become the EC's largest ever food aid programme. Nor, for that matter, did it suddenly remove support in January 1991, following the opening of Massawa.

CHAPTER EIGHT

Stabilisation of the Crisis and the Routinisation of ERD

The events of the mid-1980s initiated a significant organisational and programmatic growth of the IAs and ERD. In operational terms, from this period ERD and the CBO became much more effective. Indeed, despite the suspension of cooperation between the Fronts from 1985 to early 1988 and the prosecution of vicious counter-insurgency measures by the Dergue, the relief management systems developed by the Fronts and IAs had stabilised the public welfare crisis by the end of the 1980s. With regard to ERD's mandate, it represents a time of organisational conflict in response to these changes and a growing concern about the possible effect that ERD assistance was having on the dynamics of the war. Organisational tensions included those between NCA and an increasingly independent ERD administration and renewed debate around the issue of relief versus development amongst ERD members. Externally, friction arose between ERD and the IAs and, increasingly, the Sudanese government. The result of these various contradictions was to lead, in April 1989, to the second re-establishment of ERD. This time, however, an ERD clearly under NCA administrative control.

The Split Between the EPLF and TPLF

Between mid-1985 and early 1988, the EPLF and TPLF were in a state of formal non-communication. This split was based on political and ideological differences, and although not erupting into armed conflict, the level of opposition over the period did vary in intensity. Since the split also affected relations between ERA and REST, which for a long period broke off all communications, it represented a major crisis for ERD.[1] Given ERD's neutral mandate, however, it is significant that the event is little reported in the minutes of the period. Apart from the breakdown in coordination and communication between the IAs, one of the main effects of the split on the CBO was that for much of the period the EPLF prohibited REST convoys travelling from Kassala in Sudan and through Eritrea into northern Tigray. This necessitated REST operating out of Gedaref and involved a longer journey, essential road building and a general increase in transport costs.[2]

Chapter Two discusses some the differences between the Fronts. Briefly, the EPLF practised a more conventional and positional style of warfare while the TPLF adopted a mobile guerilla strategy. In relation to the IAs, this translated into a logistical and organisational character with regard to ERA and REST respectively. Reflecting its military growth, by 1984, the TPLF had begun to assert its political programme outside Tigray. Political and ideological differences with the EPLF, hitherto submerged, became more manifest. These differences crystallised in mid-1985 with the TPLF's establishment of a Marxist-Leninist League of Tigray (MLLT). The EPLF felt that the Albanian style policies advocated by the MLLT were a mistake and a sign of a lack of political experience within the TPLF.[3] In a joint meeting, the EPLF decided to withdraw cooperation.

The developing rift was given added shape by the fact that the TPLF was enjoying some success in countries such as Sudan, Saudi Arabia and Italy, where the EPLF had less political purchase.[4] Moreover, some left groups had begun to regard the TPLF as an alternative to the Dergue. The differences between the Fronts were strung on several ideological and rhetorical pegs. The respective positions with regard to the Soviet Union was one of these. Chapter Two discusses the EPLF analysis of the Soviet Union as a strategic friend but tactical enemy. This view related to the EPLF's endeavours to overcome international isolation by giving it an entrée to the socialist bloc. The TPLF saw things differently. For it, the Soviet Union was the main strategic enemy. At this stage the TPLF maintained the option of secession, while the EPLF argued in terms of Tigray's regional autonomy.[5] The TPLF also argued that the EPLF's positional warfare was a mistake. The EPLF was isolated in one part of Eritrea while the government was able to operate in the rest and, unlike the EPLF, it could recruit new troops. Finally, although the TPLF regarded the rank and file of the EPLF as socialist, it claimed that its leadership was bourgeois.[6]

The severing of communication between the Fronts came at a crit-

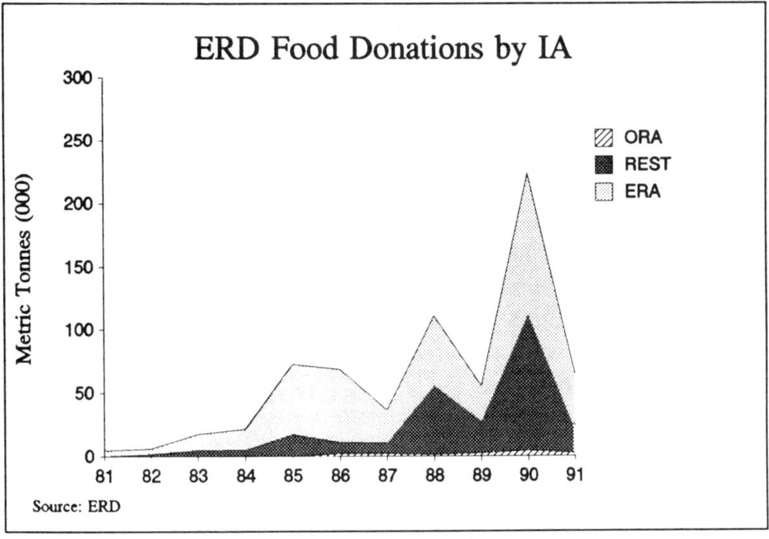

Figure 7

ical time for the TPLF. Nineteen eighty-five was the year of the mass arrival of Tigrayan refugees in Sudan and the consequent near collapse of TPLF administrative structures within Tigray. As will be discussed below, for REST it was also a period of organisational crisis and reorganisation. The rapprochement that eventually developed between the Fronts was not dependent on their sorting out the above ideological differences. It related more to the changing military balance with regard to the Ethiopian state. Following the upsurge of EPLF military activity in 1987, the Dergue adopted a policy of trying to eliminate the TPLF so that it could then concentrate its efforts on Eritrea. Consequently, although beginning its own offensive, by the start of 1988 the TPLF was under great pressure. In March 1988, however, the important EPLF victory at Ababet, which proved a turning point in the war, reduced the military threat in Tigray. Although not attempting to resolve their political differences, this event brought about a meeting between the EPLF and TPLF which forged a new period of cooperation which resulted in the eventual downfall of the Dergue in 1991.[7]

With regard to ERD, the split can be seen as vindicating its attempts to maintain political distance from the IAs. That is, although the breakdown in communication was a serious matter, ERD was not compromised in relation to one side or the other and so could continue to function on a bilateral basis. When news of the EPLF's restriction of REST convoys first became known, for example, ERD let its disapproval be known.[8] At each stage of the crisis, ERD communicated its concerns to the Fronts if it was felt their actions were endangering the humanitarian operation. Although ERA and REST were not talking, ERD continued to invite the IAs to meetings in the hope of rekindling dialogue. ORA frequently acted as a go-between.[9] On several occasions DIA intervened in an attempt to initiate discussions. In one case, after a six month silence, ERD organised a garden party complete with a private room so that ERA and REST representatives could meet discretely. Throughout the split, ERD attempted to maintain an even handed approach. Indeed, one result of this experience was that it reinforced the move away from relating to the IAs in terms of their capacity, to a more equitable division of available resources.

The Organisational Growth of the IAs

The growing activity of the CBO and the effectiveness of their programmes forced significant organisational development and change of the IAs. Contrary to the expectations of conventional wisdom, in this case war was accompanied by significant internal development. Since the mid-1980s, the IAs had been increasingly successful in developing bilateral links and securing the support of other consortia. This was synonymous with a broadening of the public welfare programmes run by the Fronts and the IAs to include a range of rehabilitation inputs. With regard to ERD, a change in support policy also took place. Previously, largely through the prevalence of earmarked funding and having the larger capacity, ERA had tended to be the main beneficiary. From 1986, as Figure 7 clearly indicates, assistance was divided equally between ERA and REST.[10] It should be noted that Figure 7 also suggests that ERD was never able to meet the IA demand in an objective sense. That is, according to alleged need. During the first half of the 1980s it was limited, amongst other things, by IA capacity, and in the latter part of the decade when other agencies were involved in the CBO, it was based on the division of available resources. During 1986 ERD progressively met more of the IA demands for assistance with transport and administrative costs.[11] From this period there was also a noticeable increase in direct cash payments to the IAs, an important change over the pre-1985 situation.

(a) REST

Evidence for organisational growth is more readily available for REST. Meeting the challenge of the mid-1980s instigated a major institutional change within REST. This development was concomitant with important changes in relief policy discussed below. The mid-1980s was a traumatic period for REST. The effects of the mass migration of Tigrayan refugees into Sudan almost saw the breakdown of internal civilian administration.[12] Almost immediately, it was faced with the daunting task of organising the massive repatriation programme. The split between the EPLF and TPLF also meant that REST was denied shorter northern access routes to Tigray.

During 1985, the deterioration in REST's administrative capacity was noted by ERD.[13] At this stage, ERD was not engaged in any institution-building activity with the IAs. REST's problems were partly manifest in its inability to absorb all ERD assistance. Discussion began as to how this situation could be improved and, in August 1985, REST and the TPLF considered the matter within Tigray. The strategy which emerged from these negotiations involved (a) the restructuring of REST's administration in Khartoum and Tigray (b) the establishment of new departments of accountancy and logistics (c) the appointment of Project Officers in Khartoum and Tigray to better coordinate activities (d) the appointment of new personnel (e) strengthening the Port Sudan office and (f) the completion of new roads.[14] It is also alleged that an additional aspect of this re-organisation was that all REST staff had to be ex-TPLF fighters.[15] ERD was supportive of these administrative changes and by May 1986 an improvement in REST's administrative performance was noted.[16]

The Growing Effectiveness of the IAs and ERD

By 1986, ERD's ability to increase the flow of food aid and funds was beginning to have a beneficial impact on the relief situation within Eritrea and Tigray. Monitoring reports indicated improved health, reduced internal migration and some indication of increased herd sizes.[17] Increased relief assistance alone, however, was not the only factor. The IAs had undergone a period of organisational growth and development enabling them to begin to stabilise the situation in Eritrea and Tigray.

(a) The Situation in Tigray

During the course of 1986, building on REST's reorganisation in 1985, REST and the TPLF radically redeveloped their disaster management policies. The success of this process can be judged from the fact that although food aid movements during 1986 were insufficient to meet estimated need, there was no repeat refugee influx into Sudan. Moreover, the returnees from the earlier migration were able to remain within Tigray. Apart from USAID, this apparent anomaly drew a concerned request for clarification from ERD in February 1987.[18] Apart from the fact that REST's request could have been an over-estimate, the picture that emerged was that within Tigray, there had been a significant change of relief policy compared to 1984-85. In relation to this earlier famine, three quarters of the population had been affected in some way, many had been dispossessed of their assets, leaving large-scale migration into Sudan as the only option. In 1986, the basis of an integrated approach to disaster management was laid which proved resilient enough to withstand the return of famine conditions in 1987.

The basis of this integrated approach was for REST and the TPLF to improve relief capacity and provide the affected population with several alternative survival strategies in their village or as near to their place of origin as possible.[19] These included:

Transport:

Transport capacity greatly increased from 27 trucks in 1984 to around 150 in 1986. In addition, new roads had been built by the TPLF rendering the worst affected areas accessible.

Rehabilitation:

In 1986, 53,000 families were provided with basic agricultural inputs. In 1987, similar measures were applied.

Food Aid:

Using the Baito system of community recommendation (as described earlier), REST assigned food aid for differing periods according to need. The primary aim was to enable people to meet food shortfalls arising from poor cultivation. In 1986, 26,000 mt (of which 9,200 mt was supplied by ERD and 9,000 mt from internal purchase) was mobilized. This supplied 348,411 people for between 2-5 months and 226,510 for 2-3 months.[20] By 1987, REST was moving 5,000 mt per month and, in addition, internal purchase had expanded to 27,000 mt. This supported 386,000 people on full ration. Rations being given on a 12, 6 and 3 month basis according to need.

Food For Work:

In 1986, some food aid was made available on food for work projects in Central Region which attracted people able to migrate from adjoining areas.

Wage Labour:

Beginning in 1986, the TPLF encouraged wealthier farmers to increase the area they cultivated through provision of agricultural inputs in exchange for taking on as labourers those not receiving food aid. In 1987, 500,000 were assisted in the Western Region in finding work.

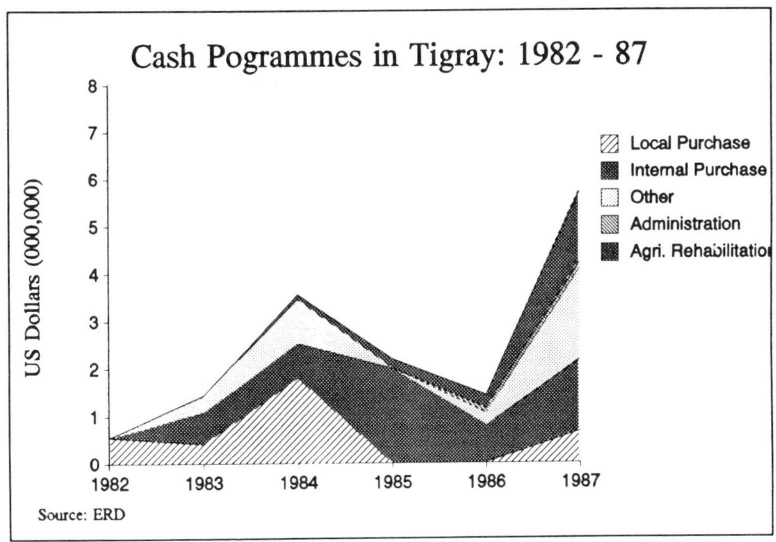

Source: ERD

Figure 8

Migration:

With the return of famine conditions in 1987, the TPLF took a policy decision not to re-establish the refugee pipeline into Sudan. The transit camps of the mid-1980s had already been abandoned on the grounds of their being vulnerable to air attack and susceptible to the spread to contagious disease. In its place, the TPLF encouraged the internal migration of only the worst affected populations. Migrants were absorbed amongst the local communities in the Central and Western Regions. The Baito system, together with utensils and other inputs provided by REST, helped this process.

Assistance from Government Towns:

In 1987, peasants in the East were encouraged to seek assistance in government held towns. The TPLF advised such people on the timing of aid deliveries, the NGO involved and the disposition of government troops in an endeavour to reduce the risk of harassment.

The emergence of an integrated approach is partly evinced in the diversification of REST cash programmes supported by ERD. Figure 8 indicates that compared to the beginning of the 1980s, when local purchase in Sudan predominated, by 1987 a wider and more balanced range of programmes existed. The "Other" category included such things as medical rehabilitation, transport, storage and locust control. This diversification of ERD cash programmes is partly the result of the international community more or less taking responsibility for CBO food aid from 1984.

(b) The Situation in Eritrea

It has already been mentioned that by 1986, the donor community felt that the emergency was over. As is shown below, ERD's conflict with ERA also began with the former's concern over lack of detailed information on food production and actual food aid needs in Eritrea. The outcome was the contracting of Leeds University to carry out its first food assessment mission (June-October 1987).[21] In many respects, this was a landmark study. It was the first detailed study of food productive capacity and aid requirement to be undertaken in Eritrea. Indeed, in terms of NGO relief operations generally, it is unusual to find such a detailed assessment. The Leeds study went far beyond the limitations of previous monitoring missions. That is, rather than detailing the actual number of beneficiaries and the impact that food aid was having, reports tended to show the tonnages of food moved and the numbers of people that would have been fed on the assumption of an average ration. The Leeds study was also important in that it tackled the issue of a structural food deficit and how, in such circumstances, food aid could have a wider role than just keeping people alive by helping reduce asset loss and promoting recovery of the productive base. For example, by reducing the pressure on pastoralists to sell animals from a recovering herd to obtain grain. Despite the optimism of the donor and NGO community, that famine conditions again prevailed toward the end of 1987, underscored the existence of a structural problem.

The study found that Eritrean crop production was sufficient for only about five months annual consumption with normal rainfall in the context of continuing warfare. Yields were also found to be much lower than those in Ethiopia and the rest of Africa. The war had impacted profoundly on agricultural production due to such things as the conscription and killing of able men; mining of fields and pastures; destruction of crops and livestock; and restrictions on movement of people and grain. Even without war, however, it was felt that food production was "far from sufficient to supply basic needs."[22] In this context, the 1983-85 famine was seen as playing a role in the emergence of a structural deficit. Animal herds had been severely reduced, restricting options for those faced with having to make up shortfalls in home production. Depletion of oxen for ploughing also greatly affected the ability of families to maintain production.

Although the Leeds study laid out the long term nature of food insecurity in Eritrea, it also clearly indicated that the CBO and ERA had been successful in stabilising the short term food requirements of the population. Indeed, on an issue which was to divide the team and cast an air of controversy over the report, it was felt by one member that the Liberated Areas as opposed to the Contested Areas had been over-supplied relative to actual need.[23] While agreeing that food aid during 1986 and 1987 had been adequate, the remaining team members were of the opinion that insufficient hard evidence existed to be able to describe the situation in the Liberated Areas as one of over-supply and, moreover, that no negative or productive dis-incentive could be shown to have resulted. The merits of this debate need not detain us here. What is important is that in terms of stabilising the situation within Eritrea, by 1987, the CBO had increased its capacity to the extent that it was now meeting immediate food aid requirements, especially in the Liberated Areas.

As in the case of Tigray, during the mid-1980s, ERD's cash-supported programmes within Eritrea also went through a stage of diversification. Figure 9 indicates that compared to the early 1980s, when the local purchase of sorghum in Sudan predominated, by 1987, a wider range of activities were supported. The "Other" category included such things as transport, locust control, medical supplies and storage.

The External Significance of Stabilisation

By the end of 1987, the IAs and the Fronts, through the CBO, had begun to get to grips with the public welfare situation in Eritrea and Tigray. Despite re-emergence of famine conditions and the Dergue's continuation of an aggressive counter-insurgency strategy, that it was possible to stabilise the populations within these areas was a remarkable

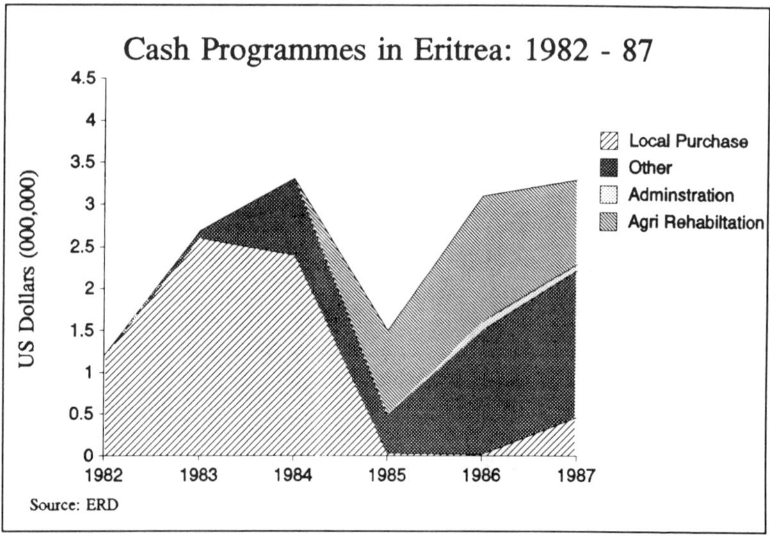

Figure 9

achievement. In the case of REST, this had involved a major re-organisation of relief policy producing a singular example of an integrated community based approach. In terms of ERD, an important factor which emerged from this period, as indicated in the TPLF's advice to seek assistance in government towns, was the pressing need to coordinate the CBO with relief assistance in government areas.[24] Up until this period, there had been few contacts and no serious attempt to coordinate activities, or even share information, between agencies working on different sides. Towards the end of 1987, propelled by the growing military success of the Fronts, increasing contact began to develop. This itself, is an indication of the growing impact of ERD and the CBO.

One of the first clear examples of the need to coordinate aid across the lines was the Alamata incident in Tigray during March 1986. This has already been described. The outcry that this unfortunate event caused amongst Addis Ababa based agencies was indicative of the continuing hostility in these quarters to anything that resembled recognition of the Fronts. Ethiopia based donor representatives, who had seen their regional position undermined with the growth of the CBO during the mid-1980s, made much of this incident. Local USAID officials, for example, claimed that it had been deliberately aimed at World Vision and that the TPLF had declared war on humanitarian aid.[25] In considering this incident, ERD, in a declaration which was delivered to the TPLF but never made public,[26] voiced its great concern regardless of who was to blame and reaffirmed that aid should be made available to "civilians in conflict areas, and that relief workers from all humanitarian organisations within accepted risks, should be given the opportunity to carry out their tasks."[27] The fact that this declaration was not made public is indicative of the continuing belief that ERD had to maintain a low profile. Within the next eighteen months, during which the Front's military push began to gain momentum, ERD's posture on such incidents would change.

ICRC and the 'Open Roads for Survival' Initiative

Generally speaking, ICRC had followed a policy of attempting to meet the humanitarian crisis in Tigray and Eritrea by working from the government side. The main exception to this was the 74 trucks it ran from Kassala in the mid-1980s into Tigray. ICRC's relationship with Eritrea had been more difficult. By 1987, however, despite the return of famine conditions and objections of ERD, ICRC felt that REST's trucking capacity was now sufficient for it to scale back its own operation. During the 1986 locust campaign, ICRC had attempted to coordinate eradication efforts from the government side. Despite what was often seen by CBO agencies as efforts at appeasement, ICRC was disliked by the Dergue and, on several occasions, was placed under pressure to curtail its operations.

Towards the end of 1987, in a move which was seen as having more to do with the organisational difficulties it faced in Ethiopia than pragmatic relief management,[28] ICRC launched a public campaign to support an 'Open Roads for Survival' initiative. With the backing of Addis Ababa based donors, this initiative was aimed at securing access to the Front areas of Eritrea and Tigray from the government side. In this campaign, ICRC saw ERD activities as a threat to its aims on the grounds that the existence of the CBO, especially when it was gaining momentum, weakened its bargaining position with the Dergue.[29] It therefore began to allege, amongst other things, that ERD was not able to reach the Central Region of Tigray and therefore the CBO should be closed in order to maximize donor pressure on the Dergue. This was the first example of Addis Ababa based agencies attempting to close or curtail the CBO. Several more would ensue in the coming years.

The ICRC's 'Open Roads' initiative did not come to fruition. The nature of the organisation's behaviour is indicative, however, of the changing nature of humanitarian politics. The de facto recognition gained by the Fronts as a result of the enhanced mid-1980s relief operation, and their growing military ascendancy, had completely changed the equation. The ICRC's plan was, effectively, a throwback to an earlier approach which, rather than seeking an agreement between equal parties, laid emphasis on the government granting permission to work in Eritrea and Tigray. One can only surmise that if the ICRC initiative had been successful, it would have caused massive disruption to the relief operation.

The 1987 Truck Incident in Eritrea and the Attempt to Coordinate Relief

At the time the ICRC was campaigning for its 'Open Roads' policy, in October 1987, the EPLF destroyed a convoy of 30 trucks to the south of Asmara. Since 24 of these were Band Aid trucks carrying relief supplies, it was widely condemned by the aid community. Although never admitted at the time, the EPLF regarded this event as a mistake. As with the Alamata incident, international condemnation was especially marked amongst Addis Ababa based donors, such as the UN, USAID and the EC. They, and the government, played up this incident as proof of the alleged real nature of the Fronts.[30] For a time, this event elevated the position of the ICRC's plan in Addis Ababa. ERD's response to the truck incident was to condemn the action, this time publicly, and use it to call for both sides to allow unobstructed humanitarian relief. Furthermore, it requested the international community to help develop "practical mechanisms to ensure that such incidents do not happen again."[31]

In November 1987, ERD arranged a meeting in Khartoum the purpose of which was to allow the EPLF to put their version of the truck incident to the donor and NGO community.[32] Although few donors attended, it did give rise to a series of discussions which produced a draft agreement with the EPLF, co-signed by ERD, Band Aid and OXFAM UK, establishing a mechanism to coordinate the movement of relief trucks entering EPLF controlled areas of Eritrea from the government side. Although ICRC had been involved in the initial discussions, it pulled out from the final stages since the plan conflicted with its 'Open

Road' proposal. The EPLF/CBO agency plan for coordinating relief movements was sent to the UN in Addis Ababa via the British Embassy in Khartoum. The good offices of the UN was requested in helping carry the plan forward: it rejected this request. Although the events of the mid-1980s had represented a form of de facto recognition, the response of the UN was symptomatic of the strong, and continuing, aversion by donors to any moves, such as aid coordination, which would effectively represent a formal recognition of the Fronts.

Donor policy was clearly contradictory at this stage. Although humanitarian support for the CBO represented an historic political shift and the beginnings of the emergence of a new paradigm of humanitarian politics, many donors, or at least their local representatives, were unable to keep pace with the changing events. Indeed, in Addis Ababa at least, they were now playing an increasingly reactionary role in attempting to carry on as if the CBO was of limited significance while the Fronts, for their part, remained little more than 'rebels'.

The Growing Independence of ERD's Administration

The demands of 1984 saw the first significant increase in ERD's Khartoum staff. In mid-1984, the first USAID shipment prompted the opening of ERD's Port Sudan office. In response to these demands, the re-establishment of ERD in October 1985 allowed for the appointment of an expatriate Assistant Executive Secretary. By mid-1987, ERD employed six senior staff, mostly expatriate, together with 11 local staff in Khartoum and 30 local staff in Port Sudan.[33] The expansion of CBO activity also saw the move to attract other ecumenical partners to join ERD. Towards the end of 1986, for example, membership was offered to agencies in Australia and Iceland.[34] In total, ERD would only attract three new members and these relatively late: Canadian Lutheran World Relief (CLWR) joining in 1989 and the Mennonite Central Committee (MCC) and Finchurchaid (FCA) in 1990.

Following the publicity of the mid-1980s and the emergence of famine conditions in Sudan, the NGO community in Khartoum grew rapidly. Despite the fact that ERD's official line remained that of keeping a low profile, by 1985, the existence of ERD was an 'open secret' in Khartoum and its activities increasingly discussed in NGO and donor circles.[35–36] The increase in ERD's size, both in organisational and programme terms, and its links with what were increasingly seen as effective and innovative indigenous agencies, produced pressures to change the profile, or at least the image, of ERD. This was also underscored by the growing effectiveness of ERD as a consortium. ERD emerged from the mid-1980s as a powerful fund raising tool, able to secure relatively huge grants compared to other NGO operations. Its dynamism in terms of resource mobilization was much greater than the sum of its parts.[37] It also had access to unique sources of information and possessed great flexibility in terms of singular contributions that different members were able to make.[38]

These attributes, together with the increasing impact of the CBO, produced pressures to 'professionalize' its activities in Khartoum.[39] This endeavour was tantamount to ERD's administration seeking a more defined and independent role outside the formal rules of its establishment. In particular, from its links with NCA, Oslo. In 1987, the boundary between the administration, that is, the Executive Secretary, and the Executive Committee was more clearly drawn so that the latter only dealt with major policy issues.[40] This also involved the administration moving to direct relations with the member agencies. At this stage, NCA's Resident Representative in Sudan and ERD's Executive Secretary continued to be the same person. In January 1988, NCA split away from Sudan the responsibility for its Equatoria programme and placed it under Nairobi management. As part of its restructuring, in April ERD's Board decided to separate the NCA Resident Representative position from that of ERD Executive Secretary and, with the appointment of a Resident Representative and the moving of the Equatoria representative's office from Nairobi to Khartoum, the split between the ERD and NCA administrations was effected in September 1988.[41] The main problem here, however, was that ERD had no legal existence within Sudan outside of NCA's country agreement. Even then, this existence was the subject of an informal understanding with the government.

Before this problem is examined in more detail, several other aspects of this growing independence need to be discussed.

The Relief Versus Development Debate

Reflecting the widespread NGO and donor belief that the emergency of the mid-1980s was now over, from the end of 1986, following a change in Executive Secretary, the ERD administration increasingly began to stress the importance of rehabilitation and development.[42] In these new circumstances, it was felt that ERD needed to address more comprehensively the move from relief to long term rehabilitation. Several discussion papers were produced on this theme and, in May

1987, for the first time a Board Meeting examined the question of ERD's medium and long-term aims.[43] While it was generally agreed that food aid requirements would reduce now the worst of the famine was over (it would in fact increase), there were differences amongst members with regard to what programme changes were needed.

ERD Administration's position was that its mandate should be changed to include long-term development work. Moreover, reflecting what was the actual situation on the ground, ERD should consider working directly with the civilian departments of the Fronts.[44] The response of members, with some important exceptions, can be seen as reflecting the earlier relief versus development discussions. LWR, SCR and DDW, for example, felt such a move, especially working directly with the civilian departments, would be disastrous. Only strict neutrality could continue to guarantee the support of donor governments. Moreover, reflecting a typically American view, LWR regarded governments, and the Fronts represented political authority in Eritrea and Tigray, as having specific functions which were not the domain of NGOs. LWR was also of the opinion that little physical development work was possible in a conflict situation. Other members stuck by the earlier position that development work was best carried out through bilateral links.

Although a former member of ERD's relief lobby, a change of opinion had begun to take place in NCA. It reported that it had shifted its position in favour of development work but was still hesitant to move in this direction. Although not seeing itself in solidarity, NCA also considered the Fronts as equivalent to governments but, unlike LWR, it was not in principle opposed to establishing direct relations. Interestingly, DIA, although a relief organisation also had a differing view to LWR. It felt that the war in Eritrea and Tigray had helped to create solidarity amongst the people which could in fact be harnessed for development purposes. Although there had always been differences of opinion amongst ERD members, during the latter part of the 1980s, helped by a more provocative stance on the part of ERD's administration, these differences tended to become more sharply focused. That ERD was able to continue as a successful and dynamic consortium is a fitting testimony to the unique chemistry of the situation.

The Conflict With ERA

The growing assertion of ERD's independence was not generally liked by the IAs, especially ERA.[45] Since the inception of ERD the IAs had been concerned that ERD should not occupy a monopoly position thereby reducing their links with the outside world. As already mentioned, part of the move by the administration towards more independence arose from a concern to professionalize its image. One aspect of this was the feeling that in the past ERD had too close a relationship to ERA.[46] It needed to distance itself and, since the bulk of ERD assistance was going to ERA (see Figure 7), it was necessary to equalise the relationship with REST. In moving to this position towards the end of 1986, the opening round in a rift between ERD and ERA which marked much of 1987 and 1988 was begun. It should also be remembered that until early 1988, ERA and REST had also suspended communication.

During the 1986-87 dry season, the NGO and donor community in Sudan and Ethiopia held the belief that the famine was over. It was a period of reflection on the need and impact of food aid. In relation to both REST and ERA, it produced a more critical approach by ERD to their continuing food aid requests and prompted demands for further justification. It also encouraged ideas that Western requirements had encouraged the IAs to grow "beyond what they should have been."[47] The results of this approach have already been partly described in relation to REST and its re-organisation of relief policy. The situation with ERA was somewhat different.

The increased activities and pressures of the mid-1980s had given the ERD administration a clearer idea of the organisational differences between the IAs. By the beginning of 1987 ERD administration had formed a view in which REST, although requiring administrative support, was credited with a clearer view of its role and relationship to the TPLF compared to ERA and the EPLF.[48] ERA was regarded has having organisational difficulty in moving from relief to long-term programme management. ERA's role in development projects and its relationship to the civilian departments of the EPLF was unclear.[49] It was felt that ERD was struggling to relate to the logistical operations of the EPLF but, at the same time, it tried to play the role of a spokesman. As we have seen, this role was established with the creation of ERA in 1976. By 1987, however, the ERD administration felt that this was now creating problems.[50] In particular, ERA was thought to be "screening" the civilian departments of the EPLF from outside development assistance.

Part of this emerging conflict with ERA related to ERD's belief that the emergency had ended and that a more comprehensive operation should be established. This naturally threatened the position of the IAs which had been built upon relief assistance. In the case of ERA, the conflict was compounded by the fact that, compared to REST, it was widely believed to be more organisationally insular and less open to internal scrutiny. Questions of the targeting, allocation and use of food aid, for example, were issues of great sensitivity. Moving to a new regime in which resources were divided more equitably between ERA and REST was not appreciated by the former, yet, convincing arguments for a continuation of the status quo were not forthcoming. There was a growing feeling that ERD had channelled a lot of food aid into Eritrea on the basis of little real understanding of the situation on the ground. Monitoring reports never really got beyond gross statistics and names on a map. Lack of information led to accusations of impropriety[51] including allegations of the misuse of food aid.[52] Together with pressure from USAID, it was these allegations which provided the background for the early 1987 discussions between ERD and ERA which led to the first Leeds food assessment study in Eritrea (June-October 1987).[53] The results of this study, as we have seen, were themselves surrounded in some controversy.[54] The dispute within the team as to whether the liberated areas had been over-supplied or not was an important part of the tension between ERD's administration and ERA.

The conflict with ERA was a very serious matter for ERD. While a number of individual members were closely involved, ERD as a consortium tended to suppress such disagreement since its neutrality rested upon placing the IAs above politics with the consequent lumping of 'ERA/REST' together as basically similar organisations.[55] It was sometimes felt that most ERD members did not want to understand such conflict in case its implications may force a reappraisal of this view.[56] The administration, however, had crossed the Rubicon and had become involved.

During 1987, relations between the ERD administration and ERA continued to deteriorate. ERA, it should be pointed out, had its own complaints. In August 1987, a meeting took place in order to try to resolve their differences. ERA was of the opinion that ERD's mandate should be modified to allow greater IA representation. A position which it had held for some time. ERD, moreover, should be evaluated to ascertain what functions could be taken over by ERA itself.[57] It was felt that the ERD administration had assumed a too powerful role and that a more formal understanding was now required. ERA suggested that a new tripartite agreement should be sought defining the responsibilities and relations between ERD, ERA and the EPLF civilian departments. Since many of the ERD members had already strongly opposed any formal relationship with the Front's civilian departments in May, this suggestion was not really feasible. For its part, ERD wanted better coordination on project funding, lists of agencies approached and a regular update on how funding was progressing. The insinuation being that ERA was double funding.

A general lack of communication persisted through 1988 until there was a change of Executive Secretary towards the end of the year. For much of the period ERA stopped forwarding information to ERD. In April 1988, the issue of local purchase in Sudan became a point of contention. The charge was that ERA had confidential links with some Sudanese merchants which kept quotes high.[58] When ERD attempted to unilaterally contract different merchants, a row ensued. This led to demands for an agreement to cover local purchase. In June, the EC became involved when ERA tried to establish bilateral links with the EC outside ERD. Given that the EC was already in violation of its own mandate in aiding the CBO, this action was felt to be politically irresponsible on the part of ERA and reinforced the administration's view that ERD should continue to play a mediating role. ERA, for its part, argued that by confining its role to the field, ERD did not "encourage our development."[59]

It should be stated here that none of the allegations against ERA were ever proven. The Leeds food assessment mission, for example, was inconclusive. Some commentators have argued that personality differences lay at the heart of the problem. Despite these tensions the CBO continued to function. The contrast between the generally poor relations with ERA, however, and the good relations with REST and ORA, were marked.

The July 1988 Evaluation

The concerns and conflicts over the role of ERD which had clearly emerged by the end of 1987, fed directly into the decision to carry out a second evaluation of ERD. The Centre for Partnership in Development, Oslo, was contracted to carry out this work which was completed in July 1988. Rather than focus on the impact of ERD programmes, the terms of reference were largely concerned with ERD's structure and the appropriateness of its policies in the light of its avowed aims.[60] The evaluation recorded a generally positive impression of ERD and its work. With the exception of the Leeds study, however, the lack of systematic reporting made it difficult to verify the effect of ERD programmes. Reflecting the long standing differences between ERD and the IAs over such things as advocacy, the evaluation team also recognised that ERD meant different things to different people.

The recommendations of the team are interesting in that they reflect the growing concern that ERD's assistance may have gone beyond its humanitarian intention. With regard to the future role of ERD, continuing the debate that had begun in 1987, the evaluation recommended that ERD needed to consider its structure in the light of anticipated needs. Apart from the re-organisation of the Board and Executive Committee, a clear Mission Statement known to all parties was required. This should include its role in assessment and monitoring so that ERD placed "greater emphasis on monitoring, assessing and reporting on the implementing agency's (sic) programmes in allocation of resources."[61] In this respect, the team recommended the continuation of Leeds-type studies, including one for Tigray. With regard to food aid, apart from urging that the IAs should handle local purchase in Sudan, it was suggested that support for internal purchase in Tigray should be supported but a separate evaluation was required to ascertain if it "indirectly supports the 'liberation movements' in order to avoid...claims of partisan activities."[62] With regard to monitoring generally, the evaluation recommended a tightening up of procedures such that the amounts of food aid actually distributed were shown and not just "quantities transported and the number of people such quantities would have fed at normal ration rates."[63]

With regard to the rehabilitation programmes supported by ERD, the team recommended separate evaluation together with a general improvement of financial management and programme reporting. The differences of opinion amongst ERD members has already been noted on several occasions. The evaluation team was concerned that Board Members tended to represent their agency first and ERD second. It recommended reducing the seniority of the agency representatives serving on the Board and giving them a clear ERD brief. Although the evaluation created a good deal of interest at the time and clearly reflected current concerns, it should be noted that its major recommendations, including those concerning assessment and monitoring, were never implemented.[64] The evaluation was overtaken by events. Namely, a growing rift with the Sudanese government and the merging of ERD with NCA.

Antagonism With the Government of Sudan

During the mid-1980s, scores of NGOs entered Sudan. Until this period, Sudanese policy had been to resist the penetration of international agencies. The crisis of 1984-85, however, together with the political flux that followed the fall of the Nimiery regime, was the basis upon which this virtual humanitarian invasion took place. Since the 1970s, the Sudanese government had recognised that international NGOs operate at the limits or outside state control. With eighty or so NGOs established in Sudan within the space of a couple of years, by 1986 the NGO question had reached a critical mass sufficient to become a major domestic issue. NGOs are usually mandated to work with people not governments. Such linkages bypass the state and impact directly within the global arena of development and humanitarian politics. Chapter Five has argued that the change in policy on behalf of major donors in terms of their supporting the CBO signalled a move toward the post-cold war era. NGOs, and the challenge to sovereignty with which they are synonymous, complete the picture.

Within months of the election of a new government in April 1986, it was made clear that the government intended to control the activities of NGOs. This attitude was further hardened due to the involvement of some NGOs in attempting to provide humanitarian relief in South Sudan. Moreover, when these attempts met with resistance, several agencies had made the plight of the civilian population known to the international media. The developing antagonism between the Sudanese state and international and national Christian NGOs had important implications for ERD. NCA, for example, was aware that its programme in South Sudan could "endanger the ERD activities."[65] The geopolitical reasons for Sudan maintaining an open border remained; indeed, with Ethiopia aiding the SPLA in South Sudan they had been strengthened. The emerging difficulty, however, was the fact that ERD and the CBO was run by NGOs. The contradiction for the Sudanese government was that its external interests were underpinned by a mode of delivery which increasingly contradicted its internal sovereignty.

Although the Sudanese government made its position clear on its intention to control NGO activity in 1986, it would be several years before such measures took formal shape. This delay was mainly due to the fact that for most of this period there was intense competition between different ministries to register and control NGO resources. What was noticeable however from 1986, was a steady increase in the difficulties faced by NGOs working in Sudan. NGOs including ERD, for example, faced growing problems in terms of importing vital equipment and supplies. Earlier and more generous arrangements became increasingly restricted. Beginning in October 1986, the first inconclusive attempt to register NGOs took place.[66] At the end of the year, several NGO personnel were expelled from South Sudan for alleged unacceptable activities. Restrictions on radio communications and travel permits followed in the wake of these developments. The latter increased the difficulty faced by expatriate staff wishing to travel outside Khartoum. Although the pressure mounted on NGOs in Sudan, the IAs were not affected.[67] Having separate agreements with ministries and other bodies, they were able to import and conduct their activities as before. This difference reflects the underlying continuity of Sudanese geopolitical interests and was matched in other areas by the government's increasing attempts to indigenise NGO activity.

The Merging of ERD with NCA

During 1988, the internal political struggle around the right to register NGOs was finally settled in favour of the Ministry of Social Welfare. Within months this was followed by a change in ERD's Executive Secretary. While this change saw a normalisation of relations with ERA, it was quickly supplanted by difficulties with the government. In mid-1988, the Ministry of Social Welfare set a deadline whereby all NGOs and their activities had to be registered. This represented a great problem for ERD since, technically, it did not exist. Earlier agreements with the Sudanese government to operate had been verbal: none of the parties had wished anything to be recorded on paper. Moreover, successive changes of government and purges within State Security had changed personnel and dimmed institutional memory.

Arguing that NCA was now unable to cover for ERD, in October 1988, the new Executive Secretary pushed for the complete separation of the ERD administration from NCA.[68] The intention was for ERD to seek separate registration and, if necessary, to extend its mandate to operate within Sudan.

Over the next couple of months several meetings took place between the ERD administration and government and security officials. These meetings disclosed that the government was not particularly interested in a separate registration.[69] This was also resisted by the Executive Committee.[70] In order to resolve the matter, the General Secretary of NCA was invited to re-establish links with the government of Sudan on the basis not of separation, but of NCA taking direct responsibility for ERD.[71] Contrary to the views of the Executive Secretary, ERD members accepted that NCA was well placed to take on this role. In subsequent discussions with the Sudanese government at the beginning of 1989, NCA established that this was acceptable to the government. That NCA should establish control rather than have an independent ERD was also supported by the IAs.[72] Given the anti-NGO climate that existed in Sudan, it was appreciated that NCA was willing to take such a potentially risky move.

In April 1989, it was agreed that ERD should become a part of NCA's Sudan based programme. In a merger which became effective in July 1989, ERD's Executive Secretary was now responsible to the NCA Resident Representative with ERD activities becoming a discrete part of NCA's overall programme. The status of the Board was changed to that of Advisory Group and, in 1990, the IAs were admitted as full members. This merger represented a difficult period for all those involved. Seeing the move as a loss of position, the Executive Secretary left within months of the merger becoming effective. Through a sense of solidarity, most of the senior staff also left in late 1989 and early 1990.[73] This was a particularly difficult time given the great increase in CBO activity that was then taking place.

In many respects, this merger represented the end of ERD as a clandestine cross-border operation made necessary by the limitations of sovereignty. By 1989, its activities were public knowledge and the changing fortunes of the war would see ERD members begin to play an increasingly public role. The CBO had become so routinised that it could now be acknowledged as the responsibility of a single agency.

Peace Advocacy and Concern Over Prolonging the War

As evidence began to emerge during and after 1986 that the CBO was beginning to have an impact on the emergency, it fed an emerging concern amongst some ERD members that the CBO had gone past being a humanitarian operation and had begun to play a role in the dynamics of the war. Was it unconnected, for example, that following the restoration of a semblance of civilian stability, 1988 proved to be a year of significant military advance by the Fronts? This question is discussed in Chapter Ten. It is sufficient to mention here that while the internal management of the relief programmes in Eritrea and Tigray remained under indigenous control, from the mid-1980s the international community began to increasingly displace and substitute for those internal material resources that had previously been directed to public welfare. In other words, this material substitution can be seen as the main manifestation of the internationalisation of public welfare which gathered momentum from this period. The possible effects of this displacement and its relation to the war began to increasingly shape the debate within ERD.

It has already been mentioned that some ERD members had already been involved in peace advocacy during the first part of the 1980s. During the latter part of the 1980s, this activity continued. The SCR had first formed an NGO group to influence the Swedish government. In early 1987, NCA also embarked on a similar enterprise and brought together four other Norwegian NGOs in order to approach the Norwegian Minister of Foreign Affairs.[74] After a series of meetings the Minister agreed to become involved. With the cooperation of the Scandinavian embassies in the Horn (Norway did not have an embassy in Addis Ababa), this led to 18 months of gathering information and informal discussion. During the course of 1988, however, as the military balance swung in favour of the Fronts, it created a situation in which all parties were less inclined to seek a negotiated solution. Sensing that the position had become deadlocked, the Norwegian initiative petered out.[75]

At the end of 1988, the diplomatic standoff rekindled discussion within ERD that member agencies should, themselves, be doing more to try to bring the war to an end.[76] Because differences of opinion existed amongst members, however, the overriding concern was to maintain the integrity of the consortium and it was not until a year later that definite moves were taken. In early 1989, in an attempt to break the diplomatic inertia, ex-US president Jimmy Carter launched a round of all party discussions which became known as the Carter Initiative. This was immediately supported by the Norwegian government. In an acknowledgement of its experience, ERD was also involved on a consultative basis. Although the Carter Initiative did not achieve its aim of a negotiated settlement, it is credited with developing a better understanding within the US of the complexity of the situation.

While doubts had existed for a couple of years, this continuing deadlock served to focus within ERD the concern that humanitarian relief itself may be prolonging the war. In July 1989, LWR, which had previously taken a back seat in most internal ERD discussions, voiced its worry that since the mid-1980s the IAs had been presenting ever-increasing requests for relief assistance.[77] In relation to the issue of food aid and dependency, LWR felt that the Leeds 1987 study had been inconclusive. Attempting to meet this increasing demand for assistance, moreover, had produced a feeling of never-ending commitment and that ERD itself may be prolonging the war by feeding people today only for them to be killed tomorrow. LWR put forward the position, not then generally shared amongst ERD members, that maybe ERD should attempt to bring peace by standing up to the Fronts. LWR's approach, which it held until the end of the war, has been dubbed 'Tough Love'.[78] The argument was also extended to South Sudan. In essence, it is claimed that prolonged and expensive international relief intervention was allowing warring parties to evade their humanitarian responsibility to civilians. In such circumstances, should efforts to broker peace fail, then aid agencies should seriously consider withholding food aid.

This position was discussed at the November 1989 AG meeting in Oslo. In discussion it was agreed not to pursue a new policy, but that ERD needed to focus more clearly on longer-term issues. The background to this was the fact that UN policy in the Horn, reflecting wider changes in humanitarian politics, had begun to change. In South Sudan, for example, since April 1989, the UN had been coordinating a large scale CBO from Kenya, based upon a free passage agreement, called Operation Lifeline (OLS).[79] This made UN policy in Ethiopia appear increasingly dated. In this connection, NCA raised the prospect of publicly campaigning for the free passage of relief food, something which the ERD members had endorsed since 1984. In this respect, NCA had re-established contacts with the Norwegian Ministry of Foreign Affairs and wished to send it a note urging government support for an OLS-type operation for Ethiopia. In discussion, it was thought that focusing directly on OLS was not a good idea. This was because many donors, including USAID, had not wished to see the UN play a prominent coordinating role in South Sudan.

The letter which was eventually sent to the Norwegian Foreign Minister called for food aid to be supplied from all sides. In particular it urged support for the current peace initiatives. It also pointed out that transport costs of humanitarian relief would be cut by half if Ethiopian ports could be used instead of the CBO. The letter therefore urged that all possible relief corridors should be opened and, citing the precedent of OLS, the Foreign Minister was pressed to ask the UN General Secretary to do everything in his power to secure food for "northern Ethiopia."[80] By the end of 1989, moves were also underway to increase access for agencies working from the government side. This is discussed in Chapter Nine.

CHAPTER NINE

Replacing the Cross Border Operation with Aid from the Government Side

War and Famine Summary (1990-1993)

In February 1990, the EPLF overwhelmed the Ethiopian army at Massawa, capturing this key port after a three day battle. Almost immediately, the government retaliated with constant air strikes against the port, often targeting food stores and using napalm and cluster bombs. Frequent attacks lasted until June, and thereafter sporadic bombings served as a reminder that the government still mattered when it came to decisions about humanitarian aid flows.[1] The situation in Ethiopia in 1990 was much calmer than in Eritrea. The EPRDF consolidated its territory and helped REST expand its capabilities for relief and rehabilitation. It has been argued that Ethiopian army abuses against civilians diminished considerably because the zones of contention were increasingly majority Amhara areas, and most of the army officers were Amhara. The incidents that did take place were often the result of a breakdown in authority or morale.[2] The EPRDF launched a massive offensive in February 1991 which in only two weeks resulted in the liberation of all of Gonder and Gojjam from government control. By May 1991, the EPRDF had reached the outskirts of Addis Ababa while the EPLF had tightened its siege of the Asmara garrison. Asmara finally surrendered on 25 May. Three days later, the EPRDF marched largely unopposed into Addis Ababa.

This period of consolidation and eventual victory resulted in very uneven consequences for civilians in Tigray and Eritrea. In Tigray the potential for famine was greatly ameliorated by EPRDF actions such as the liberalisation of the grain trade and population movements, intra-regional movement of grain, and making available limited opportunities for migrant labour. The fact that Tigray was peaceful for the first time in nearly fifteen years also meant the end of government counter-insurgency measures.[3] Yet another factor was the increasing effectiveness of humanitarian relief efforts. The provision of resources for the internal purchase of grain in Tigray, the establishment of the southern line from Assab into Tigray and Wollo, and the consolidation and expansion of the cross-border operation made civilians much more accessible to relief efforts on the part of indigenous agencies and international organisations. By contrast, famine conditions worsened in many parts of Eritrea from 1989-1991. This was the result of a number of factors including (a) consecutive years of drought in 1989 and 1990 (b) the ban by the Ethiopian army on the free movement of commercial food into and of people out of Asmara (c) the requisitioning and looting of food from civilians by the government garrison in Asmara and (d) the increase in poverty of peasant households throughout Eritrea. Between 1987 and 1992, the poverty rate increased in some areas from 62% to 78% of households while livestock herds had declined by a third.[4]

After the fall of the Dergue, the EPRDF formed a transitional government which included most of the political organisations in Ethiopia, excepting those perceived to have collaborated with the former regime. In June 1992, regional elections were held throughout much of Ethiopia. These were marred by the withdrawal of the second largest contingent within the government, the Oromo Liberation Front, together with questions from international observer teams about the degree of obstruction and manipulation of the process by the EPRDF. During 1993, it is intended to draft a constitution in preparation for national elections. In post-war Eritrea, the EPLF acceded to the request by the US and other donors to allow a two year interim period before holding an independence referendum. During those two years, the Provisional Government of Eritrea allowed no political parties, the diametric opposite of the approach pursued in Ethiopia, where over 130 political parties helped create a political hurricane in Addis Ababa. In April 1993, Eritreans overwhelmingly voted for independence and received wide international recognition almost immediately. After thirty years of war, formal independence was celebrated on 24 May 1993.

The Southern Line Operation

Due to the growing military successes of the Fronts and the end of the war in May 1991, the cross border operation was gradually replaced by relief assistance channelled from the government side. Initially this was provided by Ethiopian church agencies and then the UN. Prior to the end of the war, the negotiations with the Fronts that were necessary to achieve this replacement conferred a large measure of recognition. The issue is raised, however, whether the price of victory has been a dependence upon the international community following the CBO's material substitution for the public welfare function of the Fronts.

It has already been shown that towards the end of the 1980s, ERD was increasingly involved in peace advocacy and was making contact with agencies working in government areas. Helped by the Carter Initiative, by 1989, pressure was also growing on the Ethiopian government from these agencies and their supporting donors for more action from its side. The main Ethiopian NGO consortium was the Joint Relief Programme (JRP) which had emerged from an earlier consortium in 1985. Its members were the Ethiopian Catholic, Lutheran and Orthodox churches together with the American based Catholic Relief Services (CRS). The return of famine conditions in 1989 in Tigray prompted JRP to propose a free passage plan which would require the agreement of the TPLF and the Ethiopian Government. To the surprise of the JRP agencies, the Dergue eventually agreed.[5] There is some speculation as to why the Dergue agreed to what became known as the Southern Line Operation. Some have argued that because the EPLF was putting the port of Assab under pressure at the time, the government hoped that accepting a free passage arrangement might reduce this.[6] Others, however, are at a loss to explain the Dergue's agreement since it stood to gain little from the arrangement.[7]

With the mediation efforts of ERD, representatives of JRP, the TPLF and REST met secretly in Khartoum in February 1990 to discuss the arrangements for operation. This was the first meeting of its type and coincided with the fall of Massawa. Through the JRP agencies, the Ethiopian government had laid down certain conditions which REST was unable to accept. When the JRP took up the matter in Addis Ababa, however, the government eventually reached an agreement. Although many restrictions remained, such as the exclusion of all international agencies from the operation and the limitations of TPLF movements, it began in March 1990. Special stickers were placed upon the JRP trucks to clearly distinguish them and guarantee their safe passage.

The JRP programme was seen by REST as important for the eastern areas of Tigray where the operation was mainly confined to the main roads and adjacent areas. Generally speaking, the Southern Line Operation was regarded by REST as insufficient and something of a government public relations exercise.[8] The TPLF, however, also realised that they had gained an important element of recognition.[9] It had, however, had to make a number of political and military sacrifices. The terms of the agreement, for example, meant that the Dergue could relax its defense around JRP towns and redeploy its troops in the knowledge that EPRDF forces could not attack them. Some ERD members also felt that a chance had been missed by REST's allowing the JRP agencies to set up their own distribution centres rather than insisting they work through the community based Baito system.[10] The difference in relief management systems is discussed in Chapter Eleven.

During 1990, when the CBO reached its peak, the JRP operation was also delivering an average of 9,000 mt per month to Tigray and 3,000 mt to Northern Wollo.[11]

The Northern Line from Massawa

The Northern Line Operation from Massawa involved the delivery of WFP food aid into Eritrea. The Port of Massawa fell to the EPLF in February 1990, at the same time as the JRP Southern Line negotiations were taking place. An important effect of this was that relief supplies en route to Massawa were diverted to Port Sudan with the result that the CBO reached record levels with around 250,000 mt of food aid being delivered in 1990. For USAID, 1990 was a year of record donations to the CBO and Ethiopia generally. Early in 1990 a delegation from Congress together with consultants from the Office of Foreign Disaster Assistance made an unprecedented journey into Front held territory to examine CBO needs.

Initially the Dergue tried to hide the fact that it had lost control of Massawa. US and donor pressure, however, was for the warring parties to agree to reopen the port under UN control. While face to face discussions between the EPLF and the Ethiopian government did not take place, the EPLF accepted a tripartite negotiating structure with the UN's WFP playing a mediating role. The EPLF, it is claimed, accepted this arrangement due to the starvation that was occurring in and around government controlled Asmara.[12] By July ERA had prepared an office for the UN in Massawa in anticipation of an agreement.[13] At the June 1990 superpower summit, the US and Soviet Union agreed to jointly push for the opening of Massawa, to which the Ethiopian government agreed in principle. The Dergue, however, continued to act in bad faith and, while negotiations continued, was simultaneously bombing the port. Under UN pressure, an arrangement was eventually reached whereby supplies through Massawa would be evenly divided between the EPLF and the government. In August 1990, however, the first UN ship planned to dock was turned back from the port due to a procedural dispute with the EPLF.

Largely as a result of government intransigence, it was not until January 1991 that a ship successfully docked at Massawa, nearly a year after the port had fallen, and the Northern Line Operation began. UN relations with ERA were generally poor. Despite the change in the military balance, although the EPLF had gained further de facto recognition through the Northern Line negotiations, the UN moderated its behaviour to limit this effect. Although ERA asked for UN monitoring of both its and the government supplies, for example, WFP declined the offer fearing that this would somehow make ERA's operations 'official'.[14] Reflecting normal UN procedure, at least as some would argue, the UN managed the Northern Line Operation on the basis of telling other parties as little as possible and disclosing few of its own intentions. ERA had great difficulty establishing a dialogue, obtaining reimbursement for transport costs, getting answers to inquires, and so on.

With the opening of the port in January 1991, donors in Addis Ababa began to press for the closing of the CBO and directing all assistance through Massawa and Assab. A fierce debate ensued in USAID, for example, which resulted in a decision to channel all resources through Massawa and end US support of the cross-border operation. The IAs strongly opposed this development. In the case of Eritrea, for example, its northern regions were better served from Port Sudan. USAID officials claimed that the change had been made on the basis of cost[15] and the fact that WFP provided better monitoring.[16] As we have seen, however, WFP was providing no monitoring at all. It should be noted that January was also the month in which hostilities in the Gulf War broke out. All USAID staff were evacuated from Khartoum. In the past, its Khartoum office had been supportive of the CBO. This development left USAID's Addis Ababa representative, who had long opposed the cross-border operation, in a strong position within the decision making process. The conflict between donor representatives is returned to below.

Following the withdrawal of USAID support, the level of CBO activity dropped markedly in 1991. The EC, it should be mentioned, maintained its commitment. This was more through organisational inertia, however, rather than a policy decision. Following the end of the war in May, ERA also began to route its supplies through Massawa. This, plus the closing of ERD's Port Sudan office in June and the moving of the ERD office to Asmara in October, meant that by the end of 1991 the CBO had more or less finished. Although the international community continued to be the main suppliers of food aid, the task of coordinating relief assistance was taken over by WFP. Relief operations in Eritrea and Ethiopia had been normalised so to speak. For its part, ERD had long thought that circumstances had forced it reluctantly to take on a UN style role. This takeover, therefore, was not experienced as it losing a job. Rather, the responsibility was seen as being placed where it belonged.[17] The irony, however, was that an unreformed UN, an important player in the years of denial, should now assume a role that it had long rejected.

Divisions Within the Donor Community

It would be wrong to regard donor policy in the Horn as a unified affair. There were important divisions. Chapter Three, for example, describes the major differences in the approach of USAID and the EC to Ethiopia. Following the important changes of the mid-1980s, however, another level of divergence emerged. In the mid-1980s, as Chapter Five argues, USAID and the EC changed policy and began to provide an increasing amount of assistance through NGOs, including those working the CBO. As the differences between these two strategic donors narrowed it opened up a 'headquarters' versus 'field office' division within the donor camp. Moreover, this opened the way for a regional competition between field offices having different connections with the CBO or Ethiopian relief operations. An LWR official, for example, observed that when Addis Ababa's USAID office had the upper hand, donations dropped; when the Khartoum office predominated, the opposite resulted.[18] In a period of policy uncertainty and multiple agendas, turf wars such as this take on an added importance.

One reason for this uncertainty is that the response of donor governments to complex emergencies has, since the mid-1980s, been increasingly driven by the uneven effects of the media and public opinion. This trend has increased as the economic and political significance of Africa, that is, the West's direct material interest, has declined.[19] The public concern that the 1984 media coverage of Ethiopia generated and the political bandwagon that it set rolling pushed policy beyond the bounds of conventional constraint. Indeed, it has been argued that the decision of USAID and EC to support the CBO marked the hesitant beginnings of a new and more interventionist humanitarian paradigm. These decisions, however, were taken at headquarters not field office level. With the waning of public interest in the West, one can detect during the latter part of the 1980s that power began to edge back to the field office.

To a large extent the policies of a field office of an international agency reflect the career ambitions of its resident representative. This commonly involves asserting the priority of the country of residence and its interests when key policy issues are at stake. During the latter part of the 1980s, the emergence of turf wars between donor offices in Sudan and Ethiopia often took the form of Addis Ababa based agencies attempting to reduce, or close the CBO in favour of schemes they controlled from the government side. Chapter Eight describes one of the first examples of this. That is, the late 1987 'Open Road for Survival Initiative' proposed by the ICRC. It will be recalled that in developing this proposal the ICRC claimed that ERD was reducing donor bargaining power with the Dergue. Similarly, during 1989, WFP also began to argue that the reach of ERD was limited as a means of increasing its own importance.[20]

Such pressures grew as the negotiations to open Massawa developed during 1990. In October, a donor meeting took place in Khartoum to discuss allegations made by Addis Ababa based donor representatives concerning the CBO. Although no evidence was produced, the feeling in Addis Ababa was that the CBO was poorly monitored since the monitors were biased and relief distributions stage managed by the Fronts. Moreover, relief shipments were allegedly being diverted by the Fronts for off-shore sale. The Addis Ababa donors were pushing for making Massawa a cease-fire zone under UN control. This would then allow "the cross-border operation to be limited and grain could reach Eritrea and Tigray more closely monitored by the UN and JRP."[21] The Khartoum USAID and British representatives strongly objected to these claims. Furthermore, while supporting the opening of Massawa, the limited capacity of the port was pointed out. It has already been indicated that the evacuation of Khartoum's USAID delegation in January 1991 allowed the view of its Addis Ababa representative to prevail.

While it was common to interpret the attempts by Addis Ababa based donors to curtail the CBO as a means of exerting political influence on the Fronts, this view is probably misplaced. Headquarters level donors already exerted control over the end destination of food aid whatever route it took. Since the mid-1980s, moreover, ERD had largely transferred the responsibility of supplying relief assistance to non-government areas to the international community. The reasons for field office competition are likely to be more mundane and unconnected with objective relief criteria: regardless of the circumstances, local representatives wanted to be personally involved.

The London Peace Conference

During 1990, the US convened a series of separate meetings with the Fronts and the Ethiopian government. The Reagan Doctrine had passed with the end of the Reagan administration. US interests had come to focus on such things as the welfare of Ethiopian Jews (to which American Jewish organisations had begun to pay serious attention) and the prevention of mass famine through conflict resolution. Since both of these required ongoing negotiations, the US continued to push for a diplomatic solution right up to the fall of Addis Ababa in May 1991.

For several years ERD had been concerned that its assistance may be prolonging the war. At the time of the London Peace Conference in May 1991, which in an unprecedented manner brought all parties to the conflict together, this fear had become more widespread. Newspapers had begun to carry stories on the theme that food aid was propping up warring factions which cared little for civilians caught in the fighting.[22] In addition to behind the scenes support, ERD's contribution to the conference was a letter to the delegates which reflected the earlier Tough Love theme of LWR. Apart from calling for a resolution to the war, it pointed out that as humanitarian organisations "we feel there is a limit to how long we can keep up our present level of relief assistance if no political solution can be reached."[23] It added that if a solution could be found, the agencies were ready to confirm their support for rehabilitation and long-term development.

In the event, the end to the war was nearer than many thought. By 1989, the USA had recognised that the days of the Ethiopian government were limited. The Carter initiative had gone some way in forming this view. With the forces of the EPLF and EPRDF already waiting at the gates of Addis Ababa on the eve of the Peace Conference, the Americans made an unexpected move. To the surprise of the Europeans, the USA delegate informed the government representatives that the Dergue's term of office had run its course. In consultation with the Fronts the USA set out its plans for an orderly transfer of power. This intervention, which isolated the Dergue in the international arena, is widely credited with hastening the capitulation of the Ethiopian government and preventing much unnecessary suffering.[24] The US subsequently dropped its opposition to Eritrean self-determination and defined a policy in which non-humanitarian aid would be forthcoming to the Provisional Government of Eritrea and the Transitional Government of Ethiopia in the context of the establishment of democratic systems of governance.

From Self-Reliance to Dependency?

The end of the war and the transition to peace in the Horn has brought a welcome respite to this troubled region. Many observers, however, feel that securing the peace may be just as difficult, not more so, as fighting the war. The singularity of the Fronts lay in the development of a political practice which united the provision of public welfare with political mobilization. The ending of the war has removed a potent symbol around which mobilization could be structured. Moreover, the internationalisation of public welfare in the mid-1980s, can be argued to have gradually displaced those material resources previously supplied by the Fronts and civilian populations. The degree of this substitution is unknown. Its existence, however, is represented in the handover of the relief and rehabilitation input of the CBO to the international community.

Rather than dealing with ERD and sympathetic NGOs, the new governments of Eritrea and Ethiopia have entered a novel arena. To what degree the price of victory has been a material dependence on donor governments which now can only be resolved at an international level is a topic for further study. In the transition to peace, this issue also relates to a concern as to whether the institutions exist to accomplish the difficult tasks ahead. Such questions shaped the discussions surrounding the decision to phase out ERD. Before examining this debate, however, the issue of the international substitution for indigenous public welfare capacity needs to be addressed more fully.

CHAPTER TEN

The Internationalisation of Public Welfare and the Replacement of Indigenous Capacity

Between 1981 and 1991, ERD, either through accessing from abroad or purchasing in Sudan, Tigray and Eritrea, made available around 3/4 million metric tonnes of food aid, perhaps half of the total supplied by the international community, for use within non-government areas. The cash value of this food, together with the additional relief and rehabilitation programmes supported by ERD represent a total expenditure in the order of 350 million US dollars, around 1/3 of which was raised by ERD members themselves. Rather than examining the effect of this substantial programme solely in relief terms, such as its adequacy in relation to assessed need, this history has opted to sketch a different approach. That is, by seeing sustained resource flows of such magnitude, even if deemed emergency relief, as having a definite economic and institutional impact on the recipient society. Indeed, given the amount of emergency aid relative to the limited size of the formal economy in many chronic African emergencies, it is surprising that the study of the wider economic impact of large-scale relief operations remains a neglected area.

The Question of Adequacy

The main focus of those studies which have examined the effects of food aid in Eritrea and Tigray have concentrated on the implications for rural productive systems. Apart from the significant gaps and inconsistencies in the available evidence, especially the real size of the populations at risk and the actual number of beneficiaries, this work, together with showing the complexity of estimating need, achieves agreement in several important areas.

Generally speaking, the available evidence suggests that rural households have never recovered their asset base following the process of impoverishment leading to the famine of the mid-1980s.[1] The most exhaustive study to date has been the work carried out in Eritrea by Leeds University in 1987[2] and 1991. Comparison of the data produced in these two studies indicates a serious depletion of the rural asset base over this period. In 1987, for example, 62% of households were classed as 'poor'. By 1991, this had risen to 78%.[3–4] Most provinces had also witnessed a severe reduction in herd size and, for poor farmers in particular, the lack of draught oxen was an important limitation on production. Although some of this asset loss has been the result of military action, the impression is that food aid has been insufficient in quantity to prevent this continuing erosion. This is despite the fact that in semi-subsistence conditions, food aid not directly consumed is easily monetised or converted into a medium of social exchange. Thus, although it has been argued that the CBO had helped to stabilise the humanitarian crisis by 1987, it was insufficient to prevent a continuing impoverishment.

Even when the CBO was delivering record amounts of food aid at the end of the 1980s, insufficiency necessitated the continuation of internal targeting.[5–6] Food aid, moreover, mainly consisted of staple grain with relatively few supplementary items. ERD's mix of food commodities, for example, consistently failed to reach WHO's recommendations for a balanced diet.[7–9] Besides the nutritional implications of this trend, the lack of supplementary foodstuffs reduced the ability to exchange or sell food aid for other essential commodities. Taken as a whole, the Leeds studies, together with that of Silkin and Hughes,[10] find little evidence that the sustained receipt of food aid has created dependency in rural producers in Eritrea or Tigray.

The Concept of a Relief Economy

Although the evidence would suggest that food aid was never enough and of sufficient quality, it undoubtedly played an important role in helping keep people alive. As the discussion in Chapter Five suggests, when utilised in an integrated relief strategy, it provided an additional coping mechanism which allowed the Fronts to gradually stabilise the crisis and, where possible, support the rural productive system. If food aid has to be placed in context, it is within this integrated system. Chapter Two argues that during the 1970s, the Fronts developed a political practice which linked the provision of public welfare with the politics of mass mobilization. In considering the impact of the CBO, the question that existing studies have not asked is how far the development of the relief operation substituted for the welfare programmes initially instigated by the Fronts. During the late 1970s and early 1980s, self-reliance was a key concept in the solidarity literature that grew up around the Fronts. After the mid-1980s, as the CBO became more important, this idea is encountered less frequently. The political implications of this proposition will be discussed later. Here, the evidence for substitution will be examined.

In order to analyse the extent of substitution, food aid has to be seen in a different light. That is, as part of a wider relief economy capable of impacting on the recipient society at many levels, not just the rural productive system. This includes a range of modalities, such as, the extensive creation of local employment that relief systems afford; the impetus given to the development of a transport infrastructure; the support for commercial farming through local purchase; the help given to the recipient exchequer when currency exchange rates for relief operations are pegged at artificially high levels; the support offered by sustained relief flows to the black market or parallel economy; and so on. Unlike normal NGO development projects, the scale and scope of relief operations means that these economic impacts can be of regional, if not national significance. How relief economies develop and, with the run-down of a long-term operation, what type of transitional crises emerge is a little-understood process. It suggests that dependency, should it occur, may not be within the rural productive system. Rather, it should be looked for at the institutional and national economic level. Given the consolidation of a number of large-scale relief operations in Africa since the internationalisation of public welfare, it is a phenomenon which urgently demands more attention.

The relief economy will be examined from the perspective of (a) food aid (b) transport (c) exchange rates and (d) the internal purchase of agricultural surplus. This is by no means an exhaustive list.

ERD and Food Aid

In order to examine food aid as part of a wider relief economy the growing efficiency of the CBO is discussed in terms of the increasing pro-

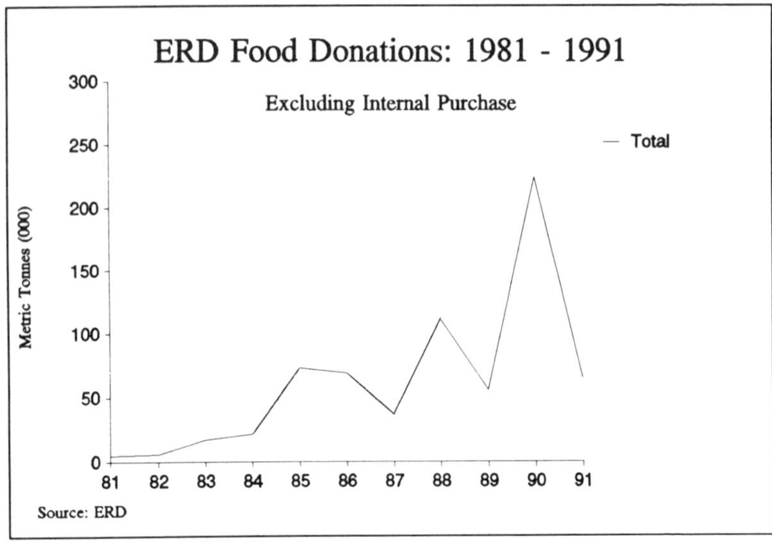

Figure 10

portion of IA requests that it was able to meet. It should be noted that IA requests are not to be confused with actual need. Estimating actual need is extremely difficult and, as we have seen, it is impossible even to ascertain the number of actual beneficiaries since monitoring reports invariably give national populations. In an environment in which estimated need always ran ahead of available food aid, for most of the period the IAs were restricted to what was available and, importantly, what they could physically truck. IA requests therefore were generally couched in relation to these considerations. Until the mid-1980s, the distribution of ERD resources reflected differences in IA transport capacity. From 1986, it adopted a policy of a more equitable division of available food aid between ERA and REST (see Figure 7). An option made possible due to the increase in REST's truck fleet. At no time was supply related to actual need. In terms of their ability to meet IA requests, however, the discussion in the preceding chapters suggests the following rough periodisation of ERD and the CBO.

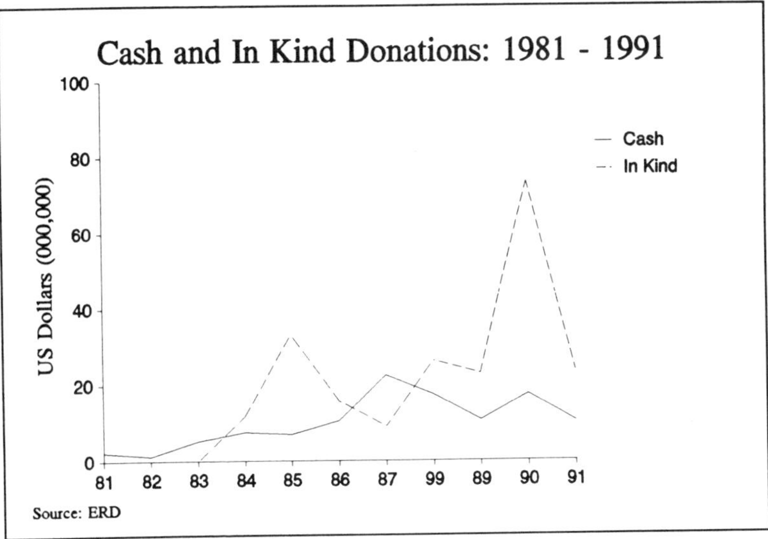

Figure 11

(a) 1978-1983: Crisis

From the late 1970s until 1983, given the developing famine, although ERD was supplying almost 100% of the CBO assistance, some 28,000 mt between 1981 and 1983, its performance dropped from 15% to around 5% of ERA's request for food aid.[11] At this stage the EPLF continued to play an important role in attempting to make good the shortfall.[12] A similar situation held for REST and the TPLF.[13] Apart from being a monopoly supplier, it should be emphasised that during this period, ERD was struggling to provide food aid mainly from its own resources.

(b) 1984-1986: Stabilisation

The significant increase in relief food during this period (around 164,000 mt was delivered, mainly to Eritrea) allowed for the gradual stabilisation of the situation in non-government areas. It can also be argued to have reduced the pressure on the EPLF. In the case of Tigray, the refugee exodus to Sudan in 1984, their repatriation and the development of an integrated relief management strategy eventually laid the ground for stabilisation there. At this stage ERD was still the monopoly supplier for the CBO. In 1986, for example, ERD was providing 75% of the total food aid.[14] An important change had taken place, however, in that supporting the food aid programme had largely become the responsibility of donor governments. This allowed the diversification of ERD's cash-supported projects into such things as rehabilitation. Figure 11 illustrates this transition. 'In kind' donations were roughly equivalent to government provided food aid. ERD cash expenditure again became important in 1987, following the temporary reduction of donor support for the CBO.

(c) 1987-1991: Consolidation

The Fronts greatly increased the areas under their control during this period. At some 492,000 mt, it also represented the bulk of ERD's food aid deliveries. It was a time when two developments became apparent. Firstly, in terms of meeting the IAs requested targets, compared to the early 1980s, the CBO became more effective. Between 1988 and 1989, for example, on average the CBO met around 40% of the IA requests. This was a several-fold improvement compared to the early 1980s. In the exceptional year of 1990, following the closure and diversion of food aid from Massawa, the CBO met 58% of ERA's request and an astonishing 92% of REST's.[15] With the increasing involvement of other NGOs in the CBO, however, the period was also one in which ERD had lost its position as monopoly food aid supplier by 1988. Although the CBO was becoming more effective, in relation to 1989, ERD's share of the total food aid delivered to Eritrea had declined to 16% and for Tigray to 26%.[16] That ERD improved its share in 1990, to an average of around 40%, was an exception to the trend.

In reviewing this periodisation of the CBO, it is clear that ERD played a major role during the early and mid-1980s. Being the only CBO food aid consortium at the time, the first part of the 1980s was important in helping stabilise the crisis and develop the relief infrastructure which allowed the increased aid of the mid-1980s to find access to non-government areas. From this perspective, it was only after the situation had been stabilised with the help of ERD that other food aid NGOs became involved.

It has already been argued that the direct appropriation of food aid was not part of the Front's political practice. In this context, however, one has to consider the scope for the fungibility of resources. That is, the ability to free-up resources from one area or one particular use and to redirect them to another area or use. The increasing efficiency of the CBO from the mid-1908s would have allowed fungibility to operate in aid of the war effort. Stabilisation, for example, preceded the turning point of the war in 1988. It was this type of concern that underpinned the growing disquiet amongst some ERD members when it was realised that military success had made the Fronts less inclined to a negotiated solution. It was only in 1990, however, when the CBO reached the peak of its effectiveness that anecdotal evidence suggests that some relief commodities may have been directly diverted to the military.[17–19] The occasion for this was the regrouping of EPLF and EPRDF forces preparatory to the final assault on Addis Ababa. The mobilization of unprecedented numbers of soldiers had reduced rural productive capacity and the Front's scope for self-generated economic activity. In these exceptional circumstances fungibility may have been insufficient, or else food aid supply was in excess of actual humanitarian requirements.

Transport Capacity

Throughout most of the 1980s, the lack of trucks and suitable roads was a major constraint on the relief programme. Indeed, transport capacity rather than estimated need, especially with regard to REST, often governed the level of the IA's requests and ERD planned commitment. The increased flow of food aid in 1985 and 1986, for example, was directly linked to an improvement of the IA's transport capacity. The development of trucking capacity in the areas controlled by, or accessible to the Fronts presented a changing situation. The development of maintenance facilities, roads and truck fleets were linked in a dynamic relationship. A transport infrastructure was also a dual use facility. Indeed, both ERA and REST's truck fleets originated from the Fronts. While IA trucks were restricted to relief purposes, the internal road and maintenance facilities were shared with the Front's military and civilian departments.

During the latter part of the 1970s and early 1980s, the IAs lacked any significant trucking capacity and relied on the Fronts. By 1979, the EPLF had established extensive maintenance facilities within Eritrea and had embarked upon a major road building programme.[20] In this year, for example, it constructed a 1,500 km Liberation Road. The TPLF's road building began in earnest from 1982, involving mass civilian participation.

(a) ERA's Truck Fleet

The evidence concerning the growth of ERA's truck fleet is patchy.

The available material would suggest that up until 1984, ERA was heavily reliant upon EPLF trucking capacity[21] having few of its own trucks.[22] In mid-1985, this reliance was such that reports speak, perhaps misleadingly, of a combined ERA/EPLF fleet of 200-300 trucks, half of them Russian Zils, and between 100-200 Toyota Land Cruisers.[23] At this stage, the EPLF had 6 major garages and 15-20 smaller facilities within Eritrea. In late 1985, through LWR, ERA was supplied with 65 new

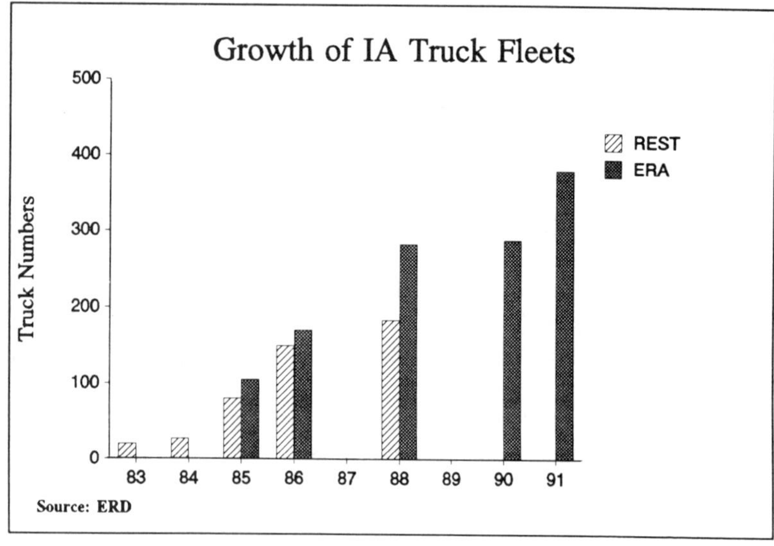

Figure 12

Mercedes trucks. In the first half of 1986, this is reported to have increased ERA trucking capacity by 61%.[24] This suggests a 1985 fleet of around 105 trucks and an early 1986 fleet of around 170. Other reports, however, speak of a late 1985 fleet of 261 with a monthly capacity of 12,272 mt.[25] There is reason to believe that this figure may include Sudanese commercial trucks which ERA also used for transport to the border. The monthly capacity also probably makes no allowance for breakdowns. By 1988, the size of ERA's truck fleet is given as 282 plus Sudanese commercial lorries with a more realistic monthly capacity of

7,970 mt. By this time most of the lorries were Mercedes. In mid-1990, the truck fleet had increased marginally to 288[26] but, by the end of 1991, the fleet was said to be 380.[27]

(b) REST's Truck Fleet

Although following a similar pattern, the growth of REST's trucking capacity is a little easier to document. In 1983, REST had 20 trucks donated by the TPLF in response to growing famine conditions.[28] These gave a monthly capacity of 360 mt. By early 1984, this had increased to 27 although still woefully inadequate to the need.[29] These trucks had a monthly capacity of 500 mt.[30] In late 1985, in addition to help from other agencies, another 75 trucks were added by ICRC and ERD.[31] This improved REST's transport capacity during 1986 by 89%. This suggests a 1985 fleet of around 80 trucks and a 1986 fleet of around 150. This period was also one of an expansion in TPLF road building, making it possible to travel from Sudan to the main Gondar/Asmara highway. By March 1988, REST's lorry fleet had grown to 170 with a monthly capacity of 5,000 mt.[32] Towards the end of 1988, the operation fleet was 183 trucks plus 100 Sudanese commercial lorries giving a capacity of 6,000 mt per month.[33]

During the dry season of 1989-1990, the combined IA capacity had increased to between 17-20,000 mt per month, indicating the continued growth of trucking capacity and road infrastructure. In the cases of both ERA and REST a similar pattern is discernable. That is, an early reliance upon the Fronts for transport which, especially from the mid-1980s, was progressively taken over by the international community, both in terms of the provision of trucks and the payment of their running costs.

Transport Costs

Although ERD was only involved on a few occasions in supplying trucks to the IAs, transport and the provision of spare parts being one of the main concerns of EIAC and TTAC, it was a major conduit for transport costs, that is, fuel, oil, tyre and other consumables in relation to the IAs own trucks, together with hire charges for Sudanese commercial lorries. Until the mid-1980s, ERD met the cost of transporting food from Sudan or the port of entry to the border. Internal running costs were the responsibility of the IAs. From this period, due to the great increase in food aid provision and pressure from the IAs, transport costs were provided to the point of distribution. Thus relieving the IAs and, in the last analysis, the Fronts of this burden.

Given the rough terrain, transport costs were a major item of expenditure. Because they were usually included in the cash value of food aid, and this is especially the case with regard to local and internal purchase, it is not easy to separate out exactly how much ERD spent on transport. In 1983, the cost of fuel and other consumables on a return journey from Kassala to Tigray, for example, was estimated to be $1,241 per trip or, for REST's 27 trucks, $33,507 for the fleet.[34] During 1983 transport costs represented 16% and 26% of all ERD's assistance to REST and ORA respectively.[35] In 1988, the value of ERD's total programme was around $75 million of which it was estimated that 1/2 was food aid, 1/4 was ERD's cash supported programme and the remaining 1/4 represented transport costs.[36] On this sort of reckoning, ERD could have spent over $100 million on transport running costs during the 1980s. Certainly, during the latter part of the 1980s, there was an upward pressure on costs which was underpinned by the fact that the IAs strategy was to distribute food as near to the beneficiaries' home locations as possible.

The high cost of transport, especially in Tigray, had a number of consequences. Expensive transport, for example, was one reason why the internal purchase of grain from areas of surplus production within Tigray was begun in 1983. At the end of 1984, in setting ERD's budget for 1985, due regard had to be made for transporting the anticipated increase in external food aid.[37] When ERD was re-established in October 1985, its new mandate officially recognised that ERD should meet transport costs, including cash transactions, thereby bringing it in line with what was already happening in practice. The manner in which these costs were paid was in the form of a flat rate based on an estimated price per tonne for internal transport. In 1986, these were $53 per tonne in Eritrea and $154 per tonne in Tigray. For moving 100 tonnes of food aid within Tigray, for example, REST would have charged ERD $15,400. In order to reimburse the IAs, and to overcome the problem of the over-valuation of the Sudanese and Ethiopian exchange rates, separate accounts were opened in Europe for ERA and REST. ERD was thereby able to reimburse the IAs in hard currency. The sums involved were considerable. In 1988, for example, the 54,600 mt of relief food delivered to Tigray represented a transport cost of over $10 million. When, in 1988, the ERD auditors wanted to curtail all hard currency transactions outside Sudan on the grounds that for services received within Sudan they were illegal, there was a considerable and understandable resistance from the IAs.[38]

Throughout the period, the question of transport costs, in particular the calculation of the flat rate, was a sensitive issue. Many members felt that ERD was paying more than the actual cost involved but lacked the information to defend alternative figures. USAID, for example, used high transport costs as one reason to reduce its food aid contribution in 1986. At the end of the 1980s, when REST attempted to increase the flat rate, it was rejected by ERD. When the external payment of transport costs ceased, the concern over high costs was compounded by the over-valued exchange within Sudan.

The Significance of Exchange Rates

In March 1983, a Bank of Sudan circular (No. 116) restricted all NGO transactions, including humanitarian relief, to an official exchange rate which then stood at Ls1.28 to $1.[39] Private citizens were able to obtain the market exchange rate which was then Ls1.78 to $1. From this period, the value of the official exchange rate began to deteriorate. In particular, the black market value of the Sudanese Pound, its real value, began to drop against the dollar. On several occasions the Sudanese devalued the market exchange rate in an attempt to attract foreign currency, especially from Sudanese migrants working in the Gulf. The black market value of the Sudanese Pound, however, continued to drop faster than the devaluations of the market rate. Aware of this overvaluation of the official rate, from the mid-1980s, NGOs operating in Sudan became increasingly concerned about their terms of exchange and made frequent representations to the government. By 1988, for example, the official rate stood at Ls4.4 to $1 while the market rate was Ls12.2. The black market or real value, however, was more than Ls17 to $1.[40] This was the equivalent of a 300% relief tax imposed by the Sudanese government on all NGO internal transactions requiring Sudanese currency, for example, rents, telecommunications, local salaries, fuel, transport costs, local purchase of food aid and supplies, import duties, licensing fees, and so on.

Sudan was not alone in this practice. The Ethiopian government maintained an official exchange rate of 2.07 Birr to $1 throughout the 1980s until devaluation in 1992. During most of the 1980s the real value of the Birr was around 6 to 7 Birr to $1. This was the equivalent of a 200% relief tax.[41] The contribution of the over-valued Birr to the Ethiopian exchequer can be judged from the fact that the total value of relief aid exceeded $1 billion in 1989. In the case of Sudan no overall figures are available. With regard to ERD, however, in 1989 the total value of ERD's cash programme, excluding money for internal purchase in Tigray which was exchanged on the open market in Jeddah, was around $10 million. Assuming that most of this involved currency transactions within Sudan, a 300% relief tax would suggest that around $7.5 million went to the Sudanese exchequer. ERD was, of course, not the only NGO operation within Sudan at this time. Several other large undertakings were ongoing in the North and, importantly, the UN's Operation Lifeline had been established in South Sudan. The taxing of all of these operations must have netted the Sudanese government a considerable source of hard currency. Sufficient to justify speculation that international humanitarian programmes were indirectly funding the North's war effort in South Sudan.[42]

Internal Purchase

Internal purchase (IP) was a major component of cross-border assistance in Tigray and, later and to a lesser extent, areas accessed by ORA. Internal purchase is the buying of locally produced grain for distribution in deficit areas or to food deficit families. In Tigray, IP was supported by ERD since 1983 (see Figure 9) with over $16 million being spent by 1991 (Figure 13). The programme arose out of ERD's willingness to be flexible in response to the humanitarian crisis that was facing Tigray. As the rainy season approached in 1983, little relief food was crossing the border. REST presented internal purchase as the only alternative. Since it then involved changing Sudanese Pounds to Birr on the Sudanese black market, few other NGOs would have touched such an operation at this time. Within Tigray grain was purchased in western and southern surplus areas such as Shire, Raya, and Kobo, and distributed in deficit areas.[43] Topographical, land tenure and population conditions allow western Tigray to be a surplus-producing area during most years, whereas even in good years, eastern and central Tigray usually are not self-sufficient, necessitating seasonal migration to the west to supplement family income. Even after this, many families are prevented from meeting their food needs by lack of sufficient funds, restricted private transport, and an undeveloped market infrastructure which prevent efficient private distribution. The war also greatly restricted the movement of grain and market activity which increased food insecurity.

The original request for internal purchase from REST to ERD arose from the links between Tigrayan merchants and the TPLF. From its early days, the TPLF had aligned itself with merchant and commercial farmer interests for political reasons and in order to help finance its own projects. In so far as the TPLF could establish conditions in which merchant capital could develop, it had a strategic ally within Tigray. In

1983, one merchant reported that,

> ...if we get money that circulates in the economy of our country, then that involves us in the struggle. We want to increase our capital to meet the needs of our people for food, clothing, anything.[44]

Seen in this light, it made political as well as relief management sense for the TPLF and REST to pursue external financing for internal purchase.

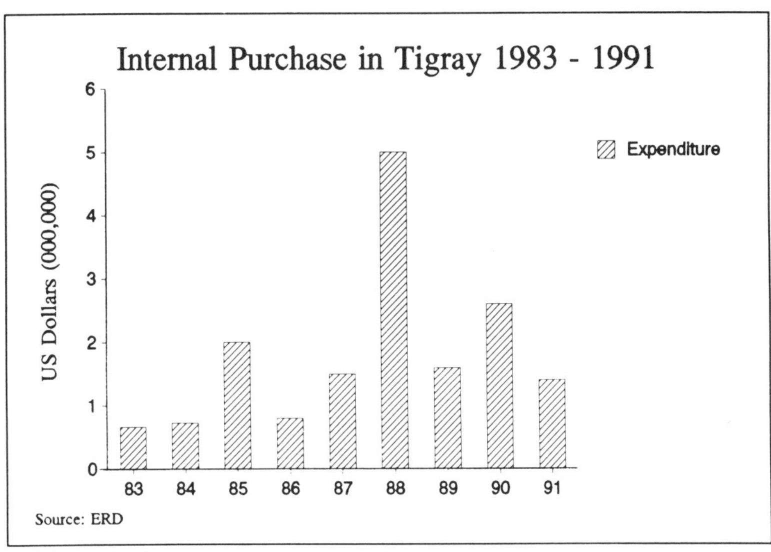

Figure 13

For ERD financed IP programmes, REST contracted local merchants who purchased, bagged, stored and transported the grain to distribution sites. They usually charged five percent for overheads and claimed a five percent profit. Merchants were required to pay farmers the current market price, and they usually charged REST a small premium over the market rate to overcome the later loss of profit when producer prices would go up as the post-harvest season progressed.[45] While the initial programmes were financed by Birr purchased on the Sudanese black market, from the mid-1980s, REST established an office in Jeddah for the conversion of hard currency into Birr on the Saudi market. The sums exchanged were considerable. In 1988, ERD alone exchanged $5 million and, by this time, other agencies were also contributing to the programme. It is even thought that the transactions attracted the attention of the Ethiopian government: Birr was obtained still in its Bank of Ethiopia wraps.[46]

Internal purchase has a number of advocates who have argued a case for its positive and developmental impact compared to the importation of food aid.[47–50] This includes (a) it stimulates local agricultural production and marketing structures (b) it provides farmers with cash and seasonal labourers with work (c) it offers a far quicker emergency response than imported food aid (d) it increased the capacity of REST to reach people in their home areas thus reducing migration (e) it does not alter local consumption patterns and (f) it offered a competitive, if not more cost-efficient alternative to CBO food aid if transport costs were added to the equation. IP has also been criticised, however, largely in terms of the relatively high cost of such programmes and fears of excessive merchant profits.[51–53]

Supporters of IP have offered convincing counter-arguments against such criticisms. The effects of the war, high transport costs, seasonal fluctuation of prices, the risk factor, and so on, have been used to explain the apparent high cost and profit margins.[54–56] Whatever negative aspects the programme may have had, moreover, is more than outweighed by the positive impact that this innovative programme achieved. Millions of dollars were channelled into the rural productive system, thereby helping to keep it functioning under the most extreme circumstances. The many employment, commercial and relief spin-offs that this programme generated were vital to the integrated disaster management system that REST developed. By 1990, IP accounted for nearly one-third of all donated food aid to Tigray. Relative and absolute transfers were much smaller in ORA areas. NGO funding dominated the programme from its inception, although in 1990 12% of funding came from the US Office of Foreign Disaster Assistance.

Following the collapse of the Dergue, the transitional government in Ethiopia maintained the official exchange rate at its previous level until a devaluation in 1992. In the period immediately following the peace, since all transactions now took place within Ethiopian, ERD was concerned that the continuing relief tax was placing the cost of IP beyond a level that members could reasonably support. In Jeddah, ERD had obtained Birr at the free market rate. While devaluation reduced this problem, ERD agencies began consideration of proposals to reorient internal purchase towards much greater emphasis on rehabilitation rather than only as an emergency response mechanism.[57]

Concluding Remarks

This discussion of the relief economy indicates that from the mid-1980s the international community progressively assumed financial and material responsibility for a growing proportion of the Front's public welfare programmes. Until this period these programmes had been largely self sufficient. This substitution is both complex and of vital importance. In reviewing the politics of liberation, Chapter Two argues that during the 1970s and early 1980s the Fronts in Eritrea and Tigray had overcome the conventional antithesis between war and development. Indeed, they had arrested and in many important respects had reversed an earlier process of decay. In the case of Eritrea, however, the Leeds studies indicate a steady erosion of the rural asset base from the mid-1980s following the re-emergence of a process of underdevelopment due to the combined effects of drought and war. The paradox is that this process is chronologically associated with the growing effectiveness of the CBO following the internationalisation of public welfare. In some respects, this connection re-affirms the argument at the beginning of this chapter that cross-border assistance, despite becoming more effective, was never enough. On the other hand, given the earlier close involvement of the Fronts in public provision, one can reasonably ask what is their relationship to the apparent transformation of development into underdevelopment that occurred during the 1980s?

This study does not have the information to answer this question in any detail. The necessity, however, of the Fronts pursuing their military aims, at the same time as having to relinquish some responsibility for public welfare to the international community, can be argued to have established the framework of the post-war political agenda. Military success would not have been possible without this relinquishment. Given its more homogeneous character, the case of Eritrea can be more readily grasped. The increasing importance of international humanitarian aid during the war can be argued to have had the effect of deferring a whole set of socio-economic problems which now have to be faced by the new government. The case of the estimated 450,000 refugees awaiting repatriation from Sudan is a good example. If one takes the Leeds 1992 estimate of the total population of Eritrea as around 2 million, this represents a potential population increase of some 20%, most of whom will require extensive public support. Eritrea's food deficit is another example. Estimates vary from the Leeds suggestion (which underestimated the 1992 harvest) that 80% of Eritrea's 1992 food needs should have been met by external food aid to FAO's guess for 1993 of 25%.

In many respects, such problems are the price of victory. They also indicate the scale of the responsibility which was shifted to donor governments and multilateral agencies with the phasing out of the CBO. Unlike many African countries, however, what distinguishes Eritrea and Tigray was that despite international material substitution, the relief system remained firmly under indigenous management. Elsewhere, NGO penetration has seen both material and managerial responsibility pass to external agencies. Following the end of the war, a key issue in Eritrea and Ethiopia is whether the political authorities have the strength and skills to maintain their managerial independence or will this also be compromised by an unresolved material and financial deficit in the face of growing popular demand?

CHAPTER ELEVEN

Neutrality Or Involvement? The End of the War and the Phase Out of ERD

Initial Response to the End of the War

It was during the AG meeting of May 1991 that the first news of the imminent end of the war reached ERD members.[1] The collapse of the Dergue had not been expected so soon and earlier ideas had envisaged ERD keeping going until the end of 1991 but based in Massawa rather than Khartoum. This dramatic change of events opened the possibility of moving the ERD office direct to Asmara. Although the logistics had to change, the initial intention was to maintain ERD's current policies.[2] The resulting move to Asmara took place in record time. ERD's Port Sudan office was closed in June, an Asmara office was applied for in August and, by October 1991, the transfer from Khartoum had been effected.[3] Given the historic change of circumstances the CBO had lost its rationale. The move to Asmara more or less decided the fact that ERD should divide its remaining programme responsibilities between Eritrea and Ethiopia. Reflecting this division, the AG meeting of November 1991 took place in Addis Ababa and Asmara. They were historic occasions, being the first time an ERD meeting had been held in Ethiopia and Eritrea respectively.

The Proposal for Ethiopia

The policy discussion at the November AG meeting in Addis Ababa centred on the new environment that had emerged.[4] The victory of the EPRDF had created a context which, as yet, was potential rather than real. In these circumstances, the majority in the aid and NGO community were sitting on the fence, waiting to see what happened next. Before the EPRDF had entered Addis Ababa, it had decided to establish a Relief Coordination Committee, consisting of REST, ERD and the former RRC, to manage the continuing relief operations. At the same time, REST was mandated to oversee the JRP operations in Tigray and Wollo.[5] The Coordination Committee was dissolved after six months and, upon leaving, REST began to assume the role of a regional NGO amongst other indigenous and international agencies within Tigray and Ethiopia. In these circumstances ERD felt that a forum for agency discussion which would allow the sharing of experience and bridge building between those that had worked on different sides of the line was required. Against the background of these concerns, the meeting accepted a "Statement of Principle" which provided guidelines for ERD's future in Ethiopia.[6]

The life of ERD within Ethiopia was tied to the political transition period with the phasing out of ERD activities no later than 1 June 1993. A similar agreement was reached in the case of Ethiopia and, in both situations, it came as something of a surprise to the IAs. Indeed, it would be fair to say that the closure of ERD was reluctantly accepted by the IAs rather than encouraged or sought. Part of the phase out would involve members gradually moving into bilateral relations with the traditional IAs and other agencies as required. During this transition period, ERD would continue to provide a number of functions. These included support for institution building with the IAs to promote bilateral linkages and continuing to provide a forum for coordination and debate. Importantly, however, the transitional role also included advocacy of ERD experience within the wider NGO community and the initiation of a dialogue between ERD members, traditional IAs and the Ethiopian church agencies in order to develop cooperation and greater understanding. A key feature of these proposals was the appointment for a six month period of a Liaison Officer attached to NCA's Addis Ababa office. Although NCA provided administrative support, the Liaison Officer would work separately from NCA's Ethiopia programme in pursuit of the above aims.

The Proposal for Eritrea

The November 1991 AG meeting in Asmara noted the differences between the situation in Eritrea and Ethiopia.[7] In comparison, Eritrea was held to be more politically united and the Church agencies spoke with one voice. Despite the great needs, many donors had yet to make their funding intentions clear. The UN, however, in advance of the international status of Eritrea being decided had already opened an office. The relationship between NGOs and the RRC in Ethiopia was also different to that between ERD, the Eritrean Relief and Rehabilitation Association (ERRA) as ERA became known following the end of the war, and the Provisional Government of Eritrea (PGE). Although other indigenous agencies were active, ERRA was distinguished by its experience and broad national reach. Unlike REST, moreover, its status as an 'NGO' was not clear. In a speech to the meeting, after thanking ERD for its assistance to Eritrea during the long days of the war, the Secretary General of PGE outlined the shape of future policy toward ERRA. While the details were still under discussion, it was envisaged that ERRA would expand its mandate to include rehabilitation and development work and, in addition, it would take on the national responsibility of a coordinating body for the programmes of indigenous and international NGOs. In many respects, the potential future of ERRA, rather than being that of an NGO, had more resemblance to a para-statal. It can be argued, as Chapter Eight indicates, that the question of ERRA's status and relationship to the body politic has been an issue since at least 1986.

As in Addis Ababa, the AG meeting adopted a "Statement of Principle" governing the future of ERD in Eritrea.[8] Again, ERD would phase out its activities during the transitional period of the government and close no later than 1 June 1993. During this period it would continue to support ERRA and also identify other indigenous agencies with which to work. ERD members, however, would gradually move towards bilateral relations. Areas of possible work included, relief, institution building, health, agricultural rehabilitation, refugee repatriation and construction. Like Ethiopia, ERD would play an advocacy role. In this case, however, rather than other agencies, the main focus would be the donor community. NCA, which by this time had opened an office in Asmara, would continue to provide administrative support.

At this stage, the ERD administration consisted of a Liaison Officer in Addis Ababa, a small ERD/NCA office in Asmara and a secretary based in NCA Oslo. This was a marked reduction relative to the days of the CBO.

The Argument for Liaison Function in Ethiopia

Compared to Eritrea, the political difficulties faced by ERD in terms of passing on its experience to the established NGO community in Addis

Ababa were bound to be great. It has already been mentioned that most agencies adopted a wait and see attitude. Few NGOs had an easy time in Ethiopia under the Dergue and, amongst the Church agencies, the Lutheran EECMY had a particularly difficult experience. It had, however, survived and had played an important role in the relief programmes of CDAA/E and JRP. There was little real knowledge in Addis Ababa of operating conditions or methods in the former non-government areas. EECMY, for example, having a large Oromo and southern following, had never really understood the basis of the Eritrean struggle and opposed the demand for independence.[9] Moreover, seeing the IAs and the Fronts as the same, it felt that the ERD members, some of whom were EECMY partners, had forged links with suspect and secular agencies.

More generally, following the collapse of the Dergue, there was a widespread suspicion amongst NGOs that had been operating under the Dergue that the EPRDF would exact some form of retribution. This was not helped by the fact that for a few months REST became part of a temporary Relief Coordination Committee established by the new government. There were frequent silences and other forms of non-communication at inter-agency meetings when ERD or REST representatives attended. Furthermore, widespread misconceptions prevailed concerning the role of ERD. Many thought, and to a great extent still think, that ERD was politically linked to the 'rebels' and led by a few powerful personalities whose agencies were not representative of mainstream NGOs.[10] In some cases, ERD is cast as a tool of the donors and, so it is claimed, it was allowed to operate with little or no reporting requirements.[11] For a time, there were also widespread rumours that the EPRDF would systematically transfer all resources from the rest of Ethiopia to Tigray. Even donors were not immune from this syndrome. The EC, for example, whose Addis Ababa office had campaigned against the CBO, was seen as being particularly keen to highlight any perceived shortcomings of the new government.

This general antipathy concerning ERD and the new government lay at the heart of the decision to appoint a Liaison Officer in November 1991 with a bridge building mandate. Within weeks of this appointment, however, the sensitivity of the position had become apparent. REST, for example, also undergoing a process of reorganisation, stayed in the background during negotiations. Even the NCA Addis Ababa representative had expressed reservations about the liaison role. NCA in Ethiopia has programme links with EECMY which is thought to have influenced this critical position.[12] By January 1992, not only was it thought by ERD that Ethiopia lacked an overall coordinating body but, importantly, the evident lack of interest amongst the Church agencies concerning liaison led to the concerned question "...do they have a wish for ecumenical cooperation?"[13] One can understand that the ending of a vicious civil war would leave a legacy of mutual misunderstanding and suspicion. In grasping the subsequent failure to develop the Liaison Officer role, it is important to realise that the proposal faced both external and internal difficulties. With regard to the former, it is necessary to examine the major organisational differences between the relief operations in the former government and non-government areas. In many respects, these differences reflect the wider political challenge that the EPRDF currently faces.

Differences Between Relief Operations in Former Government and Non-Government Areas

Chapter Two outlined the origins and nature of the humanitarian policies of the Fronts and the participatory, community based relief programmes they gave rise to. While these operations were developing in non-government areas, contrasting forms of organisation were emerging in the rest of Ethiopia.

(a) Government Operations

Until the mid-1980s, the bulk of international relief assistance was channelled through the government and the RRC. Rather than being used as a means of reciprocity with the general population, some of this relief was diverted to the military and the families of soldiers. The RRC was established by the Dergue in the mid-1970s in order to coordinate and implement relief activities on a national basis. By the mid-1980s it had a staff of over 12,000 and trucking fleet of around 1,000 lorries. In contrast to the situation in Eritrea and Tigray, this huge operation functioned on a highly centralised basis. Even decisions concerning local level food distributions were taken in Addis Ababa.[14] Rather than empowering populations, the RRC concentrated power within itself. After the mid-1980s, its share of relief commodities declined as donors began to switch to NGOs.

(b) NGO Operations

From the mid-1980s, when independent NGO relief operations began to develop, one can again detect contrary forms of organisation compared to non-government areas. These programmes include the large USAID operations run by such agencies as World Vision and the Church based consortium behind the Churches Drought Action Africa/Ethiopia (CDAA/E) which changed its name to the Joint Relief

Programme (JRP) in November 1985. The relief methods employed by the CDAA/E and later JRP are described by Solberg.[15] Although based upon methods first developed by the US based Catholic Relief Services (CRS) during the Sahelian famine of the 1970s, they are comparable with those still in general use by other major international relief agencies. During the early 1980s, CRS fashioned in Ethiopia its Nutrition Intervention Programme (NIP) which subsequently became the model for the church agencies in CDAA/E and then JRP, that is, the Ethiopian Catholic Secretariat (ECS), the Ethiopian Evangelical Church Mekane Yesus (EECMY), Lutheran World Federation (LWF) as well as CRS. In 1986, the Ethiopian Orthodox Church (EOC) also became part of JRP.

Unlike the integrated community based relief systems developed by the Fronts, NIP is based upon the family or, at least, a particular definition of the family. It is a 'family' regarded in isolation from any wider community and consisting of no other members except mothers with children under five years of age.[16] In so far as it targets this 'vulnerable group', NIP is defined as a family oriented food distribution system which operates through a network of distribution centres. Unlike the peer group targeting in non-government areas, NIP depends upon NGOs themselves defining the 'at risk' population. This is achieved by the more remote method of analysing such things as official agricultural forecasts and census data. CDAA/E staff, for example, estimated need and advised each distribution centre of its allocation. The at risk population is then registered at a distribution centre. During the time of registration, each child is weighed and measured to assess its nutritional status. Nutrional stress indicators, which trail the onset of famine conditions, are the only indicators which NIP can properly address. Family groups that have healthy, or reasonably healthy children are given a monthly take home ration which acts as a supplement to food obtained through other channels. Weak or malnourished children are given intensive remedial support at the distribution centre.

Compared to the relief management systems developed by the Fronts, what strikes one about the NIP approach is the disempowering effect it has upon the community and its individual members. It is NGO representatives who make all the key decisions concerning entitlement. The more powerless and dependent the beneficiaries become the more important and essential the NGO staff are made to appear. This is evinced in Solberg's eulogising of the sacrifices and dedication of agency staff.[17] In NIP relief systems there are no relations of political accountability between the NGO representatives and the beneficiaries. It is an act of charity for which the recipient should be grateful. In contrast, within Eritrea and Tigray, relations of accountability existed between the elected village committees, the IAs and the political administration. In NIP systems, the only relations of accountability that usually exist are between the NGO and the donor. Typically, this assumes the form of a relief sub-contracting relation. As a power relation, it enhances the strength of the NGO at the expense of the beneficiaries and, in many cases, the host government. In the case of CDAA/A and JRP, the relief operation that they ran, and continue to run, operated to augment the power of the Ethiopian Church agencies.

(c) Relations Between NGO Consortia and Government

The Christian Relief and Development Association (CRDA), which was established in the mid-1970s, was a forum composed of national and international NGOs. Rather than being in dialogue with the Dergue, it was seen as being in opposition to it[18] and was never active in terms of formulating national relief policy.[19] As consortia, CDAA/E and later JRP were also not in policy dialogue with the government. They were operational bodies whose main links were with donors. Relations with government tended to be on a bilateral basis.[20] In fact, NGOs generally within Ethiopia tended to keep their distance from the Dergue and hide, rather than discuss, their activities.[21] This is a marked contrast to the relations that pertained between the IAs and the Fronts.

Involvement in Ethiopia and the ERD Membership

Besides differences in relief systems, there were also internal difficulties facing the proposal to develop a liaison function in Addis Ababa. When it was agreed to merge ERD with NCA in April 1987, NCA was already pushing for a wider advocacy role for ERD.[22] This was based upon the idea that ERD should work for peace in the region by providing a forum for advocacy on behalf of the different organisations within the ERD Board. This general position had been supported by the IAs throughout the 1980s. Other ERD members, for example, DDW, ICCO and LWR opposed this proposal on neutrality grounds. This division fed directly into the issue of the Liaison Officer in Addis Ababa.

Following the end of the war, ERD as a consortium began to fragment and lose coherence. Some of the differences between members have already been outlined. With the advent of peace, ERD ceased to have a function for a number of members.[23] For these, the resumption of traditional bilateral relations as quickly as possible was the desired course of events. SCR, for example, soon resumed its earlier links in Eritrea. Other agencies, for example, DIA and NCA, drawn by the political complexities of the situation, felt that ERD should attempt to develop a new supportive mandate to help the transition to peace and development.[24]

Earlier Chapters have noted some of the main differences between ERD members. Stemming from the early 1980s, one of these had been the relative merits of relief or development as a mandate for ERD. Over the course of time, some agencies had changed their position on these issues. By 1987, for example, NCA had begun to move from a low key, relief posture to a more pro-active approach through its experience with ERD. That ERD members should be divided on the question of a liaison or advocacy role in Ethiopia is, therefore, not surprising. In this instance, however, agency positions can, to a varying extent, be related to their links with Ethiopian partners. Only a few ERD members, such as DIA, had no, or limited contacts with Ethiopian Church agencies.[25] The majority had various relations. SCR, DDW and LWR, for example, related to EECMY through the Lutheran structures.[26] CA is notable for its wide ranging links including membership of the other main CBO consortia, EIAC and TTAC. The trend that can be discerned during the course of 1992 was for many of the members with Ethiopian church links to be wary of adopting a liaison role, preferring instead the establishment of bilateral relations with all agencies. This represented the bulk of ERD members. One can discern in this posture a re-assertion of a conventional NGO even-handed or neutral approach in the face of political complexity. The demand for a wider advocacy role, on the other hand, can be seen as growing out of the recognition that peace had not created a level playing field.

The Collapse of the Liaison Role in Ethiopia

At the beginning of 1992, the NCA-appointed Liaison Officer, whose post was due to expire in August, was of the opinion that in seeking a wider liaison and informative role, the traditional IAs, CRDA and other Church agencies were obvious partners in this search for dialogue.[27] Those supporting a wider role saw Eritrea as having to be built from scratch. Ethiopia was different. In Addis Ababa, it was speculated that NGO institutions already existed, ERD did not have to pioneer new organisations. There was, for example, the possibility that ERD could join the EOC Round Table or CRDA.[28] The background to this position was the awareness that two different forms of NGO operation, that is, participatory structures as opposed to more centralised forms, as outlined above, had been brought together as a result of peace.[29] In these circumstances the need for bridge-building, merging and educating across these divisions was felt to be a real one.

It was a feeling which was also reinforced by the emerging trends in post-war Ethiopia. These included the ambitious reform of the RRC which began in 1991. This involves a new Emergency Code which aims at decentralising the management of relief and taking control out the hands of NGOs by making them more accountable. Many NGOs felt threatened by these moves.[30] Also, in 1992, the World Bank began negotiating more flexible terms and conditions with the new government. There was an opportunity here for NGOs to share their global experience with the government. Finally, in June 1992, reflecting earlier differences, the OLF withdrew from the transitional government. This has contributed to a growing fear of continuing political instability within Ethiopia. It has also created difficulties for ORA in Addis Ababa and some of its project sites since it is associated by others with the OLF.[31–32] Given its links with REST and ORA, it was thought that ERD could help in promoting some degree of reconciliation. In relation to all of these developments, the Liaison Officer felt that Addis Ababa lacked an NGO forum that could input its experience in such areas. For historical reasons, what was lacking was an Ethiopian NGO working group that included national and international NGOs that could address such issues. This would not be in competition with existing consortia and, moreover, it would only require a "reasonable number" of ERD members to support such a venture.[33]

Despite these arguments, by April 1992, it was already apparent that there was little enthusiasm amongst the majority of ERD members for such a venture.[34] DDW, for example, felt the primary role of the Liaison Officer was to help the IAs change into regular NGOs.[35] It was against any attempt to resurrect the large-scale regional programmes of the past. From this "planned economy" there should be a move to a "free market" where members formed bilateral relations with IAs and other indigenous agencies. NGOs, moreover, ought not attempt to take over government tasks. Other ERD members felt that a continuing close association with REST would risk being associated with government and could jeopardize wider relations.[36] In many respects, the debate which began toward the end of the 1980s, and which was given fresh impetus by the ending of the war, was whether NGOs should remain external, even-handed bodies or, facing the challenge of the political complexity of the situation, attempt to find new ways of engagement. That is, should they remain neutral or should they become involved. At the time of writing, this debate, although using different terms, has been raging in relation to Bosnia where neutrality appears to have won the day.

As part of the attempt to increase dialogue, the Ethiopian Church agencies were invited to attend the May 1992 AG meeting in Addis Ababa. Here, the need for a new forum was put forward by the Liaison Officer. This proposal was opposed by some ERD members and the Ethiopian Church agencies on the grounds that such structures, for example, CRDA, already existed. This opposition did not go into the fact of the antipathy between such organisations and the new government, the different style of operation they represented, and their lack of experience in effective policy dialogue. In terms of attempting to inject some of the ERD/IA experience of the war into the NGO community in Addis Ababa, this meeting was a failure. For those interested in developing a wider role, such as, NCA and DIA, the May meeting was a frustrating event since it indicated that many AG members did not understand or appreciate the role of the Liaison Officer.[37] By July 1992, it was clearly realised that there was insufficient interest to justify the extension of the Liaison Officer role beyond August.[38] With the termination of this post, ERD in Ethiopia, in any practical sense, came to an end.

The December 1992 AG meeting in Addis Ababa once again served to highlight the differences of opinion within ERD. In addition, the IAs felt that the decision to phase out had been taken too quickly and urged some form of future cooperation even if not all ERD members were involved.[39] The chance for this, however, had passed. The meeting was also concerned with the changing political fortunes of ORA. It concluded by asking REST and ORA to work on a proposal to establish an NGO platform on which they could work together. It was intended that this would be presented at ERD's closing meeting in June 1993. After discussing the matter on a number of occasions, REST and ORA informed this meeting that the "complex and sensitive context" currently existing mitigated against any proposal for an indigenous NGO forum at this stage.[40] Against a background of a real potential for continuing political instability, but with the re-organisation of REST as a regional NGO well underway, ERD in Ethiopia formerly closed on 10 June 1993.[41]

The Situation in Eritrea

Compared to Ethiopia, as seen by ERD the situation in Eritrea was more straightforward. Apart from being able to construct a new government from scratch, so to speak, Eritrea is relatively more homogeneous and politically united than Ethiopia. Rather than major differences between institutional forms, in Eritrea the main issues relate to the devastated economy and the lack of material and appropriate institutional resources to achieve the transition to development. From the point of view of ERD, a central issue was the future role of ERRA.

Following the end of the war, the PGE envisaged a coordinating role for ERRA with regard to NGO activity. At the same time, however, ERRA has lost many of its experienced people to PGE although its workload was increasing due to the expansion of administrative tasks.[42] As bilateral relations began to supplant ERD, it largely responded in terms of providing resources to improve ERRA's organisational capacity. During 1993, for example, ERRA intends to implement an Institutional Capacity Building Programme. However, the difficulty of establishing a mechanism to plan and coordinate NGO activity in Eritrea remains. It is the intention of the PGE to limit the activity of international NGOs to a funding and supporting capacity for indigenous agencies. It is intended that indigenous management capacity remains in the hands of Eritreans. The policy difficulty resides in the fact that ERRA has established itself as an NGO, thus qualifying for such support, at the same time as PGE has proposed that it takes on a national coordinating function. This mixed mandate is seen as creating a number of potential difficulties.[43] At the December 1992 AG meeting, therefore, it was requested that ERRA should produce a proposal concerning the future of NGO activity in Eritrea to be considered at the final meeting in June 1993.

As with REST and ORA, the closing meeting of ERD did not produce a definite proposal for NGO coordination in Eritrea. Rather, ERRA deferred the creation of an NGO platform to some future date following "extensive discussions."[44] Like REST, ERRA has also undergone reorganisation and reviewed its links with donor governments. The formal closing of ERD in Eritrea took place on 7 June 1993.[45] Compared to the close in Addis Ababa a few days later, this event was more emotional and widely reported. Borne of political solidarity, a great optimism stands facing Eritrea's daunting economic problems. Important areas of the economy have been devastated or neglected; around half a million refugees, or some 20% of Eritrea's total population, are still living as refugees in Sudan and awaiting repatriation; the bulk of the army has yet to be demobilised and found alternative work; donor governments have so far only provided a small proportion of the aid requested; and, not least, Eritrea's structural food deficit remains threatening large sections of the population with continuing food insecurity.[46]

Postscript

In a practical sense, ERD did not survive the end of the war. Internal differences amongst members soon surfaced in the absence of this defining feature. These differences propelled ERD toward dissolution and the establishment of bilateral relations with, and beyond, the former IAs. For many former members, the rationale for phasing out ERD was to re-establish more traditional links and forms of NGO activity. The irony, however, is that the continuing crisis in Eritrea and Ethiopia is far from traditional. The move to create a liaison function in Addis Ababa by a few members of ERD was an important attempt to break new ground. It represented a willingness to find a way to positively engage the complex reality of the post-war situation. That it failed to gain wide ERD support should not detract from the fact that the attempt is, itself, part of the changing perception of NGO involvement in complex emergencies. From its inception to its close, the experience of ERD has been to the fore in this debate.

CHAPTER TWELVE

Internal War And Humanitarian Assistance

The history of ERD spans a crucial period in the development of Western humanitarianism. From a time when sovereignty was commonly regarded as sacrosanct, a period has been entered in which this is less so. Moreover, the number of people affected by protracted, complex emergencies is increasing at the same time as the policy and resource implications of this trend have pitched the international relief system into turmoil. ERD, in terms of both its external and internal relations, was always a source of controversy. Its origins as a cross-border operation in violation of Ethiopian sovereignty and providing relief in the context of Africa's longest running internal war was bound to make this so. In structuring this concluding assessment it seems prudent to concentrate on the broad issues which provided the background for much of this debate. That is, the impact of ERD's assistance on the war and the economy of the region. Finally, some lessons of ERD are drawn out in the context of contemporary relief problems. Given the increasing occurrence of complex emergencies, these lessons have a wide topicality.

The Logic of Internal War

In considering the question whether ERD's relief assistance somehow fuelled or prolonged the war, one must begin from an understanding of the nature of internal war. Internal conflict within a society where the major economy, in terms of number of people supported, is one of semi-subsistence, has a dynamic and logic quite unlike conventional war between industrialised nations.[1] Under conditions of semi-subsistence, rural producers within the agrarian system provide both the economic base and the military personnel that sustains internal war. Depending on where the line falls, producers and their assets have either to be protected and developed or, alternatively, destroyed and looted. Internal war is fought on and through the structures and socio-economic groups that make up rural society: it is a form of total war. It is for this reason that internal war sometimes takes on genocidal overtones as areas are ethnically cleansed and efforts exerted to demolish the cultural, commercial and economic infrastructure that supports rural producers in opposing areas.[2] The systematic violation of human rights as currently understood is an intrinsic feature of internal conflict. Within this logic it is impossible to be neutral in a strict sense of the term. The provision of humanitarian assistance to one side of a line will invariably be seen as a partisan and aggressive act by the other. The long history in Africa of the diversion or obstruction of relief aid, failed safe passage agreements, and so on, attests to this situation.

Within Eritrea and Tigray, the Fronts often criticised those agencies working on the government side for being complicit in their actions. ERD assistance, for its part, was channelled by the IAs to areas under the administration of the Fronts. It was, therefore, equally discretionary and felt to be so by many in Addis Ababa. ERD members were no doubt somewhat troubled when the leadership of the Fronts subsequently thanked ERD for helping their struggle.[3–4] Or when senior donor representatives say in retrospect that food aid advanced the Front's political and military agendas.[5] The problem here is not with the rights or wrongs of this situation, it is that the notion of neutrality in the context of internal war is itself problematic. Because internal conflicts are fought on and through rural producers, the very same people humanitarian aid seeks to sustain, relief assistance can never be neutral in relation to the ongoing conflict: it has an impact. The fact of keeping people alive in an internal war is a political act and deserves to be recognised as such.

Fungibility and the Substitution of Indigenous Capacity

A singular feature of the Fronts was that they developed a political practice which directly combined public welfare with political mobilization. In so doing they established locally managed famine mitigation systems with few parallels in Africa. There is little doubt that the Fronts provided the bulk of the public welfare assistance within Eritrea and Tigray until the mid-1980s. Significant cross-border assistance did not begin to flow until the Eritrean conflict had raged for nearly 25 years, and the war in Tigray for 10 years. Moreover, when international aid did increase, it is widely held to have significantly lagged demand in non-government areas.[6] By comparison, far more aid was directed to the government side where it is credited with strengthening, or at least subsidising, state institutions and programmes.[7–8] The internationalisation of public welfare, however, also effected a process of substitution in terms of the material input of food, trucks, medicines and cash in non-government areas. Until the mid-1980s, the Fronts had taken the lead role in providing such items as part of their political practice. While the extent of substitution is difficult to quantify, that it took place is beyond doubt. ERD alone made available around $350 million in cash and goods in kind, almost all of it from 1984. The singular feature that defines it as different from the process of substitution going on elsewhere in Africa was the fact that it took place on the basis of indigenous management.

As popular movements, the diversion of relief assistance was not part of the Fronts' political practice. The principle of fungibility, however, underpinned by popular support, would suggest that substitution did allow the Fronts to concentrate their available resources in securing their defence and ultimate military victory. Despite being unable to halt continuing impoverishment, the CBO did help to stabilise the food crisis within Eritrea and Tigray by 1987. It can be argued that this stabilisation was a necessary precondition for the great military advances of 1988. Furthermore, when the CBO peaked in 1990, it was a time of mass mobilization in preparation of the final move on Addis Ababa the following year. While the question of degree remains, that the CBO had an impact on the dynamic of the war would appear hard to contest. It should be stated again, however, that any impact, perhaps with the exception of the closing stages of the war, was not as a result of direct diversion. Substitution meant that the Fronts could sustain and marshal the support of the growing numbers of people under their expanding areas of administration with the help of international humanitarian assistance. In the sense that both the Fronts and ERD wished to sustain life and livelihoods, although their political motives differed, their humanitarian intentions were one.

The process of substitution which the CBO allowed is an important development. For the Fronts, the CBO was their connection with the international community. With the gradual suspension of development assistance Ethiopia itself increasingly relied upon emergency aid. While creation of dependency amongst rural producers is generally discounted, the process of substitution may have created an aid dependence within the institutions of society. Ethiopia was already formally locked into the world economy. With Eritrea, however, one can see a clearer transfer of responsibility from the CBO to the international aid community. It is ironic that, after years of denial and obstruction, it was an unreformed UN which took over the place of the CBO during 1990 and 1991. In relation to Eritrea, it could be argued that the material dependence upon the international community to resolve the problem of its devastated economy has been the price of victory. Nor is it certain that the connection between public welfare and political mobilization can be maintained during the transition to peace. What is clear is that in Ethiopia and Eritrea peace has brought opportunity as well as a host of new difficulties.

The Importance of Indigenous Political Structures for Successful Humanitarian Intervention

That ERD members should have been concerned that their assistance may have been supporting the war is understandable. Given the complexity of internal war, however, and the fact that relief assistance in such situations cannot be neutral, perhaps this concern should be redirected. If it is accepted that the bottom line is to protect life and livelihoods, it would be better to ask whether ERD's assistance was channelled through indigenous political structures which, regardless of motive, maximized its effect. The answer to such a question is undoubtedly affirmative. It also indicates how important, determining even, the nature of indigenous political structures is for the provision of effective relief. The tendency for NGOs to depoliticize situations means that this is often overlooked. The importance of indigenous structures can be illustrated by a brief description of the Sudan Peoples Liberation Army (SPLA).

In relation to the SPLA, evidence suggests a more predatory relationship with rural producers compared to the EPLF or TPLF. Little can be discerned of efforts to secure the welfare of the civilians under SPLA authority which is comparable to what happened in Eritrea or Tigray. To understand this difference one must examine the political economy of the SPLA.

(a) The Political Economy of the SPLA:

The emergence of politico-military groups and movements is fought out on a terrain of semi-subsistence economies. One cannot therefore emphasise enough the enormous price in dislocation and human suffering that this implies. Groups and movements not only require conscripts to fight; they need porters to carry weapons, supplies and booty; sappers to clear mines; informants to disclose enemy positions; and importantly, a ready access to food and sustenance. How such goods and services are secured in the field is not something simply for quartermasters to worry about: to the contrary, it is a central dynamic of internal warfare. To appreciate this fact one has to develop an appreciation of the political economy of violence. The idea of food as a weapon in internal conflict has become popular in recent years. What is less frequently recognised, however, is that food and sustenance can also be a necessary goal of conflict.

Until 1989, the SPLA consolidated its presence in South Sudan in a roughly three stage process. Emerging from its alliance with the Dergue, during the mid-1980s, the first stage involved the formation of tactical alliances with local groups and, where necessary, the military defeat and looting of opponents. The local opposition to the resettlement and villagisation programme in South West Ethiopia, for example, gave the SPLA the pretext to loot, especially in Illubabor Province.[9] In order to secure a safe base and access to food in this region, the SPLA strategy was to play on the differences and traditional hostility between the two linguistically related branches of the Nilo-Saharans: the Chai and Mursi on one side, and the Nyangatom, Toposa and Turkana on the other.[10] The selective arming of these groups by the SPLA not only helped to form alliances, but the increased scale and ferocity of attacks upon their relatively unarmed rivals provided, in the form of looted grain and cattle, a vital means of subsistence. In 1987, for example, the SPLA's arming of the Nyangatom allowed it to mount a devastating attack upon the Mursi.[11] In this attack between 500-1,000 Mursi (10-20% of the entire population) were killed. Killing on this scale destroys the traditional system of checks and balances between groups.

As the SPLA extended its influence along the Sudan, Kenya and Uganda border areas, a similar strategy of playing on group enmities, selective arming and the formation of complex patterns of local alliance occurred. One consequence was the widespread displacement of the losing populations throughout the area. In 1986, for example, in order to establish a secure base and provisions in South Sudan near the Uganda border, the SPLA made use of the long-standing hostility between the Acholi and the Madi.[12] The Madi had been associated with the Amin regime and following its collapse, Madi refugees were settled in international camps across the border in Sudanese Acholi territory. These camps were attacked and looted by local Acholi and SPLA causing thousands of Madi to stream back into Uganda, sparking off one more in a succession of population displacements.

Evolving from this process of alliance and defeat, the second stage involved the recruitment from allied groups and the training of recruits in the SPLA's Ethiopian base camps. Using this local cadre, by the end of the 1980s an attempt at consolidation was taking place involving establishing a structure of internal taxation. The advent of the UN's Operation Lifeline Sudan in April 1989, in so far as significant amounts of relief food were appropriated by the SPLA, reduced tension in some areas by relieving SPLA tax pressure on non-combatant populations. In other words, the diversion of relief supplies has, ironically, made it easier for rural producers to cope.

By 1989, the SPLA had significantly transformed the socio-political system over large areas of South Sudan. It has done so, however, by increasing the imbalances within that system through the selective strengthening of some groups at the expense of others. In a number of cases, ethnic groups, in the sense of distinct socio-economic units, have ceased to exist. Just as the use of government backed militia along the North/South border has driven ethnic differences to new depths, the SPLA alliance which had emerged was unstable and fractious. Following the fall of the Dergue in 1991 the SPLA fragmented, and in so doing, has unleashed a fresh round of looting and destruction of the subsistence economy.

Neutrality as a Problem For Policy Development

The contrast between the political dynamic of predatory military movements and the EPLF and TPLF is marked. An examination of RENAMO in Mozambique, for example, would reveal similar characteristics to the SPLA.[13] In the case of the EPLF, it has already been argued that it emerged during the 1960s from a process of internal political struggle with the ELF which had some sectarian and non-reciprocal attributes. Evidence from Eritrea and Tigray would suggest that existing predatory movements, and sectarian states for that matter, need to undergo a process of reform which simultaneously embraces public welfare and political emancipation. In the case of the EPLF, this was helped by the fact that the ELF was able to attract a wide range of socio-economic groups. It was from this diverse base that political struggle and development ensued. It may be the case that contemporary predatory movements are unable to draw on sufficient social diversity, or have been successful in limiting intake, to allow this process to take place. In the absence of reform, however, the provision of humanitarian relief is problematic.

It is at this juncture that the problem for analysis and policy development represented by the Western construct of neutrality can be demonstrated. In Chapter Four it was suggested that when the non-political credentials of ERD were drafted in the early 1980s, it was done on the basis of asserting the independence of ERA and REST from the political milieu which had produced them. ERD's neutrality depended to a large extent on depicting ERA and REST as the determining agents in the relief and rehabilitation programmes which developed in non-government areas and, at the same time, minimising the fact that they both needed the support and political structures of the Fronts in order to work. Indeed, without this they could not have functioned. ERD's position is summed up in the phrase 'implementing agencies' with which it later defined ERA and REST. During most of the 1980s, this construct undoubtedly played a useful role in that it allowed ERD a platform from which it could access the assistance of wary donors. What it also did, however, was to mythologise ERA and REST and establish an unrealistic yardstick against which other indigenous NGOs, especially in the Horn, have since been judged.

The effects of this can be seen in relation to the Sudan Relief and Rehabilitation Association (SRRA) which was established in 1985 as a humanitarian wing of the SPLA. Since this period successive international NGOs have looked upon SRRA as an fledgling ERA or REST. It is only more recently that a cautionary attitude has emerged. Given the absence of a public welfare mandate within the SPLA, and the tenuous links between it and the SRRA, a fledgling view is only possible if the SRRA is seen as capable of operating independent of the political environment of which it is part. In other words, it is only possible by transposing the construct of neutrality onto the SRRA. This extraordinary view is widely held and has led to several institution-building programmes with the SRRA which have met with limited success. Unlike Eritrea and Tigray, the neutral approach to humanitarian relief in South Sudan has met with limited success because the dominant political structures are not supportive.

In humanitarian terms the CBO must be judged a success. In the last analysis, however, it owes this state of affairs to the political practice of the Fronts. That ERD was able to help appears more to be the result of historic association, even accident, rather than an ability to correctly analyze the situation. Most complex emergencies are less accommodating.

Some Lessons From ERD in Today's Changed Humanitarian Environment

In a conclusion to a history of this type, implementing agencies used to evaluative procedures will look for bottom line recommendations. In many respects, however, ERD's day to day experience was unique and cannot narrowly be reproduced in the changed environment of the present. But this is not to say that there are not broad lessons in what has happened. They do exist and they have great relevance. Some of the more important ones include the following.

(a) NGO Relief Consortia:

In recent years, NGO consortia and the comparative advantage in terms of flexibility and resource mobilization they demonstrate has gathered a growing interest. While this comparative advantage is a real attribute, consortia themselves appear to emerge only under special circumstances. It is these circumstances, moreover, rather than improved performance, which appear as a defining influence. In the case of ERD, the injustice of the war and the silence of the international community to the suffering in Eritrea and Tigray brought its members together. Despite all being ecumenical agencies, which helped, ERD members had marked differences of philosophy and approach. These differences meant that it was primarily the exigencies of the war together with a minimal relief mandate on which a consensus of sorts could be reached to keep the consortium together. Comparative advantage arose from these limiting conditions. At times of rapid social change, such as during the mid-1980s and following the end of the war, agency differences surfaced and threatened the integrity of the operation. Indeed, although not formally closing until June 1993, in a practical sense ERD did not long survive the ending of the war in May 1991.

ERD's history as a fractious consortium is not unique. Most successful NGO consortia have been relief oriented precisely because emergencies provide a minimal humanitarian platform on which they can cooperate. It should be noted that development work has always been a far more contentious area for NGO cooperation. All things being equal, NGOs are primarily lone actors. Having to compete in the charity and aid markets to attract private and government funding is a strong incentive to maintain and project an individual competence. In the past, however, all things have not been equal. ERD stands at the end of a line that stretches via Afghanistan and Cambodia back to Biafra. That is, it is an example of an NGO relief consortium which emerged during the cold war in response to the tragic humanitarian consequences of the failings of the international emergency system that this era engendered. Today, the situation has changed. Humanitarian considerations have now joined a growing list of factors in relation to which sovereignty is no longer sacrosanct. Although enhanced UN and military intervention in support of humanitarian aims has proved to be uneven and problematic, to say the least; it nonetheless marks a new departure.

In these changed circumstances the future of relief consortia cannot be taken for granted. In the past the 'illegality' of many relief situations demanded the comparative advantage that only NGO consortia could then supply. The emergence of a more interventionist climate has altered the terms of NGO engagement. In the case of Kurdistan and Somalia, for example, a high profile relief operation has worked against the formation of NGO consortia. Instead, comparative advantage has appeared in the form of individual competition between agencies for large donor contracts.[14–15] One can speculate that such competition will be encouraged by the growing trend for donor governments and UN agencies to spend more of their generally declining aid budgets on emergency relief.[16] It has created a feeling that consortia are now out of fashion, or at least they can be alright providing your NGO is the lead agency. Cases of dire international neglect exist and will remain. They will, however, be cast alongside large scale operations in conflict zones that attempt to provide relief to all sides using a series of individual NGO sub-contractors. NGO relief consortia of the future, if they are to succeed, could demand a greater degree of political agreement and determination between members than has been the case in the past.

(b) The Importance of Indigenous Political Relations:

ERD experience has clearly demonstrated the fact that effective relief in a complex emergency demands the full participation and approval of local political parties and institutions. Indeed, this support was a determining factor in the success of ERA and REST. Although this is an unremarkable conclusion, it is a point which NGOs and donors appear to forget time and again. Perhaps it is because it invites NGO policy makers to examine the quality of the relationship between rulers and ruled in the countries or situations in which they operate. For many this is a step too far. It lies at the heart, however, of the role of indigenous NGOs and international institution-building pretensions. If the quality of internal governance is poor or sectarian, what indigenous NGOs can achieve will be correspondingly constrained. In such situations care has to be taken that institution-building is not doing precisely that: institution-building in the worst sense of the term.

In complex emergencies the nature of the internal political relations becomes paramount. In circumstances when they are also of a predatory or problematic character, it is perhaps time that NGOs came to terms with the difficult task of developing new forms of involvement. In response to the mounting criticism of the international relief operation in South Sudan and Somalia, the argument has been gaining ground that the political structures and religious organisations of civil society should be strengthened in order to assist the development of a popular alternative to predatory militia groups.[17] This is a far cry from the political distance that has usually characterised agency activity. When the full gamut has been run, however, what other long term solution exists which is also capable of encouraging wider indigenous development? Such arguments can be seen as part of the same paradigm which emerged in ERD in connection with the call for liaison and constructive engagement in Ethiopia.

(c) The Contrast Between Relief Management Systems:

The Horn of Africa is singular in that it has produced two very different and contrasting modes of relief management. At the risk of oversimplification, there were decentralised and participatory organisations in Eritrea and Tigray compared to centralised and non-participatory systems in Ethiopia. In the former, moreover, the provision of public welfare was at the heart of a process of emancipation, while for the latter it was a means of preserving a sectarian regime and, although Ethiopia is not a particularly good example, it also served as a bridgehead for the extension of foreign management into internal affairs. These differences are very real and in the case of Eritrea and Tigray have had a proven effect. The integrated and participatory relief systems that emerged in the non-government areas have few parallels in Africa. Their efficiency and flexibility meant that the Eritreans and Tigrayans did far more with the relatively little international assistance they received than would have been possible using conventional relief practices. The question is therefore raised, why have these exemplary practices with their strong developmental orientation not supplanted less effective international methods? The answer is partly given above in (b). They are dependent upon the quality of the relationship between rulers and ruled and, where this is in question, sympathetic international agencies have yet to find a successful way of encouraging their formation.

There is, however, another facet to this problem. Centralised and non-participatory relief management systems are a means of maintaining political distance. In many respects, they are a counterpart of neutrality and therefore useful to donor governments. Recent events suggest that the tension between neutrality and involvement that characterises Western humanitarian politics is developing in a way which even a couple of years ago would not have been possible. Paradoxically, the erosion of sovereignty appears to have strengthened the need for political distance at the same time as humanitarianism has become more interventionist. This can be seen, for example, in Kurdistan, Bosnia and Somalia. The response of the international community has been the attempt to insert the non-participatory and non-accountable institutions of conventional emergency relief, by armed protection if necessary, within such complex emergencies. In these circumstances, political distance is achieved by defining this form of humanitarianism as the only type of intervention that is possible.[18] Military humanitarianism has proved itself to be distrustful of indigenous political relations and institutions.[19] In these circumstances, it cannot provide a long term solution.

(d) Relief Assistance and Complex Emergencies:

Emergency assistance in the context of an internal war cannot help but impact on the dynamics of the conflict. The manner in which internal wars are fought dictates that this is so. Perhaps the only way that this could be minimised would be for relief agencies to encourage a refugee exodus so that populations could be quarantined in some safe haven. As a policy, however, few would seriously support this measure. But, the implications of its just rejection demands that the reality of internal war is squarely faced. For a long time ERD agonized over the possible effect that it might have on the war. Amongst other things, this led to a restricted list of inputs, such as food aid, which were deemed non-political and therefore admissible. It has been argued, however, that the distinction between political and non-political aid in a complex emergency "is largely externally manufactured."[20] Food aid, for example, can be monetised or diverted, but seed, tools and other agricultural resources have limited military use. The debate over providing development assistance in the midst of a conflict was never satisfactorily resolved by ERD. Concern over its impact limited ERD's scope to assist the locally managed relief process to the best of its ability. Some members, for example, feel that more support could have been given to community organisation.[21]

Accepting that all relief has an impact on internal war would free the agency to make rational input decisions based upon an actual analysis of the situation. The call to strengthen the political structures of civil society has already been mentioned. Food aid can also play a part in this process but even this needs to be rethought. Where a predatory militia, for example, taxes and loots rural producers to the extent of promoting famine, it may be better to legalise the diversion of food aid that undoubtedly takes place and directly feed the group concerned. The trade off would be that rural producers be allowed to keep more of their own produce as well as developing other coping strategies. Such a ploy would not solve the problem but is an example of the radical change of approach that is currently needed. In understanding the real nature of the success of the relief programme in Eritrea and Tigray, one can better grasp the problems which now beset other operations.

The period of rapid change that we have entered together with the increasing internationalisation of public welfare since the mid-1980s may have threatened the emergence of future NGO relief consortia on the model of ERD. This does not mean, however, that collective action by NGOs in humanitarian matters is no longer required. This is far from the case. Apart from the world's many neglected and abused peoples, problems are being thrown up by ill-conceived and short term interventionism together with the growing aversion of donor governments to support long term rehabilitation and reconstruction programmes. Collective action on these issues represents the themes of the 1990s. With some justification the emergence of military humanitarianism following the Gulf War was generally well received.[22] Given earlier problems, it fostered the idea that the world was entering a more humanitarian age. Somalia and Bosnia have highlighted the problems with this analysis. Indeed, such is the complexity of these situations, it would appear that military humanitarianism as a credible solution has reached a watershed. The post-Gulf War euphoria of the past couple of years has drawn to an end. In relation to our current difficulties, there is one aspect of ERD which is of enduring importance: it always provided a critical, if not subversive, reflection on conventional practice. Such criticism is needed today more than ever.

References And Notes

Chapter One

Introduction: The Historical Significance of the Emergency Relief Desk

1. The term internal war is used here in a loose sense to denote conflict situations other than conventional war between states. It includes civil war as well as counter-insurgency operations and regionally defined zones of insecurity.

2. de Waal, A. "A Re-assessment of Entitlement Theory in the Light of Recent Famines in Africa." *Development and Change*; 990;21: 469-490.

3. Downs, R E; Kerner, D O; Reyna S P, eds. *The Political Economy of African Famine. Food and Nutrition in History and Anthropology*, Vol 9 ed. Philadelphia: Gordon Breach Science Publishers; 1991.

4. Duffield, M. *Sudan at the Cross Roads: From Emergency Preparedness to Social Security*. Institute of Development Studies Discussion Paper; 1990; (277).

5. Keen, D. "A Disaster For Whom?: Local Interests and International Donors During Famine Among the Dinka of Sudan." *Disasters*; 1991; 15(2): 58-73.

6. Smith, G (ERD/DIA). "Counting Quintals: Report on a Field Monitoring Visit to Tigray," Northern Ethiopia; July 1983.

7. Clay, J. "Ethiopian Famine and the Relief Agencies". in: Nichols, B; Loescher, G, eds. *The Moral Nation: Humanitarianism and US Foreign Policy Today*. South Bend, Indiana: University of Notre Dame Press; 1989: 247-8.

8. Pateman, R. *Even the Stones are Burning*. Trenton, New Jersey: Red Sea Press; 1990.

9. Africa Watch. *Evil Days: 30 Years of War and Famine in Ethiopia*. New York: Africa Watch; September 1991.

10. Ferris, E. *Humanitarian Politics: Cross-Border Operations in the Horn of Africa*. Uppsala: Life and Peace Institute; 1992: 6.

11. Silkin, T; Hughes, S. "Food Security and Food Aid: A Study From the Horn of Africa." London: CAFOD/Christian Aid; September 1992: 13.

12. *ibid*: 14.

13. Clough, R E. *Free at Last? US Policy Toward Africa and the End of the Cold War*. New York: Council on Foreign Relations; 1992: 12.

14. Duffield, M. "War and Famine in Africa." Oxfam Research Paper No 5; 1991.

15. Korten, D C. *Getting to the 21st Century: Voluntary Action and the Global Agenda*. Connecticut: Kumarian Press; 1990.

16. Habte-Selassie, Bereket. "Eritrea and the United Nations." in: Research and Information Centre on Eritrea, ed. *The Eritrean Case*. Rome: RICE; 1982: 115-166.

17. Smith, G. "Past and Future Approaches to Relief and Rehabilitation in Ethiopia." Presented at: Donors' Conference on Relief and Rehabilitation; Addis Ababa; May 1992: 5.

18. Ferris. *op.cit*. 1992: 18.

19. US House of Representatives. Select Committee on Hunger. "Renewed Challenge in Ethiopia." Washington, DC; 8 October 1987.

20. Bondestam, L; Cliffe, L; White, P. An Independent Evaluation of the Food Situation in Eritrea Submitted to the Emergency Relief Desk: Eritrea Food and Agricultural Assessment Study, Final Report. University of Leeds: Centre of Development Studies; March 1988.

21. Centre for Development Studies (University of Leeds). An Independent Evaluation of the Food Situation in Eritrea in 1991. Submitted to the Emergency Relief Desk, 2 May 1992: Eritrea 1991: A Needs Assessment Study; Final Report, August 1992.

22. *Africa Rights*. "Somalia, Operation Restore Hope: A Preliminary Assessment." London: *Africa Rights*; May 1993.

Chapter Two

Public Welfare and the Politics of Liberation

1. Kaplan, R. *Surrender or Starve: The Wars Behind the Famine*. Boulder: Westview Press; 1988.

2. Varnis, S. *Reluctant Aid or Aiding the Reluctant: US Food Aid Policy and Ethiopian Famine Relief*. New Brunswick: Transaction Publishers; 1990.

3. Minear, L. *Humanitarianism Under Siege: A Critical Review of Operation*

Lifeline Sudan. Trenton, NJ: Red Sea Press; 1991.

4. Life and Peace Institute. *The Challenges to Intervention: A New Role for the UN?* Uppsala: Life and Peace Institute; 1992.

5. Bimbi, G. "The National Liberation Struggle and the National Liberation Fronts." in: RICE, ed. *The Eritrean Case*. Rome: Research and Information Centre on Eritrea; 1982: 181.

6. *ibid*: 183.

7. EPLF. *The Cause of Famine in Ethiopia*. From, Dimtsi Hafash, June 1980: EPLF, ed. Selected Articles From EPLF Publications (1973-1980). Rome: Eritrean People's Liberation Front; May 1982: 59-61.

8. Wright, K. Tigray: *A Political Report;* September 1979.

9. EPLF. "Victories Won by the EPLF in 1976." From, *Vanguard*, March 1977: EPLF, ed. Selected Articles From EPLF Publications (1973-1980). Eritrean People's Liberation Front: Rome; May 1982: 77-87.

10. EPLF. Department of Social Affairs. Eritrean People's Liberation Front; November 1982.

11. Duffield, M. "War and Famine in Africa." Oxfam Research Paper No 5; 1991.

12. Araria, G. *The Politics of Famine and Strategies for Development in Ethiopia*. Ann Arbor: University of Michigan; 1990: 169,180.

13. Eisenloeffel, F N (DIA/ERD). "The Eritrean Durrah Odyssey 1983;" July-August 1983.

14. Wright, K. "Relief For Tigray:" Report on a Visit, February-March 1979; 2 May 1979.

15. EPLF. *op.cit.* March 1977.

16. Dines, M (Euro Action Accord). "Eritrea: The Current Situation." London; June 1979.

17. REST. ERD Evaluation. Khartoum; 1 February 1984.

18. Roso (RICE). Interview; Asmara; 3 February 1993.

19. EPLF. *op.cit.* March 1977.

20. Smith, G (DIA/NCA). Interview; Addis Ababa; 29 January 1993.

21. EPLF. *op.cit.* June 1980.

22. Smith, G (ERD/DIA). Counting Quintals: Report on a Field Monitoring Visit to Tigray, Northern Ethiopia; July 1983.

23. Bimbi. *op.cit.* 1982: 204.

24. The TPLF developed a different perspective on the Soviet Union. This divergence formed part of the background to the split between the EPLF and TPLF in the mid 1980s. This is discussed in Chapter Five.

25. EPLF. *op.cit.* November 1982.

26. Gebremedhin, R (ERA). Memo on ERA and its Activities: Eritrean Relief Association; March 1976.

27. *ibid.*

28. *ibid:* 21.

29. *ibid.*

30. Normark, S (ERD). Report on Visit to Eritrea. Khartoum; 4-15 June 1982.

31. EPLF. *op.cit.* November 1982.

32. Normark, S (SCR). Report on a Visit to Sudan and Eritrea: 19 February-12 March 1978. Skelleftea; March 1978.

33. Wright. *op.cit.* 2 May 1979.

34. EPLF. *op.cit.* November 1982.

35. Smith. *op.cit.* 29 January 1993.

36. Smith. *op.cit.* July 1983.

37. Jacobsen, A (ERD). Report on a Field Trip to Eritrea: 16 September-16 October 1984. Khartoum; 24 October 1984.

38. Vaux, T. "Famine in Eritrea." Oxford: OXFAM; March 1990.

39. Nerayo Teklemichael (ERRA). Interview; Asmara; 3 February 1993.

40. Eisenloeffel. *op.cit.* July-August 1983.

41. Silkin, T; Hughes, S. "Food Security and Food Aid: A Study From the Horn of Africa." London: CAFOD/Christian Aid; September 1992.

42. Gebremedhin. *op.cit.* March 1976: 26.

43. Abubaker, G M. *Sudan's Attitude Towards the Eritrean Revolution*. Khartoum: University of Khartoum; April 1983.

44. Karadawi, A (Community Aid Abroad). Interview; Addis Ababa; 26 January 1993.

45. Stabrun, O (NCA). Report on a Visit to Eritrea; 24 February 1978.

46. Weaver, J L; Kontos, J F (USAID). "Refugee Situation in Sudan." Khartoum; December 1982.

47. Karadawi. *op.cit.* 26 January 1993.

48. *ibid.*

49. Abubaker. *op.cit.* April 1983.

Chapter Three

The Horn and the Divergence of Donor Policy

1. Africa Watch. *Evil Days: 30 Years of War and Famine in Ethiopia*. New York: Africa Watch; September 1991: 141-2, 147.

2. Bennett, J [and others]. "Tigray 1984: An Investigation." Oxford: OXFAM; 1984: 16-18.

3. Africa Watch. *op.cit*. September 1991: 130-134.

4. Babb, T. Organisation and Structure of Aid: Task Force Report for the Administrator. Washington DC: Agency for International Development; 1977: V:2-3.

5. McPherson, M P. Administrator's Message to Employees: State of the Agency. Washington DC: Agency for International Development; 1884: 1.

6. Lappe, F [and others]. *Aid as an Obstacle*. San Francisco: Institute for Food and Development Policy; 1980: 93-105.

7. Nelson, H; Kaplan, I, eds. *Ethiopia: A Country Study*. Washington DC: Government Printing Office; 1981: 222.

8. Finney, L. "Development Assistance: A Tool of Foreign Policy." *Case Western Reserve Journal of International Law*; 1983; 15: 232.

9. Varnis, S. *Reluctant Aid or Aiding the Reluctant: US Food Aid Policy and Ethiopian Famine Relief*. New Brunswick: Transaction Publishers; 1990: 42.

10. *ibid:* 43,100.

11. US General Accounting Office. *The US Response to the Ethiopian Food Crisis*. Washington DC: General Accounting Office; 1985: 16, 20.

12. Varnis. *op.cit*. 1990: 65.

13. Clay, J. "Ethiopian Famine and the Relief Agencies." in: Nichols, B; Loescher, G, eds. *The Moral Nation: Humanitarianism and US Foreign Policy Today*. South Bend, Indiana: University of Notre Dame Press; 1989: 233.

14. Shepherd, J. "The Politics of Food Aid." *Africa Report*; April 1985: 51-52.

15. *Africa Watch*. *op.cit*. September 1991: 363.

16. Varnis. *op.cit*. 1990: 69.

17. Ferris, E. Humanitarian Politics: *Cross-Border Operations in the Horn of Africa*. Uppsala: Life and Peace Institute; 1992: 14.

18. "The Main Provisions of the New ACP-EEC Convention." *The Courier*; November 1979; (58): 26-37.

19. Van Woudenberg, W. "Ethiopia and the European Community." *The Courier*; January-February 1980; (59): 19-20.

20. Piper, I. "Overcoming the Feudal Past." *The Courier;* January-February 1980; (59): 12-17.

21. Mengistu Haile Mariam. "The Major Objective of Our Revolution Remains Development With Equity." *The Courier;* January-February 1980; (59): 9-11.

22. Piper. *op.cit.* January-February 1980.

23. Clapham, C. *Transformation and Continuity in Revolutionary Ethiopia.* Cambridge: Cambridge University Press; 1988: 121-23.

24. Van Woudenberg. *op.cit.* January-February 1980.

25. EPLF. "The Cause of Famine in Ethiopia." From, Dimtsi Hafash, June 1980: EPLF, ed. *Selected Articles From EPLF Publications (1973-1980).* Rome: Eritrean People's Liberation Front; May 1982: 59-61.

26. Firebrace, J (War on Want). Statement to the European Parliament Re: Tins of EEC Butteroil Observed at Sheraro, Tigray Province, Ethiopia 12/4/82. London: War on Want; 29 November 1982.

27. Smith, G (Free Lance Journalist). Observations in Eritrea and Tigray During 1982. Somerville, Massachusetts; 30 November 1982.

28. Bennett, J (University of Durham). Statement Regarding Abuses of Food Aid: Tigray, Northern Ethiopia. Durham: Department of Sociology and Social Policy; 25 January 1983.

29. Hailemikael, Abreha (RRC). Sworn Statement; 7 November 1983.

30. Smith, G. "Past and Future Approaches to Relief and Rehabilitation in Ethiopia." Presented at: Donors' Conference on Relief and Rehabilitation; Addis Ababa; May 1992.

31. South; February 1983.

32. Willemse, J (DIA). Travel Report Visit, Rome: 3-7 March 1984. Utrecht; March 1984.

33. Pisani, E (EC Commission). [Letter to Marshall, J, MEP]. Brussels; 1 February 1984.

Chapter Four

Neutrality, Humanitarianism and the Formation of ERD

1. Sprunger, J (LWR). Interview; New York; 18 November 1992.

2. Solberg, R W. *Miracle in Ethiopia: A Partnership Response to Famine.* New York: Friendship Press; 1991: 77.

3. Erichsen, J (NCA). Interview; Oslo; 16-17 March 1993.

4. Willemse, J (DIA). [Letter to Renshaw, P, CA]. Utrecht; 13 June 1984.

5. Normark, S (SCR). Report on a Visit to Sudan and Eritrea: 19 February-12 March 1978. Skelleftea; March 1978.

6. Erichsen. *op.cit.* 16-17 March 1993.

7. Stabrun, O (NCA). Report on a Visit to Eritrea; 24 February 1978.

8. Erichsen. *op.cit.* 16-17 March 1993.

9. Jacobsen, A (NCA/ERD). Interview; Asmara; 4 February 1993.

10. NCA and SCC, Signatories. Agreement Concerning Formation of an Emergency Relief Desk. Khartoum; 21 February 1981.

11. Jacobsen. *op.cit.* 4 February 1993.

12. ERD. Evaluation Report: 30 January - 8 February 1984. Oslo; 5 March 1984.

13. Padt, R. "The Meaning of Neutrality and its Consequences: The Medecins Sans Frontieres Experience." in: Wackers, G L; Wennekes, C T M, eds. *Violation of Medical Neutrality*. Amsterdam: Thesis Publishers; 1992: 48-54.

14. ERD. *op.cit.* 5 March 1984.

15. ERD. Minutes of ERD Board Meeting. Geneva; 26 January 1982.

16. ERD. Minutes of ERD Board Meeting. Khartoum; 16 April 1982.

17. OXFAM. Briefing Paper: "UN Response to Humanitarian Emergencies: A Challenge to the International Community." Oxford: OXFAM; August 1991.

18. DIA. "The Right to Humanitarian Assistance in Emergency Situations: Protocol on the Roles and Responsibilities on Non-Governmental Organisations." Utrecht: Dutch Interchurch Aid; 23 November 1992.

19. Boutrous-Ghali, B, UN General Secretary. "An Agenda for Peace: Preventive Diplomacy, Peacemaking and Peace-Keeping." New York: United Nations; 17 June 1992.

20. Erichsen. *op.cit.* 16-17 March 1993.

21. ERA. ERA's Position on ERD. Khartoum; 1 February 1984.

22. Abadi Zemo (REST). Interview; Addis Ababa; 28 January 1993.

23. ERD. Minutes of a Meeting of Representatives of Agencies Associated With the Sudan Council of Churches Emergency Relief Desk. Geneva; 28-29 May 1984.

24. ERD. Minutes of ERD Meeting. Khartoum; 19 February 1981.

25. ERD. Minutes of Board Meeting. Khartoum; 14 November 1981.

26. Hendrie, B (Former ERD). Interview; Asmara; 5 February 1993.

27. ERD. Minutes of Board Meeting. Khartoum; 6-7 October 1981.

28. Normark, S, Executive Secretary (ERD). Report: April-June 1982. Khartoum; 30 June 1982.

29. Overby, T (Former ERD). Interview; Asmara; 8 February 1993.

30. ERD. Minutes of Interim Executive Committee Meeting. Khartoum; 8-10 July 1985.

31. CA. Strictly Confidential: Notes on ERD Board Meeting: 14th/15th October 1985. London; October 1985.

32. ERD. *op.cit.* 19 February 1981.

33. Willemse, J (DIA). Interview; Utrecht; 24 February 1993.

34. ERD. *op.cit.* 26 January 1982.

35. Normark, S (ERD). Report: January - March 1982. Khartoum; April 1982.

36. ERD. Minutes of Board Meeting. Khartoum; 30 June 1982.

37. Willemse, J (DIA). Interview; Utrecht; 24 February 1993.

38. ERD. Minutes of Board Meeting. Khartoum; 12 September 1983.

39. Jacobsen, A, Executive Secretary (ERD). Annual Report No 1: 1983. Khartoum; 7 February 1984.

40. Willemse, J (DIA). Travel Report Visit, Rome: 3-7 March 1984. Utrecht; March 1984.

41. Euro Action Accord. Confidential: Report of Euro Action-Accord Mission to Eritrea: December-January 1978; January 1978.

42. Billanou, M (EIAC). Interview; Asmara; 2 February 1993.

43. Bennett, J (University of Durham). Statement Regarding Abuses of Food Aid: Tigray, Northern Ethiopia. Durham: Department of Sociology and Social Policy; 25 January 1983.

44. Robinson, C; Hughes, S (Christian Aid). Interview; London; 6 January 1993.

45. Willemse, J (DIA). [Telex to Renshaw, P, CA].Utrecht; 1 October 1984.

46. Normark, S (ERD). Emergency Relief Desk 01.08.81 -30.09.81. Khartoum; 1 October 1981.

47. Normark. *op.cit.* 30 June 1982.

48. ERD. *op.cit.* 5 March 1984.

49. Barth, N (LWR). Interview; New York; 5 October 1992.

50. Willemse. *op.cit.* 13 June 1984.

51. Karadawi, A (Former COR). Interview; Addis Ababa; 26 January 1993.

52. ERD. *op.cit.* 5 March 1984.

53. *ibid.*

Chapter Five

The Internationalisation of the Crisis

1. Shepherd, J. Ethiopia: *The Use of Food as an Instrument of US Foreign Policy. Issue, A Journal of Opinion*; 1985; 14: 5.

2. Cuny, F. "Politics and Famine Relief." in: Nichols, B; Loescher, G, eds. *The Moral Nation: Humanitarianism and US Foreign Policy Today*. South Bend, Indiana: University of Notre Dame Press; 1989: 278-287.

3. Clay, J W; Holcombe, B K. *Politics and the Ethiopian Famine, 1984-1985*. Cambridge, MA: Cultural Survival; 1985.

4. Korn, D. "Ethiopia: The Dilemma for the West." *World Today*; January 1986: 5.

5. Kaplan, R. *Surrender or Starve: The Wars Behind the Famine*. Boulder: Westview Press; 1988: 41, 52, 68.

6. Hutchinson, R, ed. *Fighting for Survival*. Gland, Switzerland: International Union for Conservation of Nature and Natural Resources; 1991: 76.

7. Hendrie, B. "The Tigrayan Refugee Repatriation: Sudan to Ethiopia, 1985-1987." in: Cuny, ed. *Repatriation During Conflict: Africa and Asia*. Dallas: Centre for the Study of Societies in Crisis; 1992: 293.

8. Clay, J. "Ethiopian Famine and the Relief Agencies." in: Nichols, B; Loescher, G, eds. *The Moral Nation: Humanitarianism and US Foreign Policy Today*. South Bend, Indiana: University of Notre Dame Press; 1989: 232.

9. Ferris, E. *Humanitarian Politics: Cross-Border Operations in the Horn of Africa*. Uppsala: Life and Peace Institute; 1992: 11.

10. US House of Representatives. Subcommittee on Human Rights and International Organisations. Human Rights and Food Aid in Ethiopia. Washington DC; 16 October 1985: 181.

11. "UN Says Food is Reaching North Ethiopia." *New York Times*; 4 August 1985: 2, Cols 1-6.

12. Clay. op.cit. 1989: 233.

13. Minear, L (Humanitarianism and War Project, Refugee Policy Group). Interview; Washington DC; 10 March 1993.

14. Varnis, S. *Reluctant Aid or Aiding the Reluctant: US Food Aid Policy and Ethiopian Famine Relief*. New Brunswick: Transaction Publishers; 1990: 93.

15. Africa Watch. *Evil Days: 30 Years of War and Famine in Ethiopia*. New York: Africa Watch; September 1991: 367.

16. Presidential Determination No 85-20. Determination With Respect to Ethiopia. Washington DC; 7 September 1985.

17. *Africa Watch. op.cit.* September 1991: 369.

18. Clough, R E. *Free at Last? US Policy Toward Africa and the End of the Cold War*. New York: Council on Foreign Relations; 1992: 16.

19. ERD. Annual Report, 1985. Khartoum; 15 May 1986.

20. Jacobsen, A (NCA/ERD). Interview; Asmara; 4 February 1993.

21. Korn. *op.cit.* January 1986: 136-7.

22. Sprunger, J (LWR). Interview; New York; 18 November 1992.

23. Jacobsen, A (NCA/ERD). Interview; Asmara; 2 February 1993.

24. Hendrie, B. "Cross-Border Relief Operations in Eritrea and Tigray." *Disasters*; 1990; 13(4): 354.

25. ERD. *op.cit.* 15 May 1986: 9.

26. Vallely, P. "Famine: Russia and US on Collision Course." *The Times*; 4 June 1985.

27. *Africa Watch*. *op.cit.* September 1991: 186-8.

28. Gill, P. *A Year in the Death of Africa*. London: Paladin; 1886.

29. Smith, G (DIA/NCA). Personal Communication; Asmara; 4 June 1993.

30. Interviews with USAID officials, October and November 1992, Washington and January 1993, Addis Ababa.

31. Karadawi, A (Former COR). Interview; Addis Ababa; 26 January 1993.

32. Gill. *op.cit.* 1886: 151.

33. Hendrie. *op.cit.* 1990: 355.

34. Sprunger. *op.cit.* 1992.

35. Hardy, D (Canadian LWR). Interview; Ottawa; 21 November 1992.

36. Cottingham, Rev. B (Former LWR). Interview; New York; 18 October 1992.

37. Clark, L. *Early Warning Case Study: The 1984-5 Influx of Tigrayans Into Eastern Sudan*. Washington DC: Refugee Policy Group; 1986.

38. Hardy. *op.cit.* 1992.

39. Culter, P. "The Development of the 1983-85 Famine in Northern Ethiopia" [PhD Thesis]: London University; 1988: 408.

40. Willemse, J (DIA). Travel Report Visit, Rome: 3-7 March 1984. Utrecht; March 1984.

41. Smith, G. Concept Paper - Cross Border Operations. Khartoum; 5 March 1985.

42. CA. [Letter to EEC Member State Development Ministers]; May 1985.

43. *ibid*.

44. Robinson, C; Hughes, S (Christian Aid). Interview; London; 6 January 1993.

45. Janda, C (SCC). [Letter to Telex to Renshaw, P, CA]. Khartoum; 19

October 1984.

46. Robinson, C (CA). Memorandum: ERD Meeting and EEC. London; 29 April 1985.

47. ERD. Minutes of Emergency Relief Desk Meeting. London; 8-9 May 1985.

48. Robinson. *op.cit.* 23 October 1985.

49. Firebrace, J. "Food as Military Aid." *New Statesman*; 7 December 1984; 108(2803): 5-6.

50. Duffield, M. "The Emergence of Two-Tier Welfare in Africa: Marginalization or an Opportunity for Reform?" Public Administration and Development; 1992; 12: 139-154.

51. Smith. *op.cit.* 5 March 1985.

Chapter Six

The Re-Establishment of ERD

1. ERD. Evaluation Report: 30 January - 8 February 1984. Oslo; 5 March 1984.

2. ERD. Minutes of a Meeting of Representatives of Agencies Associated With the Sudan Council of Churches Emergency Relief Desk. Geneva; 28-29 May 1984.

3. Kline, D. "Politics Hinders Food Aid to Starving People in Ethiopia." *The Christian Science Monitor*; 3 August 1984: 5-7.

4. Willemse, J (DIA). Personal Communication; Utrecht; 28 May 1993.

5. Willemse, J (DIA). [Letter to Renshaw, P, CA]. Utrecht; 13 June 1984.

6. Renshaw, P (CA). [Letter to Janda, C, SCC]. London; 3 August 1984.

7. Willemse, J (DIA). [Telex to Renshaw, P, CA]. Utrecht; 1 October 1984.

8. Janda, C (SCC). [Telex to Renshaw, P, CA]. Khartoum; 26 September 1984.

9. Janda, C (SCC). [Letter to Renshaw, P, CA]. Khartoum; 8 October 1984.

10. Renshaw, P (CA). [Letter to ERD Agencies]. London; 18 October 1984.

11. Jacobsen, A (ERD). [Telex to Renshaw, P, CA]. Khartoum; 28 December 1984.

12. Renshaw, P (CA). [Letter to Jacobsen, A, ERD]. London; 11 January 1985.

13. Jacobsen, A (ERD). [Letter to ERD Agencies]. Khartoum; 13 February 1985.

14. Kraemer, H R (ICCO). [Letter to Renshaw, P, CA]. Zeist; 21 December 1984.

15. Renshaw. *op.cit.* 22 April 1985.

16. Renshaw, P. *Christian Aid and the Emergency Relief Desk*. London; 22 April 1985.

17. ERD. Agencies Perspective on ERD; 8 May 1985.

18. ERD. Minutes of Emergency Relief Desk Meeting. London; 8-9 May 1985.

19. ERA. ERA's Position on ERD. Khartoum; 1 February 1984.

20. ERA. Encl. 3: To: ERD Ex. Comm. Khartoum; 7 July 1985.

21. Hensle, H (BFW). *Diakonisches Werk: Attempts to Initiate Discussions/Negotiations for Peaceful Settlement*. Stuggart; 7 May 1985.

22. Willemse, J (DIA). Interview; Utrecht; 24 February 1993.

23. Erichsen, J (NCA). Interview; Oslo; 16-17 March 1993.

24. Jacobsen, A, Executive Secretary (ERD). Annual Report No 1: 1983. Khartoum; 7 February 1984.

25. Kline. *op.cit*. 1984.

26. Hensle. *op.cit*. 7 May 1985.

27. Stanhope, H. "Mengistu Spending Shocks the West." *The Times*; 21 September 1984.

28. Renshaw, P (CA). [Telex to Normark, S, SCR]. London; 24 October 1984.

29. ERD Agencies. "Urgent Resolution on Ethiopian Famine." Press Release. *Woudschoten*, The Netherlands; 1 November 1984 (for release on 2 November).

30. Galloway, G. "The Mengistu Famine." *The Spectator*; 1 December 1984: 6-7.

31. Firebrace, J. "Food as Military Aid." *New Statesman*; 7 December 1984; 108(2803): 5-6.

32. Smith, G (Free Lance Journalist). "Observations in Eritrea and Tigray During 1982." Somerville, Massachusetts; 30 November 1982.

33. Survival International. "Resettlement: The Evidence." London: *Survival International*; March 1985.

34. Smith, G. Report on New Refugee Arrivals to Blue Nile Province Sudan: January 13 -14, 1985. Demazin, Sudan; January 1985.

35. Smith, G (REST Support Committees Information). Report on Visit to Sudan/Tigray, December 1984 - March 1985; 12 March 1985.

36. Clay, J W; Holcombe, B K. "Politics and the Ethiopian Famine, 1984-1985." Cambridge, MA: *Cultural Survival*; 1985.

37. Valley, P. "Ethiopians Admit Tegre Crisis." *The Times*; 25 February 1985.

38. Vallely, P. "Ethiopian Troops Sever Food Supply Lines to Starving Tigre." *Times*; 7 May 1985.

39. Willemse, J (DIA). [Telex to Keulemans, N, CICARWS Emerg.]. Utrecht; 13 November 1984.

40. Hensle. *op.cit.* 7 May 1985.

41. Hensle, H. Nicht Ist, "Was Nicht Sein Darf..." Diakonie Report; March 1985.

42. Renshaw, P (CA). Conversation with Hugh Mackay, Save the Children Fund: 'Ethiopia Drought'. London; 2 August 1984.

43. *Survival International. op.cit.* March 1985.

44. Clay, J W. "Western Assistance and the Ethiopian Famine: Implications for Humanitarian Assistance." in: Downs, R E; Kerner, D O; Reyna, S P, eds. *The Political Economy of African Famine*. Philadelphia: Gordan and Breach; 1991: 147-75.

45. Renshaw. *op.cit.* 22 April 1985.

46. Smith, G. "Concept Paper - Cross Border Operations." Khartoum; 5 March 1985.

47. Whisenant, J (LWR). Personal Communication; 28 May 1993.

48. ERA. *op.cit.* 7 July 1985.

49. CA. Strictly Confidential: Notes on ERD Board Meeting: 14th/15th October 1985. London; October 1985.

50. Erichsen. *op.cit.* 1993.

Chapter Seven

Front Ascendancy and the Vicissitudes of Donor Assistance

1. Africa Watch. *Evil Days: 30 Years of War and Famine in Ethiopia*. New York: Africa Watch; September 1991: 184.

2. *ibid:* 209.

3. *ibid:* 184.

4. ERD. Annual Report 1988. Khartoum; December 1988: 1.

5. *Africa Watch. op.cit.* 1991: 237.

6. *ibid:* 240.

7. de Waal, A. "Population and Health of Eritreans in Wad Sherifei." London: *Action Aid*; 1989.

8. Smith, G (DIA/NCA). Personal Communication; Asmara; 4 June 1993.

9. *Africa Watch. op.cit.* 1991: 255-68.

10. ERD. Annual Report 1989. Oslo; 22 September 1990: 4, 15.

11. Clay, J. "Ethiopian Famine and the Relief Agencies." in: Nichols, B;

Loescher, G, eds. *The Moral Nation: Humanitarianism and US Foreign Policy Today*. South Bend, Indiana: University of Notre Dame Press; 1989: 252-67.

12. ERD. Annual Report, 1986. Khartoum; 18 August 1987.

13. ERD. Annual Report, 1987. Khartoum; May 1988.

14. Paulos Tesfagiorgis (Former ERA). Interview; Asmara; 3 February 1993.

15. Whisenant, J (LWR). Interview; New York; 20 November 1992.

16. Interviews with USAID officials in Washington, November 1992.

17. Overby, T (Former ERD). Interview; Asmara; 4 February 1993.

18. ERD. *op.cit.* 1987: 18.

19. Interviews with USAID officials in Washington, Addis Ababa and Asmara, October 1992 to February 1993

20. Sprunger, J (LWR). Interview; New York; 18 November 1992.

21. Whisenant. *op.cit.* 1992.

22. Hendrie, B (Former ERD). Interview; Asmara; 5 February 1993.

23. Hauser, K (Former Eritrean Relief Committee). Interview; Connecticut; 20 October 1992.

24. Tsefai Ghermazion (Provisional Government of Eritrea). Interview; Asmara; 5 February 1993.

25. ERD. Handwritten Notes: Minutes of Extraordinary Ex Comm Meeting. Copenhagen; 30 June 1988.

26. *ibid.*

Chapter Eight

Stabilisation of the Crisis and the Routinisation of ERD

1. Smith, G (DIA/NCA). Interview; Addis Ababa; 25 January 1993.

2. Smith, G (DIA/NCA). Interview; Addis Ababa; 29 January 1993.

3. Willemse, J (DIA). Personal Communication; Utrecht; 28 May 1993.

4. Nerayo Teklemichael (ERRA). Personal Communication; Asmara; 22 June 1993.

5. ERD. Handwritten notes: Minutes of Executive Committee; August 1987.

6. Nerayo Teklemichael. *op.cit.* 22 June 1993.

7. *ibid.*

8. Hensle, H (Chairperson, ERD Board). [Letter to Abadi Zemo, REST].

Khartoum; 10 July 1985.

9. Willemse. *op.cit.* 28 May 1993.

10. Abadi Zemo (REST). Interview; Addis Ababa; 28 January 1993.

11. ERD. Minutes of Board Meeting. Stuttgart; 24-25 October 1986.

12. Smith. *op.cit.* 29 January 1993.

13. ERD. Minutes of Interim Executive Committee Meeting. Khartoum; 8-10 July 1985.

14. ERD. Minutes of Executive Committee Meeting. Khartoum; 16-17 September 1985.

15. ERD. Minutes of Board Meeting. Geneva; 14-15 October 1985.

16. ERD. Minutes of Executive Committee Meeting. Woudschoten; 21-22 May 1986.

17. ERD. Annual Report, 1986. Khartoum; 18 August 1987.

18. ERD. Minutes of Executive Committee Meeting. Khartoum; 4-6 February 1987.

19. Hendrie, B (ERD). "Disaster Management in Tigray: Report on a Visit to the Non-government Held Areas of Tigray Province From January-February 1988." Khartoum; March 1988.

20. ERD. *op.cit.* 4-6 February 1987.

21. Bondestam, L; Cliffe, L; White, P. *An Independent Evaluation of the Food Situation in Eritrea Submitted to the Emergency Relief Desk: Eritrea Food and Agricultural Assessment Study, Final Report.* University of Leeds: Centre of Development Studies; March 1988.

22. *ibid:* vii-x.

23. *ibid:* 119-20.

24. Hendrie. *op.cit.* March 1988.

25. TPLF. TPLF Dismisses World Vision's Allegations. Khartoum; 15 May 1986.

26. ERD. Minutes of Executive Committee Meeting. Woudschoten; 21-22 May 1986.

27. ERD. Declaration Agreed on by the Ex Comm on the Alamata Incident. Woudschoten; 21-22 May 1986.

28. ERD. Minutes of Board Meeting. Khartoum; April 1988.

29. Hendrie, B (Former ERD). Interview; Asmara; 5 February 1993.

30. Smith, G. "Past and Future Approaches to Relief and Rehabilitation in Ethiopia." Presented at: Donors' Conference on Relief and Rehabilitation; Addis Ababa; May 1992.

31. Overby, T (ERD). [Telex to ERD Members]. Khartoum; 2 November 1987.

32. Hendrie. *op.cit.* 5 February 1993.

33. Barth, N (LWR). [Telex to Renshaw, P, CA]. New York; 26 October 1984.

34. ERD. *op.cit.* 24-25 October 1986.

35. Jacobsen, A (ERD). Interview; Asmara; 9 February 1993.

36. Abadi Zemo. *op.cit.* 28 January 1993.

37. Overby, T (Former ERD). Interview; Asmara; 4 February 1993.

38. Hendrie. *op.cit.* 5 February 1993.

39. Smith. *op.cit.* 29 January 1993.

40. ERD. Annual Report, 1987. Khartoum; May 1988.

41. ERD. Annual Report 1988. Khartoum; December 1988.

42. ERD. *op.cit.* 24-25 October 1986.

43. ERD. Minutes of Extraordinary Board Meeting. Trondheim; 14-15 May 1987.

44. *ibid.*

45. ERD. Minutes of Executive Committee Meeting. Khartoum; 4-6 February 1987.

46. ERD. *op.cit.* 18 August 1987.

47. ERD. *op.cit.* 14-15 May 1987.

48. *ibid.*

49. ERD. Minutes of Executive Committee Meeting. Trondheim; 13 May 1987.

50. Hendrie. *op.cit.* 5 February 1993.

51. Smith. *op.cit.* 29 January 1993.

52. Overby. *op.cit.* 4 February 1993.

53. Bondestam. *op.cit.* March 1988.

54. ERD. Minutes of Board Meeting. Middlessex, UK; 29-30 October 1987.

55. Smith. *op.cit.* 25 January 1993.

56. Overby. *op.cit.* 4 February 1993.

57. ERD. Minutes of Executive Committee Meeting. Khartoum; 11-13 August 1987.

58. ERD. Handwritten notes: Minutes of Board Meeting. Khartoum; 25-27 April 1988.

59. ERD. Handwritten Notes: Minutes of Extraordinary Ex Comm Meeting. Copenhagen; 30 June 1988.

60. Westborg, J, ed (Centre For Partnership in Development). Evaluation Report, Emergency Relief Desk, Sudan: July 1988. Oslo; 14 August 1988.

61. *ibid:* ii-iii.

62. *ibid.*

63. *ibid*.

64. Overby, T (Former ERD). Interview; Asmara; 8 February 1993.

65. ERD. *op.cit*. 24-25 October 1986.

66. ERD. Minutes of Executive Committee Meeting. Khartoum; 4-6 February 1987.

67. *ibid*.

68. ERD. Minutes of Executive Committee Meeting. Khartoum; 21 October 1988.

69. ERD. *op.cit*. December 1988.

70. ERD. Minutes of Extraordinary Executive Committee Meeting. Oslo; 24 November 1988.

71. Abuoaf, I (Ministry of Social Welfare and Elzakaat). [Letter to General Secretary, NCA]. Khartoum; 29 January 1989.

72. REST; ORA; ERA. "Emergency Relief Desk: Problems Encountered, Possible Solutions." Khartoum; 9 February 1989.

73. Jacobsen. *op.cit*. 9 February 1993.

74. *ibid*.

75. *ibid*.

76. Hendrie. *op.cit*. 5 February 1993.

77. Barth, N (LWR). [Letter to Erichsen, J and Willemse, J]. New York; 26 September 1989.

78. Barth, N (LWR). "Tough Love;" n.d.

79. Minear, L. *Humanitarianism Under Siege: A Critical Review of Operation Lifeline Sudan*. Trenton, NJ: Red Sea Press; 1991.

80. Erichsen, J A (NCA). [Rough Translation of Letter to Norwegian Foreign Minister]. Oslo; November 1989.

Chapter Nine

Replacing the Cross-Border Operation With Aid From the Government Side

1. Africa Watch. *Evil Days: 30 Years of War and Famine in Ethiopia*. New York: Africa Watch; September 1991: 243-46.

2. *ibid*: 270.

3. *ibid*: 278-82.

4. Centre for Development Studies (University of Leeds). "An Independent

Evaluation of the Food Situation in Eritrea in 1991." Submitted to the Emergency Relief Desk, 2 May 1992: Eritrea 1991: A Needs Assessment Study; Final Report, August 1992.

5. JRP. Annual Report 1990 and 1991. Addis Ababa: Joint Relief Partnership; March 1992.

6. Teklewoini Assefa (REST). Personal Communication; Utrecht; 17 June 1993.

7. Willemse, J (DIA). Interview; Utrecht; 24 February 1993.

8. Tekie Beyene (Former ERA). Interview; Asmara; 9 February 1993.

9. Villumstad, S (NCA/ERD). Memorandum: Some Points Arising From Encounters With JRP Operation in Tigray; 20 October 1990.

10. Willemse. *op.cit.* 24 February 1993.

11. JRP. Annual Report 1990 and 1991. Addis Ababa: Joint Relief Partnership; March 1992.

12. Tekie Beyene. *op.cit.* 9 February 1993.

13. *ibid.*

14. *ibid.*

15. Willemse. *op.cit.* 24 February 1993.

16. Tekie Beyene. *op.cit.* 9 February 1993.

17. Willemse. *op.cit.* 24 February 1993.

18. Whisenant, J (LWR). Interview; New York; 20 November 1992.

19. Clough, R E. *Free at Last? US Policy Toward Africa and the End of the Cold War*. New York: Council on Foreign Relations; 1992.

20. ERD. Minutes of Advisory Group Meeting. Oslo; 22-24 November 1989.

21. Khartoum Donors. Crossborder Donor's Meeting. Khartoum; 9 October 1990.

22. Perlez, J. "American Dilema: Food Aid May Prolong War and Famine." *The New York Times*; 12 May 1991; 4: 3.

23. Erichsen, J A; Willemse, J (ERD/AG). [Letter to Participants of the Peace Conference, London]. Oslo; 23 May 1991.

24. Erichsen, J (NCA). Interview; Oslo; 16-17 March 1993.

Chapter Ten

The Internationalisation of Public Welfare and the Replacement of Indigenous Capacity

1. Vaux, T. *Famine in Eritrea*. Oxford: OXFAM; March 1990.

2. Bondestam, L; Cliffe, L; White, P. *An Independent Evaluation of the Food Situation in Eritrea Submitted to the Emergency Relief Desk: Eritrea Food and Agricultural Assessment Study, Final Report*. University of Leeds: Centre of Development Studies; March 1988.

3. Centre for Development Studies (University of Leeds). *An Independent Evaluation of the Food Situation in Eritrea in 1991*. Submitted to the Emergency Relief Desk, 2 May 1992: Eritrea 1991: A Needs Assessment Study; Final Report, August 1992.

4. Centre for Development Studies. Prepared for the Eritrean (sic) Relief Desk: "Peace in Eritrea: Prospects for Food Security and Problems of Policy:" University of Leeds; 8 September 1992.

5. Hoskins, E. "Eritrean Famine Update:" Report for the Canadian Cross-Border Coalition and OXFAM-Canada; 25 May 1990.

6. Btzuamlak, A (OXFAM). OXFAM/EEC "Food Aid to Tigray: Monitoring Report." Khartoum; June 1990.

7. ERD. Annual Report 1989. Oslo; 22 September 1990.

8. ERD. Annual Report for 1990 (Condensed Version). Khartoum; 1991.

9. ERD. Annual Report 1991. Asmara; 31 March 1992.

10. Silkin, T; Hughes, S. "Food Security and Food Aid: A Study From the Horn of Africa." London: CAFOD/Christian Aid; September 1992.

11. ERD. Evaluation Report: 30 January - 8 February 1984. Oslo; 5 March 1984.

12. ERA. ERD Evaluation Team, "Some Questions and Answers." Khartoum; 1 February 1984.

13. REST. ERD Evaluation. Khartoum; 1 February 1984.

14. ERD. Annual Report, 1986. Khartoum; 18 August 1987.

15. ERD. *op.cit.* 1991.

16. ERD. *op.cit.* 22 September 1990.

17. Khartoum Donors. Memorandum: Crossborder Donor's Meeting. Khartoum; 9 October 1990.

18. Erichsen, J (NCA). Interview; Oslo; 16-17 March 1993.

19. Varnis, S. *Reluctant Aid or Aiding the Reluctant: US Food Aid Policy and Ethiopian Famine Relief*. New Brunswick: Transaction Publishers; 1990.

20. ERD. Monthly Report. Khartoum; May 1985.

21. ERD. *op.cit.* 5 March 1984.

22. Hoskins. *op.cit.* 25 May 1990.

23. ERD. *op.cit.* May 1985.

24. ERD. *op.cit.* 18 August 1987.

25. ERD. Minutes of Board Meeting. Geneva; 14-15 October 1985.

26. Hoskins. *op.cit.* 25 May 1990.

27. Centre for Development Studies. *op.cit.* August 1992.

28. Smith, G (ERD/DIA). "Counting Quintals: Report on a Field Monitoring Visit to Tigray, Northern Ethiopia;" July 1983.

29. REST. *op.cit.* 1 February 1984.

30. ERD. *op.cit.* 5 March 1984.

31. ERD. *op.cit.* 18 August 1987.

32. Hendrie, B (ERD). "Disaster Management in Tigray: Report on a Visit to the Non-government Held Areas of Tigray Province From January-February 1988." Khartoum; March 1988.

33. ERD. Annual Report, 1988. Khartoum; December 1988.

34. REST. *op.cit.* 1 February 1984.

35. Jacobsen, A, Executive Secretary (ERD). Annual Report No 1: 1983. Khartoum; 7 February 1984.

36. ERD. Annual Report, 1987. Khartoum; May 1988.

37. ERD. Annual Report, 1985. Khartoum; 15 May 1986.

38. ERD. Handwritten Notes: Minutes of Extraordinary Ex Comm Meeting. Copenhagen; 30 June 1988.

39. ERD [Handwritten]. Discussion of Some Practical Issues of Current ERD Operation. Khartoum; 1984.

40. ERD. Minutes of Advisory Group Meeting. Oslo; 22-24 November 1989.

41. *Africa Watch. op.cit.* September 1991.

42. Minear, L. *Humanitarianism Under Siege: A Critical Review of Operation Lifeline Sudan.* Trenton, NJ: Red Sea Press; 1991.

43. Silkin and Hughes. *op.cit.* September 1992: 20.

44. Smith. *op.cit.* July 1983: 57-58.

45. Hendrie. *op.cit.* March 1988: 15-16.

46. Smith, G (DIA/NCA). Interview; Addis Ababa; 29 January 1993.

47. de Waal, A. "Tigray: Grain Markets and Internal Purchase." Oxford: OXFAM; February 1989: 40-41.

48. Smith, G (ERD). "Internal Purchase Programme: Implications for the Present and Future." Addis Ababa: ERD Advisory Group; April 1992: 1-2.

49. Silkin and Hughes. *op.cit*. September 1992: 20-22.

50. Gilbert, G (CAA). Report on a Field Visit to Tigray. Fitzroy, Australia: Community Aid Abroad; 1989: 18.

51. Silkin and Hughes. *op.cit*. September 1992: 20-21.

52. Gilbert. *op.cit*. 1989: 16.

53. de Waal. *op.cit*. February 1989: 40-41.

54. Silkin and Hughes. *op.cit*. September 1992: 21.

55. Gilbert. *op.cit*. 1989: 16.

56. de Waal. *op.cit*. February 1989: 40-41.

57. Smith. *op.cit*. April 1992.

Chapter Eleven

Neutrality or Involvement? The End of the War and Phase Out of ERD

1. ERD. Minutes of ERD/AG Meeting. Krogerup Hojskole, Denmark; 22-23 May 1991.

2. Willemse, J (ERD/AG Chairman). [Letter to ERD Members]. Oslo; 4 June 1991.

3. ERD. Programme Up-Date No 012; 1992.

4. ERD. Minutes of Emergency Relief Desk/Advisory Group Meeting. Addis Ababa; 4-5 November 1991.

5. Teklewoini Assefa (REST). Personal Communication; Utrecht; 17 June 1993.

6. ERD. Statement of Principle on the Future of Emergency Relief Desk in Ethiopia. Addis Ababa; 5 November 1991.

7. ERD. Minutes From Emergency Relief Desk/Advisory Group Meeting. Asmara; 7-8 November 1991.

8. ERD. Statement of Principle on the Future of the Emergency Relief Desk, Asmara, Eritrea. Asmara; 8 November 1991.

9. Erichsen, J (NCA). Interview; Oslo; 16-17 March 1993.

10. Abdul Mohammed (Inter-Africa Group). Interview; Addis Ababa; 25 January 1993.

11. Assab Tekle (JRP). Interview; Addis Ababa; 26 January 1992.

12. Solberg, K (NCA). Interview; Addis Ababa; 25 January 1993.

13. NCA. Minutes of Meeting at NCA Oslo with Jacques Willemse (DIA). Oslo; 17 January 1992.

14. Villumstad, S; Hendrie, B. "New Policy Directions in Disaster Preparedness and Response in Ethiopia." *Disasters*; 1993; 17(3): 122-132.

15. Solberg, R W. *Miracle in Ethiopia: A Partnership Response to Famine*. New York: Friendship Press; 1991.

16. *ibid*: 82-90.

17. *ibid*: 88-90.

18. Villumstad and Hendrie. *op.cit*. 1993

19. Aba Kidane, Fr; Flynn, Br G (ESC). Interview; Addis Ababa; 26 January 1993.

20. Erichsen. *op.cit*. 16-17 March 1993.

21. Willemse, J (DIA). Interview; Utrecht; 24 February 1993.

22. ERD. Minutes of Board Meeting. Woudschoten; 10 -12 April 1989.

23. Borden, J (Christian Aid). Interview; London; 6 January 1993.

24. Villumstad, S; Strand, R (NCA). Interview; Oslo; 17 March 1993.

25. ERD. Minutes From Emergency Relief Desk/Advisory Group Meeting. Addis Ababa; 4-5 May 1992.

26. Erichsen. *op.cit*. 16-17 March 1993.

27. Villumstad, S (ERD). [Telex to Haugland, R, NCA]. Addis Ababa; 18 February 1992.

28. Willemse, J (DIA). [Fax to Villumstad, S, ERD]. Utrecht; 25 February 1992.

29. Villumstad, S, Liaison Officer (ERD). "Preliminary Reflections on Possible Future Relationships Between AG Members and Local Partners in Ethiopia." Addis Ababa; 3 March 1992.

30. Villumstad and Hendrie. *op.cit*. 1993

31. Villumstad, S, Liaison Officer (ERD). Update From NCA/ERD Liaison Officer in Ethiopia For March 1992. Addis Ababa; 3 April 1992.

32. Ayyaanaa Leencaa; Addisu Beyene Kaloo (ORA). Interview; Addis Ababa; 26 January 1993.

33. Villumstad, S, Liaison Officer (ERD). Memorandum to ERD/AG Partners: Future of ERD in Ethiopia, Future of Liaison Function: Evolution of ERD (Agenda Item B). Addis Ababa; 4 May 1992.

34. Villumstad, S, Liaison Officer (ERD). Update From NCA/ERD Liaison Officer in Ethiopia For March 1992. Addis Ababa; 3 April 1992.

35. (DDW/BFW). NCA-ERD Advisory Group Meeting Early May 1992. Stuttgart; 1 May 1992.

36. Villumstad and Strand. *op.cit* 17 March 1993.

37. Willemse, J (DIA). [Fax to Villumstad, S, ERD]. Utrecht; 27 May 1992.

38. Villumstad, S (Liaison Officer). [Memo to Strand, R and Ofstad, A, NCA]. Addis Ababa; 6 July 1992.

39. ERD. Minutes of ERD/AG Meeting. Addis Ababa; 1 December 1992.

40. Addisu Beyene; Teklewoini Assefa. ERD Meeting With REST And ORA: To All ERD Members From Oromo Relief Society and Relief Society of Tigray. Addis Ababa: 11 June 1993.

41. ERD. Minutes From the Emergency Relief Desk/Advisory Group Meeting. Addis Ababa; 9-10 June 1993.

42. ERD. *op.cit*. 1992.

43. ERD. Minutes of ERD/AG Meeting. Asmara; 2-3 December 1992.

44. Nerayo Tecklemichael (ERRA). "International and Indigenous NGO's in Eritrea: What Opportunities do Exist for Future Cooperation." presented at: Workshop on International and Indigenous NGOs in Eritrea: What are the Prospects for Future Cooperation; Asmara; 8 June 1993.

45. ERD. Minutes of the Emergency Relief Desk/Advisory Group Meeting. Asmara; 6-7 June 1993.

46. Gebremichael Mengistu. Paper Presented to the ERD/AG Meeting. Asmara: 6-7 June 1993.

Chapter Twelve

Internal War and Humanitarian Assistance

1. Duffield, M. "War and Famine in Africa." Oxfam Research Paper No 5; 1991.

2. Duffield, M. NGOs, "Disaster Relief and Asset Transfer in the Horn: Political Survival in a Permanent Emergency." *Development and Change*; 1993; 24: 131-157.

3. Minear, L (Humanitarianism and War Project, Refugee Policy Group). Interview; Washington DC; 10 March 1993.

4. Whisenant, J (LWR). Interview; New York; 20 November 1992.

5. Pearson, W (USAID). Interview; Addis Ababa; 24 January 1993.

6. Silkin, T; Hughes, S. *Food Security and Food Aid: A Study From the Horn of Africa*. London: CAFOD/Christian Aid; September 1992: 12.

7. Varnis, S. *Reluctant Aid or Aiding the Reluctant: US Food Aid Policy and Ethiopian Famine Relief*. New Brunswick: Transaction Publishers; 1990: 171.

8. Clay, J. "Ethiopian Famine and the Relief Agencies." in: Nichols, B; Loescher, G, eds. *The Moral Nation: Humanitarianism and US Foreign Policy Today*. South Bend, Indiana: University of Notre Dame Press; 1989: 249.

9. Africa Watch. *Evil Days: 30 Years of War and Famine in Ethiopia*. New York: Africa Watch; September 1991: 334-9.

10. Alvarrson, J. "Starvation or Peace or Food and War?: Aspects of Armed Conflict in the Lower Omo Valley." Uppsala Research Reports in Cultural Anthropology; 1989.

11. Turton, D. Warfare, "Vulnerability and Survival: A Case From Southern Ethiopia." *Cambridge Anthropology, Special Issue: Local Warfare in Africa*; 1989; 13(2): 67-85.

12. Allen, T. "Violence and Moral Knowledge: Observing Social Trauma in Sudan and Uganda." *Cambridge Anthropology, Special Issue: Local Warfare in Africa*; 1989; 13(2): 56-66.

13. Duffield. *op.cit*. 1991.

14. Duffield, M. (Internal Agency Report) OXFAM's Emergency Response to the Gulf War: August 1990 - August 1991. Oxford: OXFAM; November 1991.

15. Borden, J (Christian Aid). Interview; London; 6 January 1993.

16. Borton, J. "Recent Trends in the International Relief System." *Disasters*; 1993; 17(3): 187-201.

17. *Africa Rights*. "Somalia, Operation Restore Hope: A Preliminary Assessment." London: *Africa Rights*; May 1993.

18. Traynor, I. "Why Mercy Fails to Bring Relief." *The Guardian*; 15 April 1993: 9.

19. *Africa Rights*. *op.cit*. May 1993.

20. Hendrie, B. "Cross-Border Relief Operations in Eritrea and Tigray." *Disasters*; 1990; 13(4): 359.

21. Whisenant, J (LWR). Interview; New York; 20 November 1992.

22. Weiss T; Campbell, K M. "Military Humanism." *Survival*; 1991; 33(5): 451-465.

Bibliography

Unpublished and Agency Material

Abubaker, G. M. *Sudan's Attitude Towards the Eritrean Revolution*. Khartoum: University of Khartoum; 1983 Apr.

Abuoaf, I. (Ministry of Social Welfare and Elzakaat). [Letter to General Secretary, NCA]. Khartoum; 1989 Jan 29.

Addisu Beyene; Teklewoini Assefa. ERD Meeting With REST And ORA: To All ERD Members From Oromo Relief Society and Relief Society of Tigray. Addis Ababa: 11 June 1993.

Babb, T. *Organization and Structure of Aid: Task Force Report for the Administrator*. Washington DC: Agency for International Development; 1977.

Barth, N. (LWR). [Letter to Telex to Renshaw, P, CA]. New York; 1984 Oct 26.

Barth, N. (LWR). [Letter to Erichsen, J and Willemse, J]. New York; 1989 Sep 26.

Barth, N. (LWR). *Tough Love*. n.d.

Bennett, J. (University of Durham). "Statement Regarding Abuses of Food Aid: Trigray, Northern Ethiopia." Durham: Department of Sociology and Social Policy; 1983 Jan 25.

Bennett, J. [and others]. "Tigray 1984: An Investigation." Oxford: OXFAM; 1984.

Btzuamlak, A. (OXFAM). OXFAM/EEC Food Aid to Tigray: Monitoring Report. Khartoum; 1990 Jun.

CA. [Letter to EEC Member State Development Ministers]. London; 1985 May.

CA. Strictly Confidential: Notes on ERD Board Meeting: 14th/15th October 1985. London; 1985 Oct.

Culter, P. *The Development of the 1983–85 Famine in Northern Ethiopia* [PhD Thesis]. : London University; 1988.

DDW/BFW. NCA–ERD Advisory Group Meeting Early May 1992. Stutggart; 1992 May 1.

de Waal, A. *Population and Health of Eritreans in Wad Sherifei*. London: Action Aid; 1989.

de Waal, A. Tigray: *Grain Markets and Internal Purchase*. Oxford: OXFAM; 1989 Feb.

DIA. *The Right to Humanitarian Assistance in Emergency Situations: Protocol on the Roles and Responsibilities on Non-Governmental Organizations*. Utrecht: Dutch Interchurch Aid; 1992 Nov 23.

Dines, M. (Euro Action Accord). *Eritrea: The Current Situation*. London; 1979 Jun.

Duffield, M. Internal Agency Report: *OXFAM's Emergency Response to the Gulf War*: August 1990-August 1991. Oxford: OXFAM; 1991 Nov.

Eisenloeffel, F. N. (DIA/ERD). *The Eritrean Durrah Odyssey 1983*. 1983 Jul.

EPLF. Department of Social Affairs. *Eritrean People's Liberation Front;* 1982 Nov.

ERA. ERA's Position on ERD. Khartoum; 1984 Feb 1.

ERA. ERD Evaluation Team, *Some Questions and Answers*. Khartoum; 1984 Feb 1.

ERA. Encl. 3: To: ERD Ex. Comm. Khartoum; 1985 Jul 7.

ERD. Agencies Perspective on ERD. Khartoum; 1985 May 8.

ERD. Annual Report, 1985. Khartoum; 1986 May 15.

ERD. Annual Report, 1986. Khartoum; 1987 Aug 18.

ERD. Annual Report, 1987. Khartoum; 1988 May.

ERD. Annual Report, 1988. Khartoum; 1988 Dec.

ERD. Annual Report, 1989. Oslo; 1990 Sep 22.

ERD. Annual Report for 1990 (Condensed Version). Khartoum; 1991.

ERD. Annual Report 1991. Asmara; 1992 Mar 31.

ERD. Declaration Agreed on by the Ex Comm on the Alamata Incident. Woudschoten; 1986 May 21.

ERD. [Handwritten]. Discussion of Some Practical Issues of Current ERD Operation. Khartoum; 1984.

ERD. Evaluation Report: 30 January-8 February 1984. Oslo; 1984 Mar 5.

ERD. Minutes of ERD Meeting. Khartoum; 1981 Feb 19.

ERD. Minutes of Board Meeting. Khartoum; 1981 Oct 6.

ERD. Minutes of Board Meeting. Khartoum; 1981 Nov 14.

ERD. Minutes of Board Meeting. Geneva; 1982 Jan 26.

ERD. Minutes of Board Meeting. Khartoum; 1982 Apr 16.

ERD. Minutes of Board Meeting. Khartoum; 1982 Jun 30.

ERD. Minutes of Board Meeting. Khartoum; 1983 Sep 12.

ERD. Minutes of a Meeting of Representatives of Agencies Associated With the Sudan Council of Churches Emergency Relief Desk. Geneva; 1984 May 28.

ERD. Minutes of ERD Meeting. London; 1985 May 8.

ERD. Minutes of Interim Executive Committee Meeting. Khartoum; 1985 Jul 8.

ERD. Minutes of Executive Committee Meeting. Khartoum; 1985 Sep 16.

ERD. Minutes of Board Meeting. Geneva; 1985 Oct 14.

ERD. Minutes of Excutive Committee Meeting. Khartoum; 1986 Feb 6.

ERD. Minutes of Executive Committee Meeting. Woudschoten; 1986 May 21.

ERD. Minutes of Board Meeting. Stuttgart; 1986 Oct 24.

ERD. Minutes of Executive Committee Meeting. Khartoum; 1987 Feb 4.

ERD. Minutes of Executive Committee Meeting. Trondheim; 1987 May 13.

ERD. Minutes of Extraordinary Board Meeting. Trondheim; 1987 May 14.

ERD. Handwritten notes: Minutes of Executive Committee. 1987 Aug.

ERD. Minutes of Excutive Committee Meeting. Khartoum; 1987 Aug 11.

ERD. Minutes of Board Meeting. Middlessex, UK; 1987 Oct 29.

ERD. Minutes of Board Meeting. Khartoum; 1988 Apr.

ERD. Handwritten notes: Minutes of Board Meeting. Khartoum; 1988 Apr 25.

ERD. Handwritten Notes: Minutes of Extraordinary Ex Comm Meeting. Copenhagen; 1988 Jun 30.

ERD. Minutes of Executive Committee Meeting. Khartoum; 1988 Oct 21.

ERD. Minutes of Extraordinary Executive Committee Meeting. Oslo; 1988 Nov 24.

ERD. Minutes of Board Meeting. Woudschoten; 1989 Apr 10.

ERD. Minutes of Advisory Group Meeting. Oslo; 1989 Nov 22.

ERD. Minutes of ERD/AG Meeting. Krogerup Hojskole, Denmark; 1991 May 22.

ERD. Minutes of ERD/AG Meeting. Addis Ababa; 1991 Nov 4.

ERD. Minutes From ERD/AG Meeting. Asmara; 1991 Nov 7.

ERD. Minutes From ERD/AG Meeting. Addis Ababa; 1992 May 4.

ERD. Minutes of ERD/AG Meeting. Addis Ababa; 1992 Dec 1.

ERD. Minutes of ERD/AG Meeting. Asmara; 1992 Dec 2.

ERD. Minutes of the ERD/AG Meeting. Asmara; 1993 Jun 6.

ERD. Minutes From the ERD/AG Meeting. Addis Ababa; 1993 Jun 9.

ERD. Monthly Report. Khartoum; 1985 May.

ERD. Programme Up–Date No 012. Khartoum; 1992.

ERD. Statement of Principle on the Future of Emergency Relief Desk in Ethiopia. Addis Ababa; 1991 Nov 5.

ERD. Statement of Principle on the Future of the Emergency Relief Desk, Asmara, Eritrea. Asmara; 1991 Nov 8.

Erichsen, J. A. (NCA). [Letter to Norwegian Foriegn Minister]. Oslo; 1989 Nov.

Erichsen, J. A.; Willemse, J. (ERD/AG). [Letter to Participants of the Peace Conference, London]. Oslo; 1991 May 23.

Euro Action Acord. Confidential: Report of Euro Action–Acord Mission to

Eritrea: December–January 1978. London; 1978 Jan.

Firebrace, J. (War on Want). Statement to the European Parliament Re: Tins of EEC Butteroil Observed at Sheraro, Tigray Province, Ethiopia 12/4/82. London: War on Want; 1982 Nov 29.

Gebremedhin, R. (ERA). Memo on ERA and its Activities. : Ertrean Relief Association; 1976 Mar.

Gebremichael Mengistu. Paper Presented to the ERD/AG Meeting. Asmara: 6–7 June 1993.

Gilbert, G. (CAA). Report on a Field Visit to Tigray. Fitzroy, Australia: Community Aid Abroad; 1989.

Hailemikael, Abreha (RRC). Sworn Statement. 1983 Nov 7.

Hendrie, B. (ERD). Disaster Management in Tigray: Report on a Visit to the Non–government Held Areas of Tigray Province From January–February 1988. Khartoum; 1988 Mar.

Hensle, H. (Chairperson, ERD Board). [Letter to Abadi Zemo, REST]. Khartoum; 1985 Jul 10.

Hensle, H. (BFW). *Diakonisches Werk: Attempts to Initiate Discussions/Negotiations for Peaceful Settlement*. Stuttgart; 1985 May 7.

Hoskins, E. Ertrean Famine Update: Report for the Canadian Cross–Border Coalition and OXFAM–Canada. 1990 May 25.

Jacobsen, A. (ERD). [Telex to Renshaw, P, CA]. Khartoum; 1984 Dec 28.

Jacobsen, A. (ERD). [Letter to ERD Agencies]. Khartoum; 1985 Feb 13.

Jacobsen, A., Executive Secretary (ERD). Annual Report No 1: 1983. Khartoum; 1984 Feb 7.

Jacobsen, A. (ERD). Report on a Field Trip to Eritrea: 16 September–16 October 1984. Khartoum; 1984 Oct 24.

Janda, C. (SCC). [Telex to Renshaw, P, CA]. Khartoum; 1984 Sep 26.

Janda, C. (SCC). [Letter to Renshaw, P, CA]. Khartoum; 1984 Oct 8.

Janda, C. (SCC). [Telex to Renshaw, P, CA]. Khartoum; 1984 Oct 19.

JRP. Annual Report 1990 and 1991. Addis Ababa: Joint Relief Partnership; 1992 Mar.

Khartoum Donors. Memorandum: Crossborder Donor's Meeting. Khartoum; 1990 Oct 9.

Kraemer, H. R. (ICCO). [Letter to Reshaw, P, CA]. Zeist; 1984 Dec 21.

McPherson, M. P. Administrator's Message to Employees: State of the Agency. Washington DC: Agency for International Development; 1884.

NCA. Minutes of Meeting at NCA Oslo with Jacques Willemse (DIA). Oslo; 1992 Jan 17.

NCA and SCC, Signatories. Agreement Concerning Formation of an Emergency Relief Desk. Khartoum; 1981 Feb 21.

Nerayo Tecklemichael (ERRA). *International and Indigenous NGO's in Eritrea: What Opportunities do Exist for Future Cooperation*. presented at: Workshop on International and Indigenous NGOs in Eritrea: What are the Prospects for Future Cooperation; Asmara. 1993 Jun 8.

Normark, S. (ERD). Emergency Relief Desk 01.08.81-30.09.81. Khartoum; 1981 Oct 1.

Normark, S. (SCR). Report on a Visit to Sudan and Eritrea: 19 February–12 March 1978. Skelleftea; 1978 Mar.

Normark, S. (ERD). Report: January-March 1982. Khartoum; 1982 Apr.

Normark, S. (ERD). Report on Visit to Eritrea. Khartoum; 1982 Jun 4.

Normark, S., Executive Secretary (ERD). Report: April–June 1982. Khartoum; 1982 Jun 30.

Overby, T. (ERD). [Telex to ERD Members]. Khartoum; 1987 Nov 2.

OXFAM. Briefing Paper: UN Response to Humanitarian Emergencies: A Challenge to the International Community. Oxford: OXFAM; 1991 Aug.

Pisani, E. (EC Commission). [Letter to Marshall, J, MEP]. Brussels; 1984 Feb 1.

Presidential Determination No 85–20. Determination With Respect to Ethiopia. Washington DC; 1985 Sep 7.

Renshaw, P. (CA). [Letter to Janda, C, SCC]. London; 1984 Aug 3.

Renshaw, P. (CA). [Letter to ERD Agencies]. London; 1984 Oct 18.

Renshaw, P. (CA). [Telex to Normark, S, SCR]. London; 1984 Oct 24.

Renshaw, P. (CA). [Letter to Jacobsen, A, ERD]. London; 1985 Jan 11.

Renshaw, P. (CA). [Letter to ERD Agencies]. London; 1985 Apr 22.

Renshaw, P. *Christian Aid and the Emergency Relief Desk*. London; 1985 Apr 22.

Renshaw, P. (CA). Conversation with Hugh Mackay, Save the Children Fund: 'Ethiopia Drought'. London; 1984 Aug 2.

REST. ERD Evaluation. Khartoum; 1984 Feb 1.

REST; ORA; ERA. Emergency Relief Desk: Problems Encountered, Possible Solutions. Khartoum; 1989 Feb 9.

Robinson, C. (CA). Memorandum: ERD Board Meeting, Geneva, 15th October 1985. London; 1985 Oct 23.

Robinson, C. (CA). Memorandum: ERD Meeting and EEC. London; 1985 Apr 29.

Silkin, T.; Hughes, S. *Food Security and Food Aid: A Study From the Horn of Africa*. London: CAFOD/Christian Aid; 1992 Sep.

Smith, G. *Addressing Relief and Repatriation Needs in Non–Government Held Areas: Implications for Policies and Programs*. Presented at: Conference on Repatriation During Conflict; Addis Ababa. 1992 Oct.

Smith, G. Concept Paper-Cross Border Operations. Khartoum; 1985 Mar 5.

Smith, G. (ERD/DIA). Counting Quintals: Report on a Field Monitoring Visit to Tigray, Northern Ethiopia. 1983 Jul.

Smith, G. (ERD). *Internal Purchase Programme: Implications for the Present and Future*. Addis Ababa: ERD Advisory Group; 1992 Apr.

Smith, G. (Free Lance Journalist). *Observations in Eritrea and Tigray During 1982*. Somerville, Massachusetts; 1982 Nov 30.

Smith, G. *Past and Future Approaches to Relief and Rehabilitation in Ethiopia*. Presented at: Donors' Conference on Relief and Rehabilitation; Addis Ababa. 1992 May.

Smith, G. Report on New Refugee Arrivals to Blue Nile Province Sudan: January 13 –14, 1985. Demazin, Sudan; 1985 Jan.

Smith, G. (REST Support Committees Information). Report on Visit to Sudan/Tigray, December 1984-March 1985. 1985 Mar 12.

Stabrun, O. (NCA). Report on a Visit to Eritrea. 1978 Feb 24.

Survival International. *Resettlement: The Evidence*. London: Survival International; 1985 Mar.

TPLF. TPLF Dismisses World Vision's Allegations. Khartoum; 1986 May 15.

Vaux, T. *Famine in Eritrea*. Oxford: OXFAM; 1990 Mar.

Villumstad, S. (ERD). [Telex to Haugland, R, NCA]. Addis Ababa; 1992 Feb 18.

Villumstad, S. (Liason Officer). [Memo to Strand, R// Ofstad, A, NCA]. Addis Ababa; 1992 Jul 6.

Villumstad, S., Liason Officer (ERD). Memoradum to ERD/AG Partners: Future of ERD in Ethiopia, Future of Liason Function: Evolution of ERD (Agenda Item B). Addis Abbaba; 1992 May 4.

Villumstad, S., Liason Officer (ERD). Preliminary Relfections on Possible Future Relationships Between AG Members and Local Partners in Ethiopia. Addis Abbaba; 1992 Mar 3.

Villumstad, S. (NCA/ERD). Memorandum: Some Points Arising form Encounters With JRP Operation in Tigray. 1990 Oct 20.

Villustad, S., Liason Officer (ERD). Update From NCA/ERD Liason Officer in Ethiopia For March 1992. Addis Ababa; 1992 Apr 3.

Weaver, J. L.; Kontos, J. F. (USAID). *Refugee Situation in Sudan*. Khartoum; 1982 Dec.

Westborg, J., ed (Centre For Partnership in Development). Evaluation Report, Emergency Relief Desk, Sudan: July 1988. Oslo; 1988 Aug 14.

Willemse, J. (DIA). [Letter to Renshaw, P, CA]. Utrecht; 1984 Jun 13.

Willemse, J. (DIA). [Telex to Renshaw, P, CA]. Utrecht; 1984 Oct 1.

Willemse, J. (DIA). [Telex to Keulemans, N, CICARWS Emerg.] Utrecht; 1984 Nov 13.

Willemse, J. (ERD/AG Chairman). [Letter to ERD Members]. Oslo; 1991 Jun 4.

Willemse, J. (DIA). [Fax to Villumstad, S, ERD]. Utrecht; 1992 Feb 25.

Willemse, J. (DIA). [Fax to Villumstad, S, ERD]. Utrecht; 1992 May 27.

Willemse, J. (DIA). Travel Report Visit, Rome: 3–7 March 1984. Utrecht; 1984 Mar.

Wright, K. Relief For Tigray: Report on a Visit, February–March 1979. London; 1979 May 2.

Wright, K. Tigray: A Political Report. London; 1979 Sep.

Published Material

Africa Watch. *Evil Days: 30 Years of War and Famine in Ethiopia*. New York: Africa Watch; 1991 Sep.

Africa Rights. *Somalia, Operation Restore Hope: A Preliminary Assessment*. London: Africa Rights; 1993 May.

Allen, T. *Violence and Moral Knowledge: Observing Social Trauma in Sudan and Uganda*. Cambridge Anthropology, Special Issue: Local Warfare in Africa. 1989; 13(2): 56–66.

Alvarrson, J. *Starvation or Peace or Food and War?: Aspects of Armed Conflict in the Lower Omo Valley*. Uppsala Research Reports in Cultural Anthropology. 1989;

Araria, G. *The Politics of Famine and Strategies for Development in Ethiopia*. Ann Arbor: University of Michigan; 1990.

Bimbi, G. *The National Liberation Struggle and the National Liberation Fronts*. in: RICE, ed. The Eritrean Case. Rome: Reseach and Information Centre on Eritrea; 1982: 167–207.

Bondestam, L.; Cliffe, L.; White, P. *An Independent Evaluation of the Food Situation in Eritrea Submitted to the Emergency Relief Desk*: Eritrea Food and Agricutural Assessment Study, Final Report. University of Leeds: Centre of Development Studies; 1988 Mar.

Borton, J. "Recent Trends in the International Relief System." Disasters. 1993 Sep; 17(3): 187-201.

Boutrous–Ghali, B., UN General Secretary. *An Agenda for Peace: Preventive Diplomacy, Peacemaking and Peace–Keeping*. New York: United Nations; 1992 Jun 17.

Centre for Development Studies (University of Leeds). *An Independent Evaluation of the Food Situation in Eritrea in 1991*. Submitted to the Emergency Relief Dest, 2 May 1992: Eritrea 1991: A Needs Assessment Study. 1992 Aug.

Centre for Development Studies. Prepared for the Eritrean (sic) Relief Desk: Peace in Eritrea: *Prospects for Food Security and Problems of Policy*. : University of Leeds; 1992 Sep 8.

Clapham, C. *Transformation and Continuity in Revolutionary Ethiopia*. Cambridge: University Press; 1988.

Clark, L. *Early Warning Case Study: The 1984–5 Influx of Tigrayans Into Eastern Sudan*. Washington DC: Refugee Policy Group; 1986.

Clay, J. "Ethiopian Famine and the Relief Agencies." in: Nichols, B.; Loescher, G., eds. *The Moral Nation: Humanitarianism and US Foreign Policy Today*. South Bend, Indiana: University of Notre Dame Press; 1989.

Clay, J. W. "Western Assistance and the Ethiopian Famine: Implications for Humanitarian Assistance." in: Downs, R. E.; Kerner, D. O.; Reyna, S. P., eds. *The Political Economy of African Famine*. Philadelphia: Gordan and Breach; 1991: 147–75.

Clay, J. W.; Holcombe, B. K. *Politics and the Ethiopian Famine, 1984–1985*. Cambridge, MA: Cultural Survival; 1985.

Clough, R. E. *Free at Last? US Policy Toward Africa and the End of the Cold War*. New York. Council on Foreign Relations; 1992.

Cuny, F. "Politics and Famine Relief." in: Nichols, B.; Loescher, G., eds. *The Moral Nation: Humanitarianism and US Foreign Policy Today*. South Bend, Indiana: University of Notre Dame Press; 1989: 278-287.

de Waal, A. "A Re–assessment of Entitlement Theory in the Light of Recent Famines in Africa." Development and Change. 1990; 21: 469–490.

Downs, R. E.; Kerner, D. O.; Reyna S P, eds. *The Political Economy of African Famine. Food and Nutrion in History and Anthropology*, Vol 9 ed. Philadelphia: Gordon Breach Science Publishers; 1991.

Duffield, M. "The Emergence of Two–Tier Welfare in Africa: Marginalization or an Opportunity for Reform?" *Public Administration and Development*. 1992; 12: 139–154.

Duffield, M. NGOs, "Disaster Relief and Asset Transfer in the Horn: Political Survival in a Permanent Emergency." *Development and Change*. 1993; 24: 131–157.

Duffield, M. *Sudan at the Cross Roads: From Emergency Preparedness to Social Security*. Institute of Development Studies Discussion Paper. 1990; (277).

Duffield, M. *War and Famine in Africa*. Oxfam Research Paper No 5. 1991;

EPLF. "The Cause of Famine in Ethiopia." From, Dimtsi Hafash, June 1980: EPLF, ed. *Selected Articles From EPLF Publications* (1973–1980). Rome: Eritrean

People's Liberation Front; 1982 May: 59–61.

EPLF. *Victories Won by the EPLF in 1976*. From, Vanguard, March 1977: EPLF, ed. *Selected Articles From EPLF Publications*(1973–1980). Eritrean People's Liberation Front: Rome; 1982 May: 77–87.

Ferris, E. *Humanitarian Politics: Cross–Border Operations in the Horn of Africa*. Uppsala: Life and Peace Institute; 1992.

Finney, L. *Development Assistance: A Tool of Foreign Policy*. Case Western Reserve Journal of International Law. 1983; 15.

Firebrace, J. "Food as Military Aid." New Statesman. 1984 Dec 7; 108(2803): 5–6.

Firebrace, J. (War on Want). "Statement to the European Parliament Re: Tins of EEC Butteroil Observed at Sheraro, Tigray Province, Ethiopia 12/4/82." London: *War on Want*; 1982 Nov 29.

Galloway, G. "The Mengistu Famine." *The Spectator*. 1984 Dec 1: 6–7.

Gill, P. *A Year in the Death of Africa*. London: Paladin; 1886.

Habte–Selassie, Bereket. "Eritrea and the United Nations." *in: Research and Information Centre on Eritrea*, ed. *The Eritrean Case* (Proceedings of the Permanent Peoples' Tribunal of the International League for the Rights and Liberation of Peoples, Session on Eritrea, Milan, Italy, 24–26 May, 1980). Rome: RICE; 1982: 115–166.

Hendrie, B. "Cross–Border Relief Operations in Eritrea and Tigray." *Disasters*. 1990; 13(4): 351–360.

Hendrie, B. "The Tigrayan Refugee Repatriation: Sudan to Ethiopia, 1985–1987." in: Cuny, ed. *Repatriation During Conflict: Africa and Asia*. Dallas: Centre for the Study of Societies in Crisis; 1992: 291-377.

Hensle, H. Nicht Ist, *Was Nicht Sein Darf*... Diakonie Report. 1985 Mar.

Hutchinson, R., ed. *Fighting for Survival*. Gland, Switzerland: International Union for Conservation of Nature and Natural Resouces; 1991.

Kaplan, R. *Surrender or Starve: The Wars Behind the Famine*. Boulder: Westview Press; 1988.

Keen, D. "A Disaster For Whom?: Local Interests and International Donors During Famine Among the Dinka of Sudan." *Disasters*. 1991; 15(2): 58–73.

Kli Kline, D. "Politics Hinders Food Aid to Starving People in Ethiopia." *The Christian Science Monitor*. 1984 Aug 3: 5–7.

Korn, D. *Ethiopia: The Dilema for the West*. *World Today*. 1986 Jan: 4-7.

Korten, D. C. *Getting to the 21st Century: Voluntary Action and the Global Agenda*. Connecticut: Kumarian Press; 1990.

Labour Party. *Labour's Programme* 1992. London: Labour Party.

Lappe, F. [and others]. *Aid as an Obstacle*. San Francisco: Institute for Food and Development Policy; 1980.

Life and Peace Institute. *The Challenges to Intervention: A New Role for the UN?* Uppsala: Life and Peace Institute; 1992.

"The Main Provisions of the New ACP–EEC Convention." *The Courier*. 1979 Nov(58): 26–37.

Mengistu Haile Mariam. "The Major Objective of Our Revolution Remains Development With Equity." The Courier. 1980 Jan(59): 9–11.

Minear, L. *Hunanitarianism Under Siege: A Critical Review of Operation Lifeline Sudan*. Trenton, NJ: Red Sea Press; 1991.

Nelson, H.; Kaplan, I., eds. *Ethiopia: A Country Study*. Washington DC: Government Printing Office; 1981.

Padt, R. "The Meaning of Neutrality and its Consequences: The Medecins Sans Frontieres Experience." in: Wackers, G. L.; Wennekes, C. T. M., eds. *Violation of Medical Neutrality*. Amsterdam: Thesis Publishers; 1992: 48–54.

Pateman, R. *Even the Stones are Burning*. Trenton, New Jersey: Red Sea Press; 1990.

Perlez, J. "American Dilema: Food Aid May Prolong War and Famine." *The New York Times*. 1991 May 12; 4: 3.

Piper, I. "Overcoming the Feudal Past." *The Courier*. 1980 Jan(59): 12–17.

Shepherd, J. "Ethiopia: The Use of Food as an Instrument of US Foreign Policy." *Issue, A Journal of Opinion*. 1985; 14: 4-9.

Shepherd, J. *The Politics of Food Aid*. *Africa Report*. 1985 Apr: 51–54.

Smith, G. "Ethiopia and the Politics of Famine Relief." *Middle East Report*. 17(2); 1987 Mar: 31-37.

Solberg, R. W. *Miracle in Ethiopia: A Partnership Response to Famine*. New York: Friendship Press; 1991.

South. 1983 Feb.

Stanhope, H. "Mengistu Spending Shocks the West." *The Times*. 1984 Sep 21.

Survival International. *Resettlement: The Evidence*. London: *Survival International;* 1985 Mar.

Traynor, I. "Why Mercy Fails to Bring Relief." *The Guardian*. 1993 Apr 15: 9.

Turton, D. Warfare, *Vulnerability and Survival: A Case From Southern Ethiopia*. Cambridge Anthropology, Special Issue: *Local Warfare in Africa*. 1989; 13(2): 67–85.

"UN Says Food is Reaching North Ethiopia." *New York Times*. 1985 Aug 4: 2, Cols 1-6.

US General Accounting Office. *The US Response to the Ethiopian Food Crisis*. Washington DC: General Accounting Office; 1985.

US House of Representatives. Subcommittee on Human Rights and International

Organisations. *Human Rights and Food Aid in Ethiopia*. Washington DC; 1985 Oct 16.

US House of Representatives. Select Committee on Hunger. *Renewed Challenge in Ethiopia*. Washington, DC; 1987 Oct 8.

Vallely, P. "Ethiopians Admit Tegre Crisis." *The Times*. 1985 Feb 25.

Vallely, P. "Ethiopian Troops Sever Food Supply Lines to Starving Tigre." *Times*. 1985 May 7.

Vallely, P. "Famine: Russia and US on Collision Course." *The Times*. 1985 Jun 4.

Van Woudenberg, W. "Ethiopia and the European Community." *The Courier*. 1980 Jan(59): 19–20.

Varnis, S. *Reluctant Aid or Aiding the Reluctant: US Food Aid Policy and Ethiopian Famine Relief*. New Brunswick: Transaction Publishers; 1990.

Villumstad, S.; Hendrie, B. "Recent Trends in Disaster Preparedness and Response in Ethiopia." *Disasters*. 1993; 17(2): 122-132.

Weiss T; Campbell, K. M. "Military Humanism." *Survival*. 1991; 33(5): 451–465.

Interviews and Communications

Aba Kidane, Fr; Flynn, Br G. (ESC). Interview. Addis Ababa. 1993 Jan 26.

Abadi Zemo (REST). Interview. Addis Ababa. 1993 Jan 28.

Abdul Mohammed (Inter–Africa Group). Interview. Addis Ababa. 1993 Jan 25.

Araia Desta (ERA Canada). Interview. Toronto. 1992 Nov 26.

Asmanaw Belay; Tsegye Berhe (Ethiopian Orthodox Church). Interview. Addis Ababa. 1993 Jan 21.

Assab Tekle (JRP). Interview. Addis Ababa. 1992 Jan 26.

Ayyaanaa Leencaa; Addisu Beyene Kaloo (ORA). Interview. Addis Ababa. 1993 Jan 26.

Barth, N. (LWR). Interview. New York. 1992 Oct 5.

Berhane Wolde Tensaie (REST). Interview. Addis Ababa. 1993 Jan 25.

Billanou, M. (EIAC). Interview. Asmara. 1993 Feb 2.

Borden, J. (Christian Aid). Interview. London. 1993 Jan 6.

Chekol Kidane (REST). Interview. Makele. 1993 Jan 29.

Constaninos Berhe (Former ICRC). Interview. Addis Ababa. 1993 Jan 22.

Cottingham, Rev B. (Former LWR). Interview. New York. 1992 Oct 18.

de Waal, A. (Africa Rights). Interview. London. 1993 Jan 8.

Elssam Yohannes (Ministry of Foriegn Affairs). Interview. Addis Ababa. 1993 Jan 30.

Erichsen, J. (NCA). Interview. Oslo. 1993 Mar 16.

Haile Gessessa (Former REST). Interview. Addis Ababa. 1993 Jan 25.

Hardy, D. (Canadian LWR). Interview. Ottawa. 1992 Nov 21.

Hauser, K. (Former Eritrean Relief Committee). Interview. Connecticut. 1992 Oct 20.

Hendrie, B. (Former ERD). Interview. Asmara. 1993 Feb 5.

Hensle, H. (BFW/DDW). Interview. Stuttgart. 1993 Mar 2.

Howie, L. (USAID). Interview. Washington DC. 1992 Nov 23.

Jacobsen, A. (ERD). Interview. Asmara. 1993 Feb 2.

Jacobsen, A. (ERD). Interview. Asmara. 1993 Feb 4.

Jacobsen, A. (ERD). Interview. Asmara. 1993 Feb 9.

Johnson, D. Personal Communication. 1992 Dec 5.

Karadawi, A. (Community Aid Abroad). Interview. Addis Ababa. 1993 Jan 26.

Kosti Manibe (Former SCC). Interview. Asmara. 1993 Feb 5.

Lilo (Provisional Government of Eritrea). Interview. Asmara. 1993 Feb 5.

Marcunas, J. (USAID Food for Peace). Interview. Rosslyn, Virginia. 1992 Nov 23.

Meehan, F. (REST). Interview. Addis Ababa. 1993 Jan 28.

Minear, L. (Humanitarianism and War Project, Refugee Policy Group). Interview. Washington DC. 1993 Mar 10.

Nerayo Teklemichael (ERRA). Interview. Asmara. 1993 Feb 3.

Nerayo Teklemichael (ERRA). Personal Communication. Asmara. 1993 Jun 22.

Olfert, E. (MCC). Interview. Akron, PA. 1992 Nov 25.

O'Neil, J. (US Consul). Interview. Asmara. 1993 Feb 2.

Overby, T. (Former ERD). Interview. Asmara. 1993 Feb 4.

Overby, T. (Former ERD). Interview. Asmara. 1993 Feb 8.

Paulos Tesfagiorgis (Former ERA). Interview. Asmara. 1993 Feb 3.

Pearson, W. (USAID). Interview. Addis Ababa. 1993 Jan 24.

Reimer, W. (MCC). Interview. Nairobi. 1993 Feb 14.

Robinson, C.; Hughes, S. (Christian Aid). Interview. London. 1993 Jan 6.

Roso (RICE). Interview. Asmara. 1993 Feb 3.

Sayers, V. (TTAC). Interview. Addis Ababa. 1993 Jan 27.

Silkin, T. (OXFAM). Interview. Massawa. 1993 Feb 6.

Smith, G. (DIA/NCA). Interview. Addis Ababa. 1993 Jan 25.

Smith, G. (DIA/NCA). Interview. Addis Ababa. 1993 Jan 29.

Smith, G. (DIA/NCA). Personal Communication. Asmara. 1993 Jun 4.

Solberg, K. (NCA). Interview. Addis Ababa. 1993 Jan 25.

Sprunger, J. (LWR). Interview. New York. 1992 Nov 18.

Tekie Beyene (Former ERA). Interview. Asmara. 1993 Feb 9.

Teklewoini Assefa (REST). Personal Communication. Utrecht. 1993 Jun 17.

Tenhula, J. (Former LWR). Interview. Philadelphia. 1992 Oct 19.

Tesfa Seyoum (Former Eritrean Relief Committee). Interview. New York. 1992 Nov 24.

Tsefai Ghermazion (Provisional Government of Eritrea). Interview. Asmara. 1993 Feb 5.

Vaux, T.; Nauman, R. (OXFAM). Interview. Oxford. 1993 Jan 5.

Villumstad, S.; Strand, R. (NCA). Interview. Oslo. 1993 Mar 17.

Whisenant, J. (LWR). Interview. New York. 1992 Nov 20.

Whisenant, J. (LWR). Personal Communication. 28 May 1993.

Willemse, J. (DIA). Interview. Utrecht. 1993 Feb 24.

Willemse, J. (DIA). Personal Communication. Utrecht. 1993 May 28

Index